The Later Medieval Inquisitions *Post Mortem*

The Later Medieval Inquisitions *Post Mortem*

Mapping the Medieval Countryside and Rural Society

Edited by

Michael Hicks

THE BOYDELL PRESS

First published 2016
The Boydell Press, Woodbridge

ISBN 978 1 78327 079 8

The Boydell Press is an imprint of Boydell & Brewer Ltd
PO Box 9, Woodbridge, Suffolk IP12 3DF, UK
and of Boydell & Brewer Inc.
668 Mt Hope Avenue, Rochester, NY 14620-2731, USA
website: www.boydellandbrewer.com

A catalogue record for this book is available
from the British Library

This publication is printed on acid-free paper

Typeset by Servis Filmsetting Ltd, Stockport, Cheshire

Contents

Illustrations

Contributors

Katie Clarke is reading for a research degree at the University of Winchester.

Dr William S. Deller, a graduate of Oxford and London universities, is an independent scholar interested in the production and use of stereotypical documents in medieval bureaucracies.

Dr Paul Dryburgh is a Medieval Records Specialist at The National Archives, with research interests in government, warfare and politics across the British Isles in the fourteenth century.

Christopher Dyer is emeritus Professor of History at the University of Leicester. His researches into medieval economic, social and landscape history have resulted in many books and articles.

Dr Janette Garrett has worked as Research Assistant and Research Associate on projects at Northumbria University.

Michael Hicks, University of Winchester, is emeritus Professor of Medieval History and Principal Investigator of the Mapping the Medieval Countryside project. He has written extensively on late medieval political, religious and social history.

Dr Matthew Holford is research officer on the Mapping the Medieval Countryside project.

Dr Gordon McKelvie, University of Winchester, is an expert in the legal, political and social history of late medieval England.

Dr Stephen Mileson, VCH Oxfordshire, is a social and landscape historian specialising in the Middle Ages.

Dr Simon Payling is a senior fellow at the History of Parliament Trust.

Dr Matthew Tompkins is a Research Officer on the Mapping the Medieval Countryside project.

Dr Jennifer Ward spent most of her career lecturing on medieval and regional history at Goldsmiths College, University of London. Since retirement, she has continued with research and writing, mainly on women's history and on East Anglia and Essex in the Middle Ages.

Glossary

Affeeror	Official (esp. in a manorial court) responsible for determining the level of fines and amercements
Assart	Woodland cleared for cultivation
Assignment of dower	Allocation of lands of deceased tenant after IPM to his widow
Attorn	Formal acknowledgement of right
Bastard	Offspring born outside marriage with no rights of inheritance
Burgage	Type of freehold tenure in towns
Cestui que use	Beneficiary of a trust (enfeoffment to use)
Chancery	Government writing department that issued writs to hold inquisitions, received returns, and ordered subsequent actions
Courtesy of England or Law of England	A widower's entitlement to all estates of a deceased heiress by whom the man had fathered a living child (who might subsequently have died)
Demesne	Property held directly by landholder; also that part of a manor held by the lord rather than the tenants
Devenerunt	Writ to inquire who was next heir of a minor heir who had died
Diem clausit extremum (dce)	Writ issued on death of a feudal tenant to initiate inquisition *post mortem*
Dower	Common law right of a widow to one-third of all lands of which husband was seised at death and/ or during their marriage
Dowry, marriage portion	Lump sum due on marriage of a gentlewoman, often payable in instalments
Enfeoff	Convey land
Enfeoffment to use	Conveyance of land to trustees (feoffees) for a third party/ designated purpose (use)
Entail	Settlement of land on recipient and heirs or on designated individuals. Could be limited to descendants of either sex (tail general), descendants in male line (tail male), or specific individuals (remaindermen)
Escheat	Forfeiture of land in default of heirs to original donor or his heirs

Escheator	Official appointed annually in rotation by the crown to administer feudal rights in a particular county
Extent	Detailed description and valuation of a property
Exchequer	Government finance department that received income from wardships and administered their estates
Fealty	Oath due from feudal tenant on succession to estate
Fee simple	Simple tenure of land that was neither entailed nor enfeoffed
Feodary	Estate official who administered feudal rights of a lord
Feoffee	One of panel of trustees granted property by donor (feoffor) to hold it to his use
Feudal aid	Archaic royal levy on all knights' fees on particular occasions
Final concord or Fine	Fictitious lawsuit that enabled land to be transferred
Forinsec	Forinsec or foreign courts were so described to distinguish them from the principal honour court. They dealt with honorial business concerning tenants and enforced decisions made in the main court
Frankpledge, view of	Type of court (usually manorial and often private) that exercised low level criminal jurisdiction
Furlong	Subdivision of an open field, containing a number of arable strips
Gavelkind	System of partible inheritance in Kent and parts of Middlesex
Homage	Formal act of submission to a feudal lord especially the king
Honour	Feudal grouping of estates and knights' fees
Knight's fee	Military service from a manor or other property due to superior lord. Also implied other service
Jointure	Land held jointly by husband and wife for life, usually from marriage, often entailed on offspring of the match
Livery	Formal delivery of seisin to property
Mandamus	Writ of reminder issued one year after a writ of *diem clausit extremum* to command its implementation
Manor	Self-contained estate that had a court and jurisdiction, often held by military service of lord
Marriage portion	Dowry or payment due from father/ brother of a bride to father/ bridegroom at marriage
Mesne lord	Tenant of tenant-in-chief who exercised lordship over others
Mortmain	Land held by the church for ever. Since the church could not die, literally in its 'dead hand'

Onomast	Place names specialist
Oyer and terminer commission	Special judicial commission in criminal cases
Prerogative wardship	Royal right to wardship of heir and all lands of an heir to property held in knight service of the crown regardless of who was lord of the other components
Primer seisin	Royal right to revenues of an estate between death of tenant and livery of the heir
Primogeniture	Normal system of inheritance, by which males take precedence in order of birth over females of the same generation, the direct line takes precedence over collaterals, and sisters inherit equally
Proof of age	Formal process whereby under-age heirs are adjudicated of age and hence able to take up their inheritance
Scutage	Archaic tax in lieu of feudal military service
Relief	Nominal payment of £5 per knight's fee on entry to inheritance
Remainder	Designated next heir
Seisin	Physical possession of land
Selion	A strip of land in an open field for ploughing
Serjeanty	A type of free tenure for particular designated service
Sheriff	Official appointed by the crown annually in rotation to administer ancient revenues (county farm), judicial and electoral business
Socage	A type of estate tenure, usually solely for rent
Tail general	Entail of property on donor's (feoffor's) heirs of whatever sex
Tail male	Entail of property on male heirs of donor (feoffor)
Tenant-in-chief	Landowner who held land directly of king
Use	A trust
Ward	Under-age heir of a feudal tenant whose wardship (guardianship) and marriage belonged to superior lord
Wardship	A lord's right of custody of lands and heir of a feudal tenant
Will	Instructions (usually written) regarding use of lands after death. (The modern will of moveable goods was called the testament.)
Writ	Written Latin instruction from central government to local officials. Formulaic: different writs for different occasions

Abbreviations

AgHR	*Agricultural History Review*
AHEW	*Agrarian History of England and Wales*, iii, iv, ed. E. Miller and J. Thirsk (Cambridge, 1967–91)
Bean, *Decline*	J.M.W. Bean, *The Decline of English Feudalism 1215–1540* (Manchester, 1968)
BIHR	*Bulletin of the Institute of Historical Research*
BL	British Library
CAD	*A Descriptive Catalogue of Ancient Deeds in the Public Record Office* (6 vols, London, HMSO, 1890–1915)
Campbell, *ESA*	B.M.S. Campbell, *English Seigniorial Agriculture 1250–1450* (Cambridge, 2000)
Campbell & Bartley, *Atlas*	B.M.S. Campbell and K. Bartley, *England on the Eve of the Black Death: An Atlas of Lay Lordship, Land, and Wealth, 1300–49* (Manchester, 2006)
Carpenter, 'Introduction'	C. Carpenter, 'General Introduction', *CIPM*, xxii
CCR	*Calendar of Close Rolls*
CFR	*Calendar of Fine Rolls*
CIPM	*Calendar of Inquisitions post mortem and other analogous documents preserved in the Public Record Office*, i–xx, 2nd ser. i–xix (HMSO, London, 1904–92); xx–xxiii (Woodbridge, 2002–3); xxiv–vi (Woodbridge, 2009–10); 2nd ser. [Henry VII] i–iii (London, 1898–1955).
CP	G.E. C[okayne], *Complete Peerage of England, Scotland, Ireland, Great Britain and the United Kingdom*, ed. H.V. Gibbs et al. (12 vols, 1910–59)
CPR	*Calendar of Patent Rolls*
dce	*diem clausit extremum*
EHD	*English Historical Documents*
EHR	*English Historical Review*
EcHR	*Economic History Review*, 2nd series
EPNS	English Place Name Society
Feudal Aids	*Inquisitions and Assessments Relating to Feudal Aids*, 6 vols (1890–1920)
Hicks, 'Between Majorities'	M.A. Hicks, 'Between Majorities: The "Beauchamp Interregnum"1439–49', *Historical Research* lxxiii (1999)

HR	*Historical Research*
Holford, 'Testimony'	M. Holford, 'Testimony (to Some Extent Fictitious): Proofs of Age in the First Half of the Fifteenth Century', *Historical Research* lxxxii (2009)
IPM Companion	*The Fifteenth Century Inquisitions post mortem: A Companion* (Woodbridge, 2012)
McFarlane, *England*	K.B. McFarlane, *England in the Fifteenth Century: Collected Essays* (1981)
McFarlane, *Nobility*	K.B. McFarlane, *The Nobility of Later Medieval England. The Ford Lectures for 1953 and Related Studies* (Oxford, 1973)
ODNB	*Oxford Dictionary of National Biography*, 64 vols (Oxford, 2004), www.oxforddnb.com
Paston L & P	*Paston Letters and Papers of the Fifteenth Century*, ed. R. Beadle, N. Davis and C. Richmond, 3 vols, Early English Text Society supplementary series 20–22 (2004–5)
Paston Letters	*The Paston Letters, 1422–1509*, ed. J. Gairdner, 6 vols (1904)
Payling, *Nottinghamshire*	S.J. Payling, *Political Society in Lancastrian England: The Greater Gentry of Nottinghamshire* (Oxford, 1991)
Plumpton L & P	*Plumpton Letters and Papers*, ed. J. Kirby, Camden 5th ser. viii (1997)
PROME	*Parliament Rolls of Medieval England*, ed. C. Given-Wilson, 16 vols (2005)
Pugh & Ross, 'Baronage'	T.B. Pugh and C.D. Ross, 'The English Baronage and the Income Tax of 1436', *Bulletin of the Institute of Historical Research* xxvi (1953)
Ross & Pugh, 'Materials'	C.D. Ross and T.B. Pugh, 'Materials for the Study of Baronial Incomes in Fifteenth-Century England', *Economic History Review*, 2nd ser. 6 (1953)
RO	Record Office
RP	*Rolls of Parliament*, 6 vols, Record Commission (London, 1783)
SR	*Statutes of the Realm* [www.heinonline.org]
Stonor L & P	*Stonor Letters and Papers of the Fifteenth Century*, ed. C.L. Kingsford, Camden 3rd ser. xxix, xxx, xxxiv (1919–24)
VCH	*Victoria County History*

All references to calendared IPMs are to IPM numbers, not pages. All original documents cited are in The National Archives (TNA) unless otherwise indicated

1

Introduction

Michael Hicks

This book celebrates the inquisitions *post mortem*, a vast and systematic source for late medieval England that has the potential to light up many topics, such as landscape and memory, that are only now being realised. It collects the papers delivered at the second inquisitions *post mortem* conference held at the University of Winchester in 2014, valuably supplemented by papers by Paul Dryburgh, Stephen Mileson and Jennifer Ward.

This second conference was organised by the university's Professor Michael Hicks as Principal Investigator of the Mapping the Medieval Countryside project (MMC)[1] funded by the Arts and Humanities Research Council. This was a collaboration with Paul Spence and his team at the Department for Digital Humanities at King's College London. The project seeks to open access to all the published *Calendars of Inquisitions post mortem* (*CIPM*s) to anyone anywhere in the world on British History Online (BHO), to enhance *CIPM*s xviii–xxi to the standard of the most recent calendars, and to create an interactive database of *CIPM*s xviii–xxvi that is more easily searched, interrogated and analysed. Despite formidable technical difficulties, several extra *CIPM*s have been posted on BHO,[2] and interactive versions of *CIPM*s xxi–xxvi on the project website:[3] the rest should be available by the time of publication of this book. Apart from electronic publication, the project seeks to make IPMs better known as a source to academics and the general public, and to demonstrate how they can be best used through the blogs and featured IPMs on its website and its Twitter account. The 2014 conference and these proceedings are part of this process of dissemination.

Many years of calendaring IPMs have generated much new knowledge that either was lost or has percolated only indirectly into general historical consciousness. It is no accident that the critical publications most cited on IPMs precede the Second World War. Professor Christine Carpenter's introduction to *CIPM* xxii established a new foundation. The 2010 IPM conference that gave rise to the 2012 *Companion* sought to bank what had been learnt from the Cambridge-directed calendaring of *CIPM*s xxii–xxvi, notably in the papers by Carpenter,

1 www.inquisitionspostmortem.ac.uk.
2 www. British-history.ac.uk/ inquisitions-post-mortem.
3 www.inquisitionspostmortem.ac.uk.

Holford, Noble and Parkin.[4] The 2014 conference and this book seek, secondly, to continue this process, bringing together independent work from research degrees (Clarke, Deller, Garrett), from other projects (Dryburgh, Mileson), from established scholars who use IPMs (Dyer, Payling, Ward) and from the project team (Hicks, Holford, McKelvie, and Tompkins). Holford and Tompkins offer first samples of what the digitisation of the *CIPMs* and the enhanced capacity for analysis and manipulation created by the MMC project will make possible in future.

I

IPMs are the records of feudal lordship in operation. Feudal rights were valuable to the king: initially for military service, but latterly for financial reasons, whether for general levies (aids and scutage) or for wards and wardships, and also as key mechanisms for political control and manipulation. The *Book of Fees* and *Feudal Aids* serve as static surveys at periodic intervals. The inquisitions *post mortem* afford a more dynamic picture. They were key elements in an effective system initiated by writs, followed by homage, fealty, livery and grants of custody, and implemented locally by the escheators and through the escheators' accounts. The operation of the system for England and the marches of Wales from c.1236 to the 1640s is recorded in many thousands of surviving inquisitions. The English IPMs – and the *CIPMs* – cover the whole of England bar the three palatinate counties, Chester and Durham throughout and Lancaster from 1377;[5] the fourth, the Cumberland palatinate of Richard Duke of Gloucester (1483), was stillborn. The counts palatine – and indeed all tenants-in-chief – needed something similar to the IPMs to maximise their feudal rights. The palatine counties all developed writs initiating processes and inquisitions *post mortem*, although not many survive. The surviving Lancaster records commence with John of Gaunt, Duke of Lancaster (1362–99): more Lancaster IPMs than now survived in the seventeenth century, when Christopher Townley transcribed them. There is only one medieval file in The National Archives (TNA) PL 4/1. Parts of a few files dating for Durham survive from 1438 (DURH 5, 168). For Cheshire the file CHES 3/50 covers Edward V and Richard III. These are tatty fragments, incomplete, but sufficient to indicate that these subsystems started also from writs of *diem clausit extremum*. Other aspects of the process are preserved elsewhere in the Cheshire (CHES) and Lancaster (PL and DL) records and in the cursitors' records of Durham, all now at The National Archives. These lie outside the

4 *The Fifteenth Century Inquisitions post mortem: A Companion*, ed. M. Hicks (Woodbridge, 2012).

5 John of Gaunt was granted the palatinate in 1377 for life, but his father-in-law Henry of Grosmont was earl palatine from 1351, R. Somerville, *History of the Duchy of Lancaster*, i (London, 1953), 56.

current IPM projects: scanty though the sources may be, they are locally important and will reward systematic study.

The records of the crown are so unmanageably vast that historians have tended to overlook mesne lordship. The partition of estates, prerogative lordship and periodic minorities of tenants-in-chief drew ever more land into the crown system. Royal lordship impinged much less on the estates of ecclesiastical tenants-in-chief and their tenants, which may have comprised a fifth of the lands of England. There were literally hundreds of mesne lords, some of whom had huge trains of feudal tenants: as Ward shows below (chapter 4), 384 knights' fees were held of the honours of Clare and Gloucester alone, 116 held by other tenants-in-chief, leaving 268 directly accountable to the lord. What proportion of English land escaped royal oversight? Scarcely anything has been published on feudal geography, on the amount of land in each county held by churchmen, let alone mesne lords. Even the marvellous *Atlas* of early fourteenth-century England created by Professor Bruce Campbell and Keith Bartley records the distribution of lands held in chief or otherwise in royal hands,[6] not even all lay land. Yet their feudal rights could be lucrative: wardships yielded the substantial sum of £122 to the archbishop of Canterbury in 1419.[7] The lords of the honours of Gloucester and Richmond continued to employ feodaries to run their feudal affairs. Whilst the records of minor tenants-in-chief (if they ever existed) generally have not been preserved, there are considerable archives for many ecclesiastical landlords and for honours that merged with the crown, such as the duchy of Cornwall and the constituent components of the duchy of Lancaster. Those for Pontefract and Richmond have been documented and in this volume, by Jennifer Ward, the honour of Clare in Suffolk is explored (chapter 4).[8] Mesne lordship is another dimension to be explored in the next phase of the project.

Moreover, the English applied their proven system to their other domains – to the marches of Wales (covered by the main system of IPMs), to Scotland in the 1290s, to English Calais and to the king's lordship of Ireland. These topics are discussed by McKelvie (chapter 2) and Dryburgh (chapter 3). Although English Scotland was short lived, the financial imperative remained, and something similar had to be developed by the Scottish kings. Although the Irish public records were destroyed in 1922, 178 IPMs survive at TNA which Dryburgh discusses below. Similarly the English exported their system to Calais. Apparently it was not taken to other English possessions abroad – to Gascony or Normandy;

6 B.M. Campbell and K. Bartley, *England on the Eve of the Black Death: An Atlas of Lay Lordship, Land and Wealth 1300–49* (Manchester, 2006); see also M. Hicks, 'The Fifteenth Century Inquisitions *Post Mortem*: The Newest Calendars 1432–47', *Southern History* xxxiii (2011), 115.

7 F.R.H. Du Boulay, *The Lordship of Canterbury: An Essay on Medieval Society* (1966), 91.

8 M. Devine, 'The Lordship of Richmond in the Later Middle Ages', *Liberties and Identities in the Medieval British Isles*, ed. M. Prestwich (Woodbridge, 2008), ch.5; S. Rose, 'A Twelfth-Century Honour in a Fifteenth-Century World: The Honour of Pontefract', *The Fifteenth Century IX: English and Continental Perspectives*, ed. L. Clark (Woodbridge, 2010).

or at least, whatever systems of feudal oversight operated in those provinces did not result in deposits of records in the English royal archive now at Kew.

II

A second group of papers take different approaches to mapping the medieval landscape. Both Dyer (chapter 5) and Mileson (chapter 6) demonstrate how much additional meaning can be extracted by forensic scrutiny of particular phrases and by the field names that feature in extents. Holford (chapter 7) and Tompkins (chapter 8) use the electronic search facilities of the new online editions of the IPMs to add substantial data to what is known on particular mills and on market days. Holford substantially supplements the recently published *Gazetteer* and contributes additions to Everitt's survey of active markets, which has stood more or less unchallenged since 1967.

Apart from inquisitions, the *CIPMs* contain assignments for dower, partitions and proofs of age. Assignments and partitions are poorly preserved, but deserve further attention, which is not systematically attempted here. (Mileson, in chapter 6, does use assignments of dower.) This book explores the utility of the proofs of age, which generally have been better preserved and contain a wider range of material. The fifteenth-century proofs of age collect testimonies by sworn jurors to the date of birth and age of a feudal tenant-in-chief. The purpose was to prove that the heir had attained the age of majority at which he or she could take seisin of their inheritance. The key focus was the public ceremony of baptism. Either the jurors remembered their participation or had been told of the event, which coincided with some memorable accident, natural or personal occurrence. Proofs of age were an indispensable mechanism for succession to land and for the administration and termination of feudal wardships. They still reveal the descent of property, aristocratic genealogy and often aristocratic demography too. To modern historians they are useful for other additional reasons. Never more than snatches of memory, sometimes extremely brief – a mere sentence long – these depositions offer insights into both the commonplace and exceptional aspects of everyday life that are often concealed from us. The whole corpus up to 1430 has been surveyed and analysed by William S. Deller, who categorises all the surviving data in chapter 9.[9] Some at least of these memories are fictitious. There certainly are particular testimonies that appear identical in different proofs, and indeed whole proofs of age that clearly copy one another.[10] This would certainly matter if such depositions were to be used for specific purposes known already, as sources for a particular murder, a specific battle, a shipwreck or some other topic treated in other records, but virtually never can any testimony be substantiated in this way. To serve their original purposes, such testimonies needed

[9] This chapter is based on the proofs of age in ten volumes of calendars, *CIPM* xvii–xxvi.

[10] Holford, 'Testimony'.

to be credible – to illustrate aspects of real life. They offer insights into their assumptions, habits and expectations across the whole range of topics that often are not available anywhere else. If representative of what did happen, they open revealing windows to the past. Almost certainly they were representative: they convey to us stock memories akin to the school exercises discussed by Nicholas Orme.[11] Viewed in that light, as Deller has done, these snippets contain a mass of miscellaneous information on subjects as diverse as the weather, broken bones, everyday religion and much else. Potentially, proofs of age can contribute to a whole range of topics for which they are not the principal sources, often in unexpected ways. Obviously they contribute more when collated with what historians already know. Clarke's treatment of churching reveals a universal and repetitive rite of passage not only in the life of every mother but in those of everyone else (chapter 10). Hicks's paper (chapter 11) assembles such material for three deliberately contrasting topics – the lower levels of bastard feudalism, the place of monks in the community and the availability locally of exotic sweet wines. Such insights to everyday life and procedures are by-products unforeseen by the jurors and far from the feudal purposes that were served by proofs of age.

All the papers are carefully critical of the sources that they use and generally agree on their value, from sceptically to enthusiastically. Garrett's paper (chapter 12) considers the effectiveness of the system in Northumberland, a distant shire, by comparison with Berkshire. In the process she contributes to the debate on the wildness and governability of the periphery. Payling (chapter 13) draws on unparalleled expertise in the technicalities of land law and a lifetime of experience writing biographies of feudal tenants to substantiate his cautionary warnings about the details and sheer fraud slipped into the IPMs.

Of course inquisitions *post mortem* and proofs of age by themselves are of limited value. There are very few topics for which IPMs are the only source. To be fully understood and best exploited they need to be set in the context of other sources and enriched by what is known from other sources. Thus McKelvie collates his Scottish IPMs with The People of Medieval Scotland database (www.poms.ac.uk), Hicks the evidence of wine in the proofs of age with that of the Overland Trade Project (overlandtrade.org), Payling his rival claimants with the biographies created for the History of Parliament, and Holford his markets and fairs with *The Gazetteer of Markets and Fairs in England and Wales to 1516*.[12] Several of these papers demonstrate how extra value can be extracted from these sources when they are set in the appropriate contexts.

11 N. Orme, *English School Exercises 1420–1536* (Turnhout, 2013).

12 www.history.ac.uk/cmh/gaz/gazweb2.html.

III

The editor gratefully acknowledges the support of all the contributors and participants in the conference and from other members of the MMC team, notably Paul Spence (Co-Investigator) and Matthew Holford (Senior Researcher). The conference and this volume are financially supported by the Arts and Humanities Research Council and the University of Winchester.

We acknowledge the kind permissions of Professors Campbell, Holt and Langdon (the authors) to reproduce images from their books, and of the publishers Oxford University Press to reproduce figures in J. Langdon's *Mills in the Medieval Economy* (2004) p. 28; John Wiley and Sons for Distribution map of windmills, 12th century, in Richard Holt's *The Mills of Medieval England* (Oxford, 1988) p. 172; and Manchester University Press for Graph 16.1(a) (p. 280), Graph 16.3 (b) (p. 297) and Map 16.10 (p. 294) originally published in Bruce Campbell and Keith Bartley, *England on the Eve of the Black Death: An Atlas of Lay Lordship, Land and Wealth 1300–49* (Manchester, 2006).

2

Records of an Imperial Administration? Inquisitions *Post Mortems* in Scotland and Calais

Gordon McKelvie

Inquisitions *post mortem* were designed to enable the king of England to keep track of his lands and feudal rights in order to exploit any potential profits or feudal incidents arising from them.[1] Their existence and survival in themselves are a testament to the ability of English royal government throughout the Middle Ages to keep track of its lands and rights which were not confined to the area which constitutes modern-day England.[2] Angevin kings held large swathes of territory in France, though by the fourteenth century Gascony was their only French territory. From 1171 until the Irish parliament declared that Henry VIII was king of Ireland in 1541, the king of England was also lord of Ireland.[3] Even before Wales was conquered by Edward I, Welsh princes had performed homage to kings of England. English kings also claimed overlordship over Scotland from the Anglo-Saxon period onwards although, with the exception of the brief conquests of Edward I, this was much more of a theory or an ideal than a political reality. These claims to territory and overlordship provided the justification for numerous military campaigns during which English kings conquered parts of Scotland, France, Wales and Ireland, with varying degrees of success and endurance.

Ideologies such as the commitment to English overlordship over the rest of the British Isles could not in themselves lead to military success. Such ideologies and beliefs could provide only the initial impetus for conquests or the *post hoc* justification for such actions. Conquests were achieved as much by administrative capabilities as they were by military superiority and ideological concepts of overlordship. As Geoffrey Barrow observed in the context of the Edward I's conquest of Scotland:

1 I would like to thank Professor Michael Hicks, Dr Jackson Armstrong, Dr Paul Dryburgh and Dr Philip Morgan for answering my various queries in the preparation of this chapter.

2 For this paragraph see in particular: R.R. Davies, *The First English Empire: Power and Identities in the British Isles, 1093–1343* (Oxford, 2000); R.A. Griffiths, 'The English Realm and Dominions and the King's Subjects in the Later Middle Ages', in *Aspects of Late Medieval Government and Society*, ed. J.G. Rowe (Toronto, 1986), 83–105, reprinted in his *King and Country: England and Wales in the Fifteenth Century* (London, 1991), 33–54.

3 J.F. Lydon, 'Ireland and the English Crown, 1171–1541', *Irish Historical Studies* xxix (1995), 281.

> The more one reads or handles some of the vast quantity of records left behind by this burst of imperialist activity, the more one admires the calm ambitiousness and the extraordinary thoroughness of the thirteenth-century English monarchy as it set about governing a foreign country.[4]

Similar sentiments can be expressed for the parts of France, Wales and Ireland conquered by various English monarchs.

IPMs were integral parts of the extensive English bureaucracy, and those taken in parts of France, Scotland, Wales and Ireland from the thirteenth to the sixteenth centuries demonstrate one method by which successive English monarchs attempted to govern their newly conquered territory. Those IPMs taken in Ireland are discussed by Paul Dryburgh in chapter 3. Wales is more complicated because 'Wales and the Marches' was a term that 'had an air of vagueness about it'.[5] Many IPMs for Shropshire, Herefordshire and Gloucestershire also cover the march of Wales. An analysis of the locations where inquisitions were taken in the Welsh marches, the places covered by them and the nature of service recorded is too large a topic for this paper to properly address and must await further research. This chapter explains the significance of the IPMs taken in two of these areas, France – or, to be more specific, Calais – and Scotland. It demonstrates their value for understanding the nature of English imperial government in the late medieval period.

Scotland

The only known Scottish IPMs date from 1296 and are for Helen[6] de la Zouche[7] and Robert de Pinkeny,[8] both of whom held lands in both Scotland and England. These documents shed further light on English attempts at governing Scotland in the immediate aftermath of Edward I's conquest in 1296. In 1970 A.A.M. Duncan lamented that 'unfortunately we know all too little of the conduct of government in the years 1296–7'.[9] Fiona Watson's subsequent study of Edward

[4] G.W.S. Barrow, *Robert Bruce and the Community of the Realm*, 4th ed. (Edinburgh, 2005), 99–100.

[5] R.A. Griffiths, 'Wales and the Marches in the Fifteenth Century', in *Fifteenth-Century England, 1399–1509*, ed. S.B. Chrimes, C.D. Ross and R.A. Griffiths (Manchester, 1972), 13, reprinted in Griffiths, *King and Country*, 55.

[6] The spelling of her forename has been published as 'Helen' and 'Elena' in various editions. Here, 'Helen' has been chosen as it is consistent with the online database The People of Medieval Scotland: http://db.poms.ac.uk/record/person/2347/# [accessed 26 March 2015]. The spellings of those persons named in the relevant IPM have been taken from this database. All citations in this paper were accessed on 26 March 2015.

[7] C133/76/3.

[8] C133/76/6.

[9] A.A.M. Duncan, *The Nation of Scots and the Declaration of Arbroath (1320)*, Historical Association, General series lxxv (1970), 12.

I and Scotland sheds an abundance of light on the operation of English government at this time but did not consider the IPMs which were taken in 1296.[10] These documents are a further contribution to our understanding of the nature of English government in the immediate conquest of Scotland and afford an opportunity to contrast the different types of royal government in the two kingdoms.

The IPMs themselves have been published on three occasions, but their significance has gone unnoticed. They were first published in the 1806 calendar, which listed only the lands that were held by tenants-in-chief,[11] and were later published in the third volume of the modern IPM calendars in 1912.[12] Between these IPM calendars Joseph Bain included them in the second volume of his *Calendar of Documents Relating to Scotland* in 1884.[13] Bain's edition even included the names of the jurors, which modern calendars did not include until the publication of volume xxii in 2003. The inclusion of the jurors by Bain reflects the differing priorities between himself and the editors of the earlier calendars of IPMs. While Bain was concerned with making available as much information as possible about Scotland, the editors of the earlier IPM volumes were primarily interested in the study of genealogy and landholding.

The first surviving Scottish IPMs are the six for Helen de la Zouche, who was the youngest daughter of Roger de Quincy, earl of Winchester and his first wife, Helen, daughter of Alan, lord Galloway.[14] Roger de Quincy was a major Anglo-Scottish landowner and although he was never the most politically active of nobles, 'at his death, he was probably the greatest Anglo-Scottish landowner of his day'.[15] Roger de Quincy died without any male heirs, and therefore his lands were divided among his three daughters. Helen therefore inherited one-third of his lands, along with her two older sisters, in both Scotland and England. The IPMs contain the same type of information that is given in IPMs taken in England and returned to Westminster, such as the land held, of whom it was held, its value and the nature of service in which it was held. Helen had modest holdings in England: one-third of the manor of Shepshed and four virgates in Leicestershire and the manor of Halse and township of Brackley in Nottinghamshire. Most of her land, however, was in Scotland, particularly Scottish towns. She held one-third of a moiety of the town and dale in Berwick and a capital messuage and eight carucates in Edinburgh in addition to various lands in Fife, Dumfries, Ayrshire and Wigtonshire. The 1806 *calendarium* did not note that there were different

10 F.J. Watson, *Under the Hammer: Edward I and Scotland* (Edinburgh, 1998), 30–60.

11 *Calendarium Inquisitionum Post Mortem sive Escaetarum*, Vol. 1. *Temporibus Regum Hen. III, Ed I & Ed II*, ed. J. Caley (London, 1806), 129.

12 *CIPM* iii. 363, 366.

13 *Calendar of Documents Relating to Scotland*, Volume 2: *A.D. 1272–1307*, ed. J. Bain (Edinburgh, 1884), nos 824, 857.

14 http://db.poms.ac.uk/record/person/2347/

15 R.D. Oram, 'Quincy, Roger de, earl of Winchester (*c*.1195–1264)', *Oxford Dictionary of National Biography*, Oxford University Press, 2004 [http://www.oxforddnb.com/view/article/22966, accessed 26 March 2015].

inquisitions for different Scottish shires, grouping all of her Scottish lands under the term '*Scotia*'.[16] The writs ordering inquisitions into her Scottish lands were made on 20 August 1296 and were addressed to the local sheriffs, who 'constituted the pivot of royal administration'[17] in thirteenth-century Scotland. The fact that the English administration initially utilised the existing personnel of Scottish royal government to conduct Helen de la Zouche's IPM fits with the claim made by later Scottish chroniclers that Edward I initially made only a few changes to the personnel of Scottish royal government.[18] From an English perspective, making wholesale changes to the personnel of royal government immediately was probably regarded as impractical and unnecessary.

In contrast to the English IPMs that were taken in the respective counties, all of Helen de la Zouche's Scottish inquisitions were held in Berwick upon Tweed. If, for example, the inquisition into her Ayrshire lands which included one-third of a moiety of Irvine[19] were to have followed English patterns, then it would be expected that the inquisition would have been taken in Irvine or the county town, Ayr, or a nearby settlement such as Kilwinning or Kilmarnock. After putting Berwick to the sword on 30 March 1296, Edward I traversed the eastern part of Scotland in a visible display of military strength before returning to Berwick by 22 August, where he held a parliament which drew up an ordinance for the governing of Scotland along English lines, including the appointment of an escheator for the north and south of Scotland, respectively. A new administration was established in Berwick which was 'much more convenient for the English than Edinburgh'. It was at Berwick, on 28 August, that the vast majority of fealties that many Scottish nobles swore to Edward I were recorded on the 'Ragman Roll'.[20] Berwick was therefore a safe place from which the English government could operate. Although it is unlikely that all of those named on the Ragman Roll were actually at Berwick on 28 August, the IPMs seem to indicate that local sheriffs and the respective jurors journeyed to Berwick at this time.

If the IPMs were conducted at Berwick at the same time as Edward I's Berwick parliament, it may be deduced that those jurors who provided information regarding Helen de la Zouche's Scottish lands had gone over to Edward I's side. This deduction can be tested by a prosopographical analysis of the jurors derived from the People of Medieval Scotland database, which contains information on every person named in any document produced in Scotland between 1093 and 1314.[21] The dearth of surviving records for medieval Scotland means that many individu-

16 *Calendarium*, i, 129.

17 Barrow, *Bruce*, 13.

18 *John Fordun's Chronicle of the Scottish Nation*, ed. W.F. Skene (Edinburgh, 1872), 320–1; Walter Bower, *Scotichronicon*, ed. D.E.R. Watt et al., 9 vols (Aberdeen, 1987–98), vi, 81.

19 C133/76/3 m. 6. The document does not state the type of holding this is – i.e. a manor or a vill.

20 M. Prestwich, *Edward I* (London, 1988), 474 (quotation); Barrow, *Bruce*, 99–100.

21 http://www.poms.ac.uk/. The figures in this paragraph are based on searching this database for the records of each of the 72 named jurors.

als are recorded in only one record or are recorded in a few records that may be years, or even decades, apart. The discussion here is limited to what is known about each juror's relations with the English government. In total, 47 out of the 72 jurors who served on the six IPMs for Helen de la Zouche in Scotland are known to have sworn homage to Edward I on 28 August 1296. Four jurors had previously sworn fealty to Edward I and did so again on 28 August 1296: Ralph of Eglinton (Ayrshire),[22] Donald, son of Cane,[23] Gilbert of Southwick[24] (both Dumfriesshire) and Thomas of Torthorwald, knight (Wigtonshire).[25] It is not surprising that those who performed homage to Edward I also participated in a crucial aspect of English government. What is unexpected is that 25 of the jurors, which equates to around 35% of them, *did not* perform homage to Edward I, yet were still utilised by the English administration. The roll of those who swore fealty to Edward I accounts for more than 1,500 tenants-in-chief of the crown, their heirs, substantial under-tenants, burgesses, heads of religious houses and a high number of beneficed clergy.[26] One possible reason why some of the jurors are not recorded on the Ragman Roll is that they were too low down the social scale and therefore did not need to perform homage. This may explain why some jurors are not recorded as having performed homage, but it does not explain why, for instance, Bernard of Keith, knight, did not perform homage to Edward I yet served on the jury for both the Ayrshire and Berwickshire inquisitions.[27] Surely someone of knightly status would have been expected to perform homage in 1296. This evidence therefore suggests that swearing fealty to Edward I was not a prerequisite for serving in local government in August 1296.

The number of jurors who performed homage to Edward I varied between the six different IPMs. Table 2.1 shows these discrepancies, with Berwickshire and Ayrshire providing the highest proportion of jurors who performed homage to Edward I and Fife the least. Too much weight, however, should not be placed on these statistics. This evidence does not indicate that Fife was more 'patriotic' to the cause of Scottish independence, since serving on a jury cannot be equated with desertion to the cause of Scottish independence or, to put it more provocatively, with collaboration. There is not enough evidence here to suggest that any one part of Scotland was more committed to the cause of Scottish independence than the rest.[28] Similarly, there is no personal correspondence to reveal the motivations of those serving on juries. It is worth emphasising that the documents were produced by the English government and therefore need to be regarded as an indication of English, not Scottish, opinion. The documents indicate either

[22] http://db.poms.ac.uk/record/person/18718/.

[23] http://db.poms.ac.uk/record/person/9931/.

[24] http://db.poms.ac.uk/record/person/17375/.

[25] http://db.poms.ac.uk/record/person/17297/.

[26] *CDS* ii, no. 823. For analysis of Ragman Roll, see: Barrow, *Bruce*, 100–1.

[27] http://db.poms.ac.uk/record/person/14116/.

[28] This is the central thrust of G.W.S. Barrow, 'Lothian and the First War of Independence, 1296–1328', *Scottish Historical Review* lv (1976), 151–71.

Table 2.1 Homage of jurors on Helen de la Zouche's Scottish IPMs

Inquisition	Date	Performed	Did not perform	% homage
Ayrshire	28 August	9	3	75.0
Berwickshire	25 August	10	3	76.9
Dumfriesshire	26 August	7	5	58.3
Edinburgh	26 August	8	4	66.7
Fife	27 August	7	6	53.8
Wigtownshire	25 August	8	5	61.5
Total		49	26	65.3
Total – duplicates		47	25	65.3

that the English government was happy to allow those who had not sworn fealty to Edward I to serve on IPM juries, or that it did not feel that it was necessary to continually check the Ragman Roll to ensure that the IPM jurors had sworn fealty to Edward I. Moreover, it is known only with hindsight that English rule in Scotland was only temporary. For contemporaries it was perfectly conceivable that, however unpalatable, English rule in Scotland would continue and therefore service on a jury may simply have been the acceptance of new realities of Scottish political life.

The lack of a correlation between IPM jurors and those who swore fealty to Edward I is further illuminated in the IPM for Robert de Pinkeny. In contrast to Helen de la Zouche, the majority of Pinkeny's lands were in England, notably the counties of Buckinghamshire, Essex and Northamptonshire. His Scottish lands, in Ballincreff and Linlithgow, were valued at £112 10*s* per annum. There is also a detailed extent of his Scottish lands, an analysis of which is beyond the remit of this article.[29] Pinkeny was one of the men who withdrew his petition claiming to be the rightful king of Scots at the Great Cause in 1292.[30] His IPM is undated and does not state where it was taken, although it was probably after 23 November 1296, when a writ was sent to Peter de Donewico (Dunwich), escheator of the south of Scotland.[31] Yet, this evidence is not certain either, because the inquisition does not state the person before whom it was held.[32] The document is nevertheless significant because it was taken at least a few months after Edward I received homage and fealty from the Scottish elite and subsequently committed the government of Scotland to John Earl Warenne. The jury was comprised of twelve men, of whom only four are known to have performed homage to Edward I. This is particularly unexpected, since the inquisition was probably taken three

29 Extents are problematic sources that require a great deal close comparative analysis with similar types of source material: M.L. Holford, '"Notoriously Unreliable": The Valuations and Extents', *IPM Companion*, 117–44. The dearth of comparable source material for thirteenth-century Scotland makes such a comparison even more problematic.

30 http://db.poms.ac.uk/record/source/7332/.

31 *CIPM* iii. 366.

32 C133/76/6 m. 3.

months after the submission of the Scottish nobility to Edward I on 28 August that year. One of those who did not perform homage, Gilbert of Drem, also served on the jury for Helen de le Zouche's Edinburgh IPM.[33] Moreover, only one of those who did perform homage to Edward in 1296, Hugh of Newton, did so again in 1304.[34] In the months after the Scottish political community swore fealty *en masse* to Edward I, such oaths were not a prerequisite for serving on an IPM jury.

There were procedural differences between the Zouche and Pinkeny inquisitions which indicate a change in English administrative practice in Scotland in autumn 1296. Two writs of *diem clausit extremum* were sent: the first to John de Warenne, as keeper of Scotland, on 26 October;[35] the second to Peter de Donewico on 23 November 1296.[36] This suggests that a decision had been made to issue a new writ to the person who was directly responsible for holding IPMs. Donewico had been appointed escheator of the south of Scotland, along with Henry de Ry for the north of Scotland, on 8 September 1296.[37] The escheators, who were appointed by Edward I for the north and south of Scotland respectively, are sparsely documented and the extent of their activities is unclear. Donewico seems to have spent only one year as escheator for the south of Scotland, as on 23 October 1297 he was given a commission, along with John de Hodelston, to raise men for the king's army in Lancaster, Cumberland and Westmoreland.[38] He was probably taken prisoner during military campaigns, as he was named on an exchange of prisoners between Scotland and England on 7 April 1299 and was swapped for an esquire of Sir Arthur de Donhou.[39] The remainder of Donewico's commissions during Edward I's reign were in East Anglia and the south, usually pertaining to military matters.[40]

One Scottish escheator whose activities are known is John de Dalile, since an account book of his escheats in the south of Scotland for 1302–4 survives.[41] He was also in receipt of nineteen rolls of extents of the king's demesne land and sheriffs' accounts north of the Forth 'in the time of the Scottish, as evidence for surveying the state of the same under a commission to Master John de Weston and Sir James of Dalagh under seal of the Scottish Chancery'.[42] Dalile was active in a range of other activities in Scotland and complained that Patrick Earl of Dunbar was preventing him performing his duties,[43] but there is

33 http://db.poms.ac.uk/record/person/19587/.
34 http://db.poms.ac.uk/record/person/18094/.
35 C133/76/6 m. 1.
36 C133/76/6 m. 2.
37 *CDS* ii, no. 853 (p. 225).
38 *CPR 1292–1301*, 313.
39 Ibid. 406.
40 *CPR 1301–1307*, 52–3, 61, 75, 89, 128, 219, 237.
41 E101/331/9; *CDS* ii, no. 1608.
42 *CDS* ii, no. 1534.
43 Ibid. no. 1427.

no record of him conducting any IPM. There is no obvious reason why no other IPMs are known to have been taken in Scotland by English escheators, although there are two credible possibilities, along with two less likely possibilities. First, that other inquisitions were taken, archived elsewhere and subsequently lost or destroyed. Alternatively, that the escheators struggled to carry out their offices in Scotland, which is plausible, considering the fact that escheators did find it difficult to account for revenue from royal lands in Scotland.[44] A more speculative possibility is that no other tenants-in-chief died in Scotland during the period of English occupation, but this seems unlikely. Another possibility is that the English administration believed that there was no clear benefit from conducting further inquisitions in Scotland and therefore the practice ceased after 1296. This is unlikely, as IPMs were being taken in Ireland around this time.

Furthermore, the survival of IPMs relating to Scotland within the English chancery affords the opportunity to consider the discrepancies between Scottish and English governmental administrations during the late medieval period. The numerous differences in the type and scale of medieval government in Scotland and England are well rehearsed: England had a much larger, centralised bureaucracy, whereas Scotland was thinly populated, decentralised and less bureaucratic. After autumn 1296 the sheriffs and constables in Scotland who were local men had been replaced by Englishmen who did not understand the traditions and limits of governing Scotland. Fiona Watson has argued that this demonstrated 'an indifference on Edward's part towards Scots law or the peculiarities of Scottish government more generally'.[45] The resultant 'fears of arbitrary and grasping rule in the localities' were important causes in the rebellions of 1297.[46] Nevertheless, by the late thirteenth century inquisitions were well established in Scotland.[47] From 1259 records survive of retours of inquests in sheriff courts to inquire into the nature of landholding which were initiated by royal writ (normally referred to as 'brieve' in Scottish historiography).[48] Although it has been assumed that such inquests were initiated by freeholders themselves as opposed to the crown,[49] they nevertheless give an indication of the means by which Scottish royal government could keep track of crown lands. On 18 August 1260 an inquest was ordered to determine what hospices and lodgings belonged to the bishop of Aberdeen 'in

44 Watson, *Under the Hammer*, 155–6.

45 Ibid. 35.

46 M. Brown, *The Wars of Scotland, 1214–1371* (Edinburgh, 2004), 181.

47 A search for 'inquest' in the People of Medieval Scotland database yields 45 records: http://db.poms.ac.uk/search/search?basic_search_type=factoid&query=inquest&ordering=factoidtype&years=1093–1296&show_all=false. The records are from various sources and a full discussion of them and their value is not possible here.

48 http://db.poms.ac.uk/record/source/4323/.

49 D. Broun, 'Rethinking Scottish Origins', in *Barbour's Bruce and its Cultural Contexts: Politics, Chivalry and Literature in Late Medieval Scotland*, ed. S. Boardman and S. Foran (Woodbridge, 2015), 168–9.

the burghs and the king's other manors'.[50] On 21 March 1262 Robert de Monte Alto, sheriff of Forfar and his bailies were ordered to hold an inquest to determine whether Margaret, Agnes, Suannoch, Christine and Marion, daughters of Simon, door-keeper of Montrose, were his nearest lawful heirs for his land of Inyaney in Kirkden, Angus.[51] One writ addressed to the sheriff of Dumbarton in 1271 ordered an inquest into the heirs of recently deceased crown tenants.[52] Another in 1262 ordered the sheriff of Lanarkshire to determine whether Henry de Wiston was a minor when he granted land in Lanarkshire to Hugh de Moravia, knight.[53] Inquests were also ordered by Alexander III to inquire regarding the claims of Robert the crossbowman to the king's garden in Elgin,[54] whether or not the peat moss of Waddenshope had been deforced by Robert Cruik,[55] and Adam de Liberacione's title to the land of Pettinain, Lanarkshire.[56] These writs were not standardised like English writs of *diem clausit extremum* (*dce*). They ordered inquests into specific events and therefore asked only for specific information. None of them asks for a level of detail comparable to that expected of a *dce* writ in England. Although the use of inquests was common in Scotland before Edward I's invasion of 1296, the surviving sources from Alexander III's reign indicate that those inquests were narrower in scope and sought only certain specific details.

Another set of sources to consider are the five recently edited medieval Scottish formularies dating from the early fourteenth century to the 1540s, which contain various example writs that are invaluable to understanding the practice of law and government in late medieval Scotland. The writs all differ slightly in their formulae and none of them are dated. The discussion here is confined to the earliest manuscript, the Ayr manuscript, since that is the closest in time to when the Scottish IPMs were taken. The manuscript dates from the reign of Robert I after Bannockburn (1314), and was owned by the Burgh of Ayr during the fifteenth century.[57] Among the various writs that order local sheriffs to conduct inquests the most striking, from the perspective of a historian of English IPMs, is the following:

> Brieve to a sheriff ordering an inquest of good men of the country to show if A de B, father *or* brother, uncle, sister, mother of B, the bearer, died in sasine as feu of the land of N, and if his son B is lawful heir of A in the land, is of lawful age, how much the land is worth annually, from whom held, by what service, in whose hands now, how, through whom, why, and since when, if he has offended against the king or kingdom whereby he ought not to recover his heritage by law, and if the king has

[50] *Regesta Regum Scottorum IV* Part 1: *The Acts of Alexander III*, ed. C.J. Neville and G.G. Simpson (Edinburgh, 2012), no. 28.
[51] Ibid., no. 36.
[52] Ibid., no. 76.
[53] Ibid., no. 221.
[54] Ibid., no. 32.
[55] Ibid., no. 40.
[56] Ibid., no. 203.
[57] *Scottish Formularies*, ed. A.A.M. Duncan, Stair Society lxiii (2011), 6–9.

> given the land to another. He is to retour to chancery the findings of the inquest under the seals of the sheriff and of some others present at the inquest, with this brieve.[58]

The information this brieve required the recipient sheriff to provide to the crown is remarkably similar to the information sought by writs of *dce* to escheators in England.

The problem with this evidence is that it is patchy because no central register of returned retours of inquest survives until the seventeenth century. It is distinctly possible that such a register existed for earlier centuries, since the acts of Alexander III contain writs ordering that the findings of various inquests were to be returned to the either king[59] or the king's chapel.[60] Scottish kings therefore had their own version of the English IPM system, though very few of the records survive. Alexander Grant found only 33 'of the countless retours that must have existed' within the estate records of Scottish nobility between 1314 and 1475. If such inquests were taken, and returned to some central location, then it can be speculated that such records were casualties of a shipwreck in 1661 in which one of the ships returning the records of the Scottish government that were moved to London on Oliver Cromwell's orders sank in the North Sea.[61] It is apparent that inquisitions were not alien concepts to the Scottish population in 1296. This argument should not be overstated to imply that Scottish and English governments were identical and that the only difference was the luck by which English sources survive. There were clear differences in the intensity of government in the two kingdoms.

The fact that inquests into landholding occurred in both Scotland and England affords the opportunity to make one further speculation about the principles that informed politics and royal administration in both kingdoms. The differences in the styles of royal government in Scotland and England are not simply historical curiosities but are fundamental for understanding the development of a distinct Scottish identity during the central Middle Ages. David Carpenter has approached the topic of Scottish royal government from an English perspective. Carpenter noted that the Scottish king in the thirteenth century imposed far lighter demands, particularly financial ones, on his subjects than his English counterpart and suggested that 'we may wonder whether the perception that, when it came to the demands of the crown, it was far better to be Scottish than to be English, was one of the driving developments of a separate Scottish identity

[58] Ibid., A22 (p. 19).

[59] *Acts of Alexander III*, nos 27, 32, 36, 40, 75.

[60] Ibid., nos 32, 76.

[61] A. Grant, 'Service and Tenure in Late Medieval Scotland, 1314–1475', in *Concepts and Patterns of Service in the Later Middle Ages*, ed. A. Curry and E. Matthew (Woodbridge, 2000), 147–8. Dr Grant thought it likely that retours were simply kept at a local level in Scotland. Since many writs include a clause ordering the inquest to be returned to chancery, it seems likely that at least some of them were so returned but have not survived.

in the thirteenth century'.[62] Although there were clear differences in terms of the specific burdens that each government placed on its subjects, in both Scotland and England justice and the law were two of the main pillars of royal legitimacy and state formation. Dauvit Broun has argued that property law – that is, the ability of the king of Scots to guarantee the property rights of everyone living within the kingdom – was an important factor that led to the formation of a sense of a distinctive Scottish identity before the Wars of Independence.[63] Retours of inquest in particular enabled the Scottish king's subjects, particularly the lesser landowners, to witness 'the king acting as guarantor of property in a new, more tangible way'.[64] From this, it is possible to detect in these inquisitions an underlying political principle that was shared in both Scotland and England, namely, that since the crown was the ultimate guarantor of property and all land was held of the crown, the king had the right to inquire about the specific nature of landholding within his kingdom. The important difference was the ways in which this principle manifested itself.

Calais

Another conquered land where IPMs were taken was in France, or, to be more precise, Calais. For almost five centuries after Edward III claimed the throne of France at Ghent on 8 February 1340,[65] kings of England also claimed to be kings of France. Successive kings of England, however, held only those French territories that were temporarily conquered during the Hundred Years' War. English kings, and in particular Henry V, were keen to stress that they were the legitimate kings of France and therefore ruled France in accordance with French customs and traditions. The existence of the Norman and Gascon rolls is a testament to the fact that English kings strove to keep their English and French territories separate. Calais was the only place in France where IPMs were taken. There are two compatible explanations for this. First, Calais was regarded as part of England, not France, and was therefore subject to English governmental practices as opposed to French ones. Edward III attempted to expel the town's French population, with only a few given leave to remain, though whether or not the entire population left Calais is uncertain at best.[66] Proclamations were sent out across eastern England encouraging new settlers in the town and, in October 1347, 189 separate grants of property in the town were recorded on the patent

[62] D.A. Carpenter, 'Scottish Royal Government in the Thirteenth Century from an English Perspective', in *New Perspectives on Medieval Scotland, 1093–1286*, ed. M.H. Hammond (Woodbridge, 2013), 117.

[63] D. Broun, 'Becoming a Nation: Scotland in the Twelfth and Thirteenth Centuries', in *Nations in Medieval Britain*, ed. H. Tsurushima (Donington, 2010), 97–100, 103.

[64] Broun, 'Rethinking Scottish Origins', 169.

[65] *EHD 1327–1485*, 66–7.

[66] S. Rose, *Calais: An English Town in France, 1347–1558* (Woodbridge, 2008), 23–4.

rolls.[67] For Edward III, Calais was part of England, with an English population, and therefore subject to English law and governmental practices. A second, more prosaic reason, for IPMs being taken in Calais as opposed to elsewhere in France is administrative ease. As David Grummitt has pointed out, Calais was as close to Westminster as the Midlands or the Home Counties, and much closer than other military frontiers such as Ireland or the Scottish marches. It was therefore 'not one of the mere peripheries of the realm'.[68] Calais' proximity to Westminster meant that it was just as easy, if not easier, to administer it as part of England, as opposed to administering it separately with Normandy or Gascony.

In total there were 47 IPMs taken in Calais during the first century of English occupation, which appear in calendars xiii to xxvi. The first inquisition taken at Calais was for Walter de Mauny, knight, on 23 June 1371 in response to a writ dated 5 March 1371.[69] The date does not coincide with any specific events or policy decisions. Calais had already been declared the staple for wool and woolfells on 9 February 1363, though the staple was removed in 1369 when the resumption of the French war was imminent. The governing of the town was handed over to a group of 26 English merchants in March 1363.[70] There is no evidence to suggest there was any formal decision to begin conducting IPMs in Calais other than the fact that a tenant-in-chief of the English crown had died holding English lands.

The common feature in all of the IPMs for Calais for the first century of English rule was the requirement of all property owners in the town to contribute towards the defence of the town by providing one or two watches each year. Here, it should be emphasised that those holding property were required to provide the watch for the whole town, not just one watchman. The clearest evidence for this is in the IPM for Thomas Lord Berkeley, in January 1537, which was recorded in English as opposed to Latin, and which states that he held several properties in the town 'by the service of fynde two watches' each year for the defence of Calais.[71] The emphasis on defence is unsurprising, given Calais' position as an English town in France turned which it into as a 'towne of were'.[72] Indeed, the grants of property that Edward III made in Calais explicitly stated that they were 'for the safe keeping of the king's town of Calais'.[73] Given the fact that most IPMs state that the tenants-in-chief were required to provide two watches per annum for the defence of the town, it is clear that the grants were to ensure that the town was defended on every night of the year. The arithmetic does not match exactly, as two vigils per grant would lead to 378 watches per year, but the correlation

[67] Ibid., 23–4; *CPR 1345–8*, 561–8.
[68] Grummitt, *Calais Garrison*, 9.
[69] *CIPM* xiii.148 (p. 118).
[70] Rose, *Calais*, 44, 46.
[71] C142/57/98 m. 2.
[72] Grummitt, *Calais Garrison*, 10.
[73] *CPR 1345–8*, 561–8.

is nonetheless suggestive. Edward's grants in 1347 were designed to ensure the continual defence of the town throughout the year. This also suggests that service required for a particular holding which is recorded in the IPMs should not simply be dismissed as outdated or anachronistic. Admittedly some services were probably never or only rarely performed, but this does not mean that all the services recorded were meaningless. The performance of services connected with defence was essential in a 'towne of were' such as Calais.

It can also be asserted with confidence that the subjects of the inquisitions were not themselves expected to go out themselves to keep watch over the town, but were expected to pay the wages of the town's watchmen for one or two nights per year. The IPM for Alice, widow of William Strerre, states that she held property to the value of 20*s* yearly 'beyond the cost of the watchman'.[74] The amount of property held probably corresponded with the level of contribution expected of an individual for the defence of the town. For instance, John Danyell's IPM from 1428 states that he held the inn called 'Oldcaleys' of the king 'by covering one watch to guard the vill',[75] which was 'provided by turns',[76] while Thomas Earl of Salisbury held an inn with two cellars and four shops in Calais by 'covering two watches yearly ... for the defence of the vill'.[77] John Darcy, knight, was required to provide only two watchmen, as opposed to an entire watch, because he held only two tenements in the town.[78] Moreover, the specific obligation tied to each property for contributing to the town's defences could form part of a widow's dower. The IPM for Thomas Mowbray, duke of Norfolk in 1399 states that he held the property in Calais 'by rent of £3 and the provision of a watchman for the [town] guard'.[79] When his widow, Elizabeth, died in 1425 her IPM stated that she was required to provide one-third of a watch yearly, which was part of her dower.[80]

Although it is clear that property was granted in Calais with the expectation that the recipients would contribute directly to the town's defences, calculating the precise financial burden of this obligation is problematic because few IPMs give an indication of the cost, all of which are incomplete. The IPM for Elizabeth, widow of William Latymer, knight, in 1389 states that she held the various properties in the town 'by service of doing two-thirds of two watches for safeguarding the town, which are estimated at 10*s* ...*d* yearly'.[81] The original is in a poor condition and it was impossible to read the number of pennies, even under UV light.[82] Rough calculations based on this incomplete evidence would suggest that the cost for two watches would be somewhere between 15*s* and 16*s*

74 *CIPM* xviii.729.
75 *CIPM* xxiii.5.
76 Ibid., 6.
77 Ibid., 262.
78 *CIPM* xix.974.
79 *CIPM* xviii.264; see also *CIPM* xix.335.
80 *CIPM* xxii.420.
81 *CIPM* xvi.714.
82 C136/55/34 m. 3.

3*d*. If one watch was half of this, then it would cost between 7*s* 6*d* and 8*s* 1½*d* for one vigil. Another IPM that hints at the financial burden and size of a specific watch is that for Thomas de Beauchamp, twelfth earl of Warwick, which states that he held the three messuages in the town 'by the service of 4*s* 2*d* rent and the provision of 3 watchmen for the safeguard of the town'.[83] The IPMs do not state how much the wages of the three watchmen were, but later evidence can provide an indication. The Calais Act of 1536, which prescribed what the composition and organisation of the Calais garrison should be, is a problematic source as it was an attempt to rectify problems in the garrison that had arisen in the late 1520s.[84] One of the Act's clauses stated that there were to be 'foure daye watches, that is to say two for the high Towre two for the Walles',[85] with another clause stating that a watchman was to be paid 6*d*.[86] It should be noted that that there were to be four 'watches', not 'watchmen', and therefore that the precise number of men required for the watch of the town is not specified. That a watchman was to be paid 6*d* a day suggests that the watchmen that the earl of Warwick was expected to find cost him 1*s* 6*d*, taking the total financial burden he faced to 5*s* 8*d*. Again, the arithmetic does not match exactly. If the 4*s* 2*d* that Warwick paid in rent was spent on watchmen paid at 6*d*, then this indicates that a further eight watchmen were recruited, but this leaves 2*d* unaccounted for. From this evidence it can be estimated that the financial burden on the tenants-in-chief in Calais for one watch was somewhere between 5*s* and 8*s* and therefore an annual burden between 10*s* and 16*s*, assuming they were required to provide two watches per annum. This compares with the 6*s* 8*d* in poll tax due in 1379 from a squire or merchant of sufficient means[87] and suggests that a not insubstantial burden was placed on the population of Calais to assist in paying for its own protection.

Evidence in IPMs taken in England indicates that this was approximately the standard cost of a watch at this time. For example, John Argentein held the manor of Little Wymondley, Hertfordshire 'by service of 6*s* 8*d* [i.e. half a mark] for watch and ward at the castle of Craven'.[88] The same amount was the service rendered for the guard of Pevensey Castle by Richard Rademelde for holding the manor of Blatchington, Sussex.[89] Edmund Earl of March held the manors of Great and Little Walsingham in Norfolk 'by service of paying 10*s* yearly to Norwich castle as watchman's fee'.[90] This obligation to pay the wages of the town's watch can be thought of as a form of indirect taxation. Medieval political

[83] *CIPM* xviii.492.

[84] Grummitt, *Calais Garrison*, 51; Rose, *Calais*, 126–8. For the full act see *SR* iii, 632–50.

[85] *SR* iii, 632.

[86] Ibid., 639.

[87] *EHD 1327–1485*, 125–6.

[88] *CIPM* xxii.282.

[89] *CIPM* xviii.371.

[90] *CIPM* xxii.503. This finding was repeated for the IPM for his widow Anne in 1432: *CIPM* xxiv.80.

doctrine held the king responsible for the welfare and preservation of the state but gave him no claims on his subjects' wealth except for 'the preservation of the state in times of exceptional need'. From the mid-fourteenth century prolonged Anglo-French warfare meant that there was a permanent need for taxation. The threat this posed to Parliament's right to refuse taxation was circumvented by recurrent grants of indirect taxes, particularly on wool exports.[91] Requiring crown tenants in Calais to contribute towards the cost of defending the town was not a tax as such, since there was no formal assent, yet it still conforms to the principle that the king's subjects were financially liable for contributing towards the defence of the kingdom. In this case the extra financial burdens were placed on those subjects who benefited the most from the expenditure of that money, i.e. those tenants-in-chief of the crown in Calais who were paying for the defence of their town.

The granting of land and property to settlers in return for military service was an established feature of English colonialism during the Middle Ages, most notably in Wales when, after the Edwardian conquest, 'generous allocations of land' were given to barons and their retainers which were held by military service.[92] Henry V adopted a similar policy in Normandy during the fifteenth century when he granted property throughout Normandy to English settlers who, in return, were expected to contribute to their own defence and security by either paying for or carrying out military service.[93] The principle behind this form of service was the same as the land settlement imposed after the Norman Conquest when William I granted lands in England to his Norman supporters, which were held in return for military service,[94] though this practice was not necessarily a Norman importation into England.[95] Recent work on the origins of bastard feudalism has argued that although more temporary bastard feudal ties were being created by nobles during Edward I's reign, more traditional feudal connections were still an important hallmark of society.[96] In terms of military service, Andrew Spencer has argued that during Edward I's reign, 'although lords had begun to act in a "bastard-feudal" way, they were still thinking in a "feudal"

91 G.L. Harriss, 'Medieval Doctrines in the Debates on Supply, 1610–1629', in *Faction and Parliament: Essays on Early Stuart History*, ed. K.M. Sharpe (Oxford, 1978), 75–7.

92 R.R. Davies, 'Colonial Wales', *Past and Present* lxv (1974), 5–7, quotation on 6.

93 C.T. Allmand, *Lancastrian Normandy, 1415–1450* (Oxford, 1983), 50–80, 187–210. For a similar discussion focused on towns throughout France see: N. Murphy, 'War, Government and Commerce: The Towns of Lancastrian France under Henry V's Rule, 1417–22', in *Henry V: New Interpretations*, ed. G. Dodd (York, 2013), 249–72.

94 D.C. Douglas, *William the Conqueror: The Norman Impact upon England* (London, 1964), 265–88.

95 See in particular: N. Brooks, 'The Archbishopric of Canterbury and the So-Called Introduction of Knight-Service into England', *Anglo-Norman Studies* xxxiv (2012), 41–62. I am grateful to Dr Ryan Lavelle for drawing my attention to this article.

96 A.M. Spencer, *Nobility and Kingship in Medieval England: the Earls and Edward I, 1272–1307* (Cambridge, 2014), 114–73.

way', since their idea of service remained bound up in land.[97] When Edward III granted property to Englishmen in return for providing for the town's defences, which the IPMs demonstrate, he was likewise thinking in a 'feudal' way, despite the fact that English armies were increasingly being recruited via indentured retainer as opposed to feudal levies.[98] One reason for the growth in bastard feudal methods of reward – that is, temporary cash payments as opposed to grants of land, which were regarded as more permanent – was that land was a finite resource and once it was granted such an act could not be undone easily.[99] Once new land was acquired via military conquest it was possible to grant that land in return for military service, as evident in those lands conquered by Edward I, Edward III and Henry V. The settlements Wales, Normandy and Calais were, like the Norman Conquest, distinctly feudal in nature. The fact that there are no known IPMs for Normandy or Gascony means that it is not possible to examine the extent to which land held in Normandy or Gascony was held by some form of military obligation, but the Calais IPMs do show this pattern in one conquered French territory.

This chapter has shown how the IPMs for Scotland and Calais shed light on different facets of the nature of English military conquest during the late medieval period. It should be emphasised that this chapter has been confined to discussing IPMs and that other aspects of English governmental activity are potentially fertile ground for further research. The Scottish IPMs show an attempt by Edward I to govern Scotland by initially using the existing local officials in Scotland before the appointment by Edward I of his own escheators in August 1296. In the case of jurors, local knowledge was required and therefore there was a necessity in using the local population. These jurors may have been familiar with the procedures of an inquisition into the nature of particular landholding even though thirteenth-century Scottish royal government conducted inquests on a more limited scale as compared to English IPMs. The Scottish IPMs differ from those in Calais, and in Wales and Ireland too, because they provide a glimpse, albeit minor, of the nature of landholding and feudal society in Scotland *before* an English invasion, whereas the IPMs in Calais, Wales and Ireland provide evidence for feudal settlements *after* an English invasion. The IPMs in Calais indicate that Calais was regarded as part of the king of England's English crown, not his French crown. In contrast to Scotland, no attempt was made in Calais to use pre-existing structures to conduct inquisitions but instead Calais was turned into an English town. Property was granted on the basis that those holding property were expected to assist in the running of the town's defences. IPMs show that this obligation remained tied to properties held in Calais throughout the

97 A.M. Spencer, 'The Comital Military Retinue in the Reign of Edward I', *HR* 83 (2010), 54.

98 McFarlane, *England*, 25–6.

99 M.A. Hicks, *Bastard Feudalism* (London, 1995), 24.

period of English occupation. Although the IPMs in Scotland and Calais reveal different aspects of English imperial government in the later Middle Ages, when taken together they highlight the fact that the process of conducting IPMs was an important means by which the king of England kept track of his lands and feudal rights in his English lands and beyond.

3

Inquisitions *Post Mortem* in Medieval Ireland

PAUL DRYBURGH

In his preface to the companion to *The Fifteenth-Century Inquisitions Post Mortem*, Michael Hicks highlights the achievements of the medieval IPMs project, arguing that 'It sets the agenda for the much fuller exploitation of a key source for many aspects of the late medieval English economy and society and sets out the rewards of more sustained study of the IPMs.'[1] As Gordon McKelvie demonstrates above, it is not just the history of medieval England which can be illuminated by improved access to and investigation of IPMs.[2] The present paper surveys those inquisitions relating to medieval Ireland filed in the English chancery between the reigns of Henry III and Henry V. It analyses the management of the IPM process between Westminster and Dublin, compares the roles of the Irish escheator and his English counterparts, examines the composition of IPM juries and assesses the significance of Irish lands to the feudal rights of the English crown during the Middle Ages. Although Irish IPMs are few in number, they supplement the broader governmental and seigneurial record and provide key data and penetrating insights into land and landed society in Ireland over two centuries. They are a valuable counterpoint to recent studies of the inquisition process in England.

The Sources and Their Publication

Inquisitions *post mortem* were legal enquiries held to answer specific questions concerning the rights of the crown to land and other feudal incidents following the death of tenants-in-chief. They were conducted in or near the locality concerned before officers of the crown, who took evidence from local witnesses to clarify the points at issue. Between 1240 and 1415, at least 178 IPM extents and associated writs and memoranda were returned to the English chancery from Ireland. These documents now survive in the main chancery IPM series (C 132–138) at The National Archives and relate to 79 individuals with possessions across Ireland. Calendared in English in 2007 alongside a similar number of Irish inquisitions in the chancery *ad quod damnum* (C 143) and Miscellaneous (C 145)

1 *IPM Companion*, xi.

2 Above, chapter 2.

series, they are now accessible with full extents and complete lists and an index of jurors.[3] In devising and compiling *Inquisitions and Extents of Medieval Ireland*, Brendan Smith and the present author aimed to create a fuller source-base in print for historians of the medieval Irish economy and society, and thereby to 'provoke new questions and encourage re-examination of familiar topics'.[4] In contrast to the main IPM calendar series, Herbert Sweetman's monumental five-volume *Calendar of Documents Relating to Ireland* prints lists of jurors and full translations of manorial extents for the reigns of Henry III and Edward I, yet the discussion and use of Irish IPMs has been slight[5] and confined mostly to local[6] rather than broader studies on society and economy,[7] although interdisciplinary studies are changing this situation.[8]

This comparative neglect may stem from several factors. Firstly, although most of the documents are legible, not all are in good condition, some having suffered significant damage from various causes.[9] Moreover, the archive is small compared with the large number of IPMs for medieval England,[10] even including the 68 inquisitions predominantly dealing with the forfeited estates of living individuals

[3] *Inquisitions and Extents of Medieval Ireland, 1240–1415* [hereafter *IEMI*], ed. P. Dryburgh and B. Smith (List and Index Society 320 (Kew, 2007)).

[4] *IEMI*, iv.

[5] *Calendar of Documents Relating to Ireland Preserved in Her Majesty's Record Office, London* [hereafter *CDI*], 5 vols, ed. H.S. Sweetman (Dublin, 1875–86).

[6] See, for example, H.F. Berry, 'The Manor of Mallow in the Thirteenth Century', *Journal of the Royal Society of Antiquaries of Ireland* [hereafter *JRSAI*] 24 (1894), 16–18 (which prints C 133/31, no. 1, m. 12); H.T. Knox, 'Occupation of Connaught by the Anglo-Normans after A.D. 1237', *JRSAI* 32 (1902), 132–8, 393–406; 33 (1903), 58–74, 179–89, 284–94 (C 135/36, nos 21–2); G.H. Orpen, 'The Earldom of Ulster', *JRSAI* 43 (1913), 30–46, 133–43; 44 (1914), 51–66; 45 (1915), 123–42; 50 (1920), 167–77; 51 (1921), 68–76 (C 135/36, nos 20, 25); D. MacIvor, 'The Estate of Benedict Pipard of Pippardeston, A.D. 1316', *Louth Archaeological Society Journal* 14(3) (1959), 165–9 (C 134/46, no. 34); M. Hennessy, 'Manorial Organisation in Thirteenth-Century Tipperary', *Irish Geography* 29(2) (1996), 116–25 (C 132/1, no. 19).

[7] A key exception is Kevin Down, 'Colonial Society and Economy in the High Middle Ages', in *A New History of Ireland II: Medieval Ireland, 1169–1534*[hereafter *NHI*], ed. A. Cosgrave (Oxford, 1987), 439–91.

[8] *The Dublin Region in the Middle Ages: Settlement, Land-use and Economy*, ed. M. Murphy and M. Potterton (Dublin, 2010).

[9] For example, C 133/32, no. 7, m. 16 – conservation work (*IEMI*, no. 54); C 133/130, mm 65–78 – large sections illegible (*IEMI*, no. 147).

[10] Campbell and Bartley, *Atlas*, 30 states that there are 9,292 IPMs for England in the period 1300–49 alone. It has proved impossible, however, to reconcile my much lower figure for the entire corpus of Irish IPMs with the authors' 324 'extant and usable' IPMs for just that period, for which I calculate only 105, excluding an assignment of dower (*IEMI*, no. 237) and a proof of age (*IEMI*, no. 113). The authors do not substantiate their figure and the situation is further confused by the number of lords with land in Ireland for which IPMs exist, which they give as nineteen. My calculations based on the published IPMs suggest this should be twenty-two: *IEMI*, nos 104, 113, 133–58, 163, 170, 178–81, 187–93, 195–219, 228–37, 240, 251–67, 273–85, 288–93.

and other regalian rights, extracted from the IPM series into the Irish subseries of Chancery Miscellanea (C 47).[11] Lastly, the material is limited in its chronological and geographical coverage. Over 75% of Irish IPMs are dated between 1280 and 1350, with no IPMs for some modern Irish counties. Patchy survival of documents provides challenges for those using IPMs to draw reliable conclusions over time of local and national circumstances.[12] Throughout the period under discussion, furthermore, the Dublin government's authority was increasingly restricted by military and social interaction between native and settler communities. It became more inhibited from pressing royal rights in a land divided into Anglicised shired and manorialised areas and liberties, frontier areas where ethnicity, identity and loyalties blurred, and into large and expanding territories owing allegiance to native potentates outside the remit of the inquisition.[13] Although many more inquisitions were commissioned and held than those for which documents survive, a closer examination of both the IPMs and records of the English and Irish administrations reveals much of the IPM process relating to the rights of the crown in Ireland.

Administration of Irish IPMs: Overview

From the accession of John in 1199, the English king was styled 'Lord of Ireland' and, over the next fifty years, military conquest and colonisation accelerated the transfer of English legal and bureaucratic institutions to Ireland under Henry II's 1177 ordinance for its governance.[14] The life grant by Henry III in 1232 of

[11] Those for Edward I's reign have been printed in *CDI*: C 47/10/13/9, 19 (*CDI 1252–84*, nos 1056, 1181, 1205, 1482), 21–3 (*CDI 1252–84*, nos 1520, 1548, 1613); 14/1–6 (*CDI 1252–84*, nos 1416, 1666, 1801, 1898, 1918, 1953), 9 (*CDI 1285–92*, no. 115), 10 (*CDI 1252–84*, no. 2344), 16, 17–18 (*CDI 1285–92*, nos 940, 967); 15/1–2 (*CDI 1285–92*, nos 1087, 1142), 3, 4 (*CDI 1285–92*, no. 1075), 5, 6 (*CDI 1293–1301*, no. 176); 17/7–8 (*CDI 1302–07*, nos 198, 239), 10–11 (*CDI 1302–07*, nos 271, 335), 14–15 (*CDI 1302–07*, nos 367, 437), 18 (*CDI 1302–07*, no. 547), 24 (*CDI 1302–07*, no. 181). Those for the next three reigns are largely unpublished: C 47/18/10, 12, 17–19; 18/14; 19/2, 5–7; 20/1–2, 4, 8, 11, 14; 22/1, 5–8, 11–12, 15–17; 23/1–5, 9–10; 24/1, 3–4, 10, 12.

[12] Assuming my calculations are reasonable, then those 105 inquisitions for the period 1300–49 make up 59% of the surviving medieval Irish IPMs in chancery, with another thirty from the final two decades of the thirteenth century making 76% of the total. But, taken globally for the 1300–49 period, 105 constitutes only 1.1% of the total calculated by Campbell and Bartley. Their 324 IPMs for Ireland in this period, and those nineteen lords for whom IPMs survive, pale in comparison, moreover, to 9,616 total IPMs (3.3%) and 1,826 total lords (1.03%) for England and Wales, respectively. My figures would reduce these percentages further.

[13] R.F. Frame, 'Power and Society in the Lordship of Ireland', in idem, *Ireland and Britain, 1170–1450* (London, 1998), 191–220; R.R. Davies, 'Frontier Arrangements in Fragmented Societies: Ireland and Wales', in *Medieval Frontier Societies*, ed. R. Bartlett and A. Mackay (Oxford, 1989), 77–100.

[14] H.G. Richardson and G.O. Sayles, *Administration of Ireland, 1172–1377* (Dublin, 1963); *NHI*, 143–4, 172.

the chancery of Ireland to his chancellor, Bishop Ralph Neville of Chichester, facilitated the development of an administrative system centred on Dublin closely modelled on that operating in England.[15] From around this time – the first surviving Irish IPM dates to 1240–42[16] – and over the next two centuries, whenever deceased tenants-in-chief held land in Ireland and England, IPMs should have been held in both countries. The Dublin government received orders from England, but also came to employ the same portfolio of writs and initiate the same inquisition processes as in England regarding the feudal rights of the English crown in Ireland. Documentary evidence for the operation of the IPM process between Westminster and Dublin is incomplete. It certainly generated, as in England, extents of property, proofs of age, assignments of dower and partitions between coheirs. Michael Hicks' assertion that the IPM documentation is merely a part of the record evidence applies equally to Ireland.[17] Much original source material held in Ireland was lost in the destruction of the Public Record Office of Ireland in June 1922.[18] Only tantalising glimpses of medieval practice remain from records in the English chancery and reconstructions from antiquarian and later calendaring.

The IPM process

Nevertheless, a reconstruction of the IPM process relating to Irish lands of tenants-in-chief of the English crown may be attempted. Inquisitions were initiated by one of a number of writs either sent into Ireland from the English chancery under the great or privy seal, or issued by the Irish chancery under the great seal of Ireland.[19] The basic writ was *diem clausit extremum* (*dce*), informing the recipient that a tenant had died (literally 'closed his last day'), providing for the seizure

[15] *Close Rolls Preserved in the Public Record Office London 1231–4* (1905), 112–13. For a recent overview of the development of the administration centred on Dublin see *A Calendar of Irish Chancery Letters, c. 1244–1509* [hereafter *CIRCLE*], ed. P. Crooks, Historical Introduction, (https://chancery.tcd.ie/content/irish-chancery-rolls#method-of-enrolment), accessed 11 May 2015. *CIRCLE* reconstructs in digital form the rolls and letters of the medieval Irish chancery. Subsequent references to CR and PR are to these now-lost Irish chancery Close and Patent rolls, not to their still-surviving equivalents produced by the English royal chancery.

[16] Extent of the lands of Richard de Burgh: *IEMI*, nos 1–2.

[17] *IPM Companion*, 5. In terms of the Irish chancery, *CIRCLE* collates a wealth of supplementary evidence from the Irish Close and Patent rolls. Those looking for information on tenants and jurors, as well as disputes of land or property, should scour Irish legal records, published in the *Reports of the Deputy Keeper of the Public Records and Keeper of the State Papers of Ireland*, 52 vols (Dublin, 1869–1920), and unpublished in Dublin, National Archives of Ireland, RC 7 & 8 and KB 2 series.

[18] For a vivid modern account see *CIRCLE*, 'Destruction of the Irish Chancery Rolls, 1304–1922' (http://chancery.tcd.ie/content/destruction-irish-chancery-rolls-1304-1922).

[19] C. Noble, 'Writs and the Inquisitions Post Mortem: How the Crown Managed the System', *IPM Companion*, 183–200.

of his lands, the empanelment of a jury to inquire into the annual value of those lands and what rights the crown had, then returning the findings to chancery.[20] Around 55 *dce* writs concerning tenancies in Ireland are filed at The National Archives (TNA), of which half a dozen were issued in Ireland.[21] Other writs include those by which heirs proved their age in order to enter their inheritance (*de etate probanda*) and by which widows claimed their dower third after the IPM had been taken (*de dote assignanda*).[22] Only five such writs survive in the English chancery material and they are therefore not considered in detail in this survey.

The issue of a *dce* writ often followed information on the death of a tenant-in-chief reaching chancery where the deceased was known, believed, or sometimes only suspected of holding lands of the crown. Further writs might be issued as the process stalled or became disputed, in many cases after the submission of a petition. In more militarised Ireland, the need for a smooth transition between deceased tenant and active heir (or keeper) often gave urgency to the transition. A writ of April 1282 demanded the taking and return by Lammas of inquisitions concerning the counties and serjeanties held by John fitz Thomas, a major magnate in southern and south-western Ireland. The writ was issued on the petition of his heir Thomas fitz Maurice, whose interests were being affected by extensive waste and destruction to John's estates in counties Waterford, Kerry and Cork. The inquisitions themselves were delayed, as the jurors could not be convened until Lammas.[23]

This particular writ was *de certiorari*, one of around 50 filed in the chancery IPM series (*c*.25–30% of the total). These writs ordered royal officials to certify the veracity of an inquisition previously compiled but not yet returned to chancery, or to establish certain facts in response to a claim from affected parties, such as the name and age of an heir, the true value of lands and rights attached to inheritances (*certiorari super vero valore*), or the extent of lands held in knight service and presentation to churches (*certiorari (super vero valore) de feodis militum et advocacionibus ecclesiarum*).[24] They often relate to elite landowners, where accurate information on the value of estates and services and what the king or others might receive was crucial to the functioning of land tenure and patronage.[25]

The number of certification writs reflects difficulties of communication. Clearly, the English chancery was sometimes starved of the information it needed from Ireland, and the issue of a *dce* writ did not always bring about the desired

20 Carpenter, 'Introduction', 2–4, 9–11; *IPM Companion*, 3–7, 117.

21 *IEMI*, nos 92, 273, 295, 309, 323, 341.

22 Dower: Marie de St Pol, 1325 (*IEMI*, no. 237); Margaret Darcy, 1415 (nos 347–8). Proofs of age: Herbert, son and heir of John de Marisco, 1299 (no. 99); Gilbert, son of Thomas de Clare, 1302 (no. 113); Maurice, son of Maurice earl of Desmond, 1357 (no. 324).

23 *IEMI*, nos 38–45.

24 As in the 1282–4 IPMs for William de Mohun of Kildare: *IEMI*, nos 46, 58; and Richard, son of Richard de Geyton, 1309: *IEMI*, no. 163.

25 *IEMI*, no. 195 – Thomas de Clare, 1321; no. 228 – Aymer de Valence, earl of Pembroke, lord of Wexford and Carlow, 1324.

results. Bruce Campbell highlights the 'very long tail of inquisitions held after a delay of months or even years' from the death of a tenant-in-chief in the early fourteenth century. He attributes this delay to remoteness, inefficiency and pressure of events, particularly in the Lordship of Ireland, although also in the northernmost and south-western shires of England and the Welsh marches.[26] He cites the case of inquisitions on Giles de Badlesmere's Cork and Thomond estates, which took a decade after his death in 1338 to be finalised, causing frustration to his four heiresses and their husbands.[27] The documentation here shows the malign intrusion of Maurice fitz Thomas, first earl of Desmond.[28] Giles had inherited lands at Ardrahin in Connacht, Kinsalebeg (co. Waterford), Mahoonagh (co. Limerick) and Youghal and Inchiquin (co. Cork) from his mother following the death of her nephew, Thomas fitz Richard de Clare, in 1321 and her own death in 1333.[29] Desmond had initially been appointed custodian of these lands in 1321, but over the next 30 years he tried to wrest control from the absentee lords. In 1342 the deputy justiciar, chancellor and treasurer of Ireland together certified the English chancery of the recent descent and tenure of these lands, having searched the rolls and memoranda of the Dublin exchequer.[30] They were responding to a writ reciting previous IPM evidence from the Irish chancery to prove Badlesmere's tenure from the king and the heirs' right. They also detailed another inquisition taken by Thomas Charlton, bishop of Hereford, then keeper of Ireland, who had returned at the suggestion of Desmond (previously granted custody of the lands by the Irish council) that these lands were held not of the king, but from Desmond himself, 'thereby plotting to disinherit the king'.[31] Despite further IPMs taken in 1343, which reasserted the heirs' claims, Desmond nevertheless entered and administered the lordships. The heirs obtained their inheritance only following Desmond's rebellion and rehabilitation in the mid-1340s and after final IPMs had been held by virtue of other writs from Westminster in April 1348.[32]

This extreme delay is not isolated. Other instances, such as the failure for over a year of Irish authorities to return to England the inquisitions taken within twelve weeks of the death of James, first earl of Ormond in February 1338, suggest an inherent inefficiency of administering IPMs across the Irish Sea.[33] Climatic factors played their part: a notification issued by the Irish chancery on

26 Campbell and Bartley, *Atlas*, 16–17.

27 *IEMI*, nos 288–9, 291–3.

28 For whom and for what follows, see K. Waters, 'The Earls of Desmond in the Fourteenth Century' (PhD thesis, Durham University, 2004), 74–80; G.O. Sayles, 'The Rebellious First Earl of Desmond', in *Medieval Studies Presented to Aubrey Gwynn, S.J.*, ed. J.A. Watt, J.B. Morrall and F.X. Martin (Dublin, 1961), 203–29.

29 *Rep. DKI* 44, 59.

30 An interesting sidelight on where IPM documentation may have been stored in Dublin.

31 *IEMI*, no. 288.

32 *IEMI*, nos 291–2.

33 *IEMI*, nos 273–84 – *dce* writ, 18 February 1338 (Naas), inquisitions, February–April, writ *de certiorari* (Kennington), 3 March 1339.

22 October 1287 to the chief justice of the king's bench at Westminster excused William Whiterel from appearance in a suit about land in the new English town of Colp, as he 'had been prevented from attending by storms at sea and contrary winds'.[34] Although the passage of information between Ireland and England may therefore have been more at the mercy of events, nevertheless an examination of the transit of writs and inquisitions gives a more positive picture.

The mean average time between the issue of an IPM writ, together with writs and inquisitions *ad quod damnum* and miscellaneous, and the holding of an inquisition in Ireland is around 143 days (20 weeks), falling to 100 days when only IPMs are counted.[35] Examining IPM writs from England only, the mean average is around 123 days (eighteen weeks),[36] but taking median averages, these figures fall to 85 days (twelve weeks), 58 days (eight weeks) and 76 days (eleven weeks), respectively. As Campbell and Bartley have shown, in fourteenth-century England, 'once a writ had been issued most escheators and their deputies acted on their instructions with remarkable promptness', often holding the inquisition by the third week.[37] Clearly, therefore, Ireland lagged behind England, but not greatly, although these figures are averages and belie variations in both transit and bureaucratic methodology and authority.

When tenants died in England, the interval between death and issue of a preliminary writ could be brief.[38] The writ of 30 August 1282, issued at Ruthin (Denbighshire), for William de Mohun, who had Kildare estates, reveals that he had died only five days before at Ottery in Devon.[39] Similarly, the extent taken at Wexford on 26 July 1324 into the lands late of Aymer de Valence, earl of Pembroke, begins by noting that the earl had died on 23 June, three days before the issue of the *dce* writ.[40] These cases relate to men of substance and suggest that government could move rapidly where the value to the crown of assertion of royal authority and opportunity to profit, or to prospective heirs in swift transition to lordship, was obvious. It is more difficult to reconstruct such information for tenants lower down the social scale. Some inquisitions were held within six weeks of the issue of the writ in England, such as that taken by Walter de la Haye, escheator, on 27 April 1292 into the lands late of Robert de Cruys at Naul (co. Dublin) in response to a writ issued at Westminster on 25 March,

[34] *CIRCLE*, CR 15 Edw. I, §4.

[35] Both sets of figures include writs issued in England and Ireland. This figure of 100 days discounts an interval of 2951 days, almost eight years between 1309 and 1317, in an inquisition *ad quod damnum* relating to Godfrey fitz Henry's messuage in Leixlip (co. Kildare): *IEMI*, nos 164–5.

[36] These two figures exclude IPMs where the date of some of the inquisitions is not certain, such as the IPM for William de Burgh in 1333: *IEMI*, nos 251–67.

[37] Campbell and Bartley, *Atlas*, 17.

[38] But see ibid. 188–9 for discussion of the often lengthy intervals between death and writ in the fifteenth century.

[39] *IEMI*, no. 46.

[40] *IEMI*, no. 228.

33 days previously.[41] Almost 70 years later, the IPM for Elizabeth, widow of Bartholomew Badlesmere, returned extents for Dundalk (co. Louth) and Duleek (co. Meath) on 18 and 20 June 1360, respectively, 37 and 39 days after the writ had been issued at Westminster.[42] In these examples, both easterly, accessible locations and transit of writs in spring and summer may have helped.[43] Of course, these timings do not reveal the entire period within which an IPM would be initiated and returned to chancery following the death of the tenant-in-chief concerned. The evidence to answer these questions is fragmentary at best and there are no examples where the process can be viewed in full.

Conversely, those IPMs which vastly exceed the average and produced the secondary writs discussed above were more troublesome. The IPM for John, son and heir of John Biset, taken at Olderfleet (co. Antrim) in August 1279 took place 284 days after the issue of the original writ,[44] and on 3 November 1385 the IPM for Marie de St Pol, countess of Pembroke, was taken at Wexford 534 days after the writ had been issued.[45] The increasingly fragile authority of the Dublin administration from the late thirteenth century, followed by decades of famine, pestilence and war, might account for this delay, although the extent of the task in assessing large, disturbed estates with officials and tenants affected by war might also be a factor. Law and politics might also conspire to delay proceedings. Only on 11 March 1280, a full 607 days after Edward I had commanded him, did the justiciar Robert de Ufford hold an inquiry into the rightful descent of lands claimed in Ardsallagh (co. Waterford) by Geoffrey de Prendergast, 497 days after the requested certification.[46] The jurors had to assess rival claims and past actions of chief governors, in this case John fitz Thomas having claimed the lands after the supposed rebellion of the original parceners. Having repeatedly petitioned the Lord Edward, whose willingness to demur was subsequently challenged by the justiciar Stephen Longespée, John had seized the lands and administered them, causing Longespée's successor Richard de la Rochelle to seize them for the king and to refuse to release them. No doubt the delay here reflected hard bargaining locally, as well as administrative correctness, all of which could weaken links in the bureaucratic chain.

The majority of Irish IPMs were held between 40 and 80 days (or between seven and eleven weeks) after the issue of the writ in England. The mean average time between a writ's arriving and an IPM's being taken is 48 days, the median

41 *IEMI*, no. 86.
42 *IEMI*, nos 328–9. Other examples include *IEMI*, 195 (Gloucester–Knockainy, 38 days); 228 (Tonbridge–Wexford, 30 days); 291 (Westminster–Youghal, 34 days).
43 An exception is *IEMI*, nos 157–8, the IPM for Geoffrey de Liziniaco, which took 34 days to get from Dover to Dublin in February/March 1308.
44 *IEMI*, no. 36.
45 *IEMI*, no. 345. Other examples of IPMs taking over 150 days between writ and inquisition are *IEMI*, nos 30, 34, 113, 187, 192, 252, 253, 256, 304, 335, 344.
46 *IEMI*, no. 34.

average 26 days.[47] The situation for tenants dying in Ireland is less clear cut, due to scanty evidence, but the interval between death and writ is assumed to be shorter. Unique evidence is provided by the IPMs for James, first earl of Ormond, who died at Gowran (co. Kilkenny) on 16 or 18 February 1338. Writs, attested by John Charlton, the justiciar, were issued at Naas, 50 miles away, almost immediately on 18 February.[48] Given the earl's status and his struggles to assert himself against the native Irish in Tipperary and south Leinster in the 1330s, the chief governor presumably initiated particularly prompt proceedings to value his castles, manors and lands for the king, to calculate dower for the countess and to install a strong custodian for the infant heir.[49] The military and financial imperative to the Dublin government in managing Irish IPMs efficiently may have dictated swift action upon receipt of information, particularly for magnate inheritances. Those imperatives would otherwise have been countered by the disturbed state of the Lordship, the need to prioritise military campaigns to assert feudal rights and the growing inability of the fourteenth-century exchequer to pay officials and operate efficiently.[50]

Undoubtedly, the IPM process relating to Irish lands of tenants-in-chief is now obscured by centuries of Irish archival losses. The chancery fine rolls (TNA series C 60) record *dce* writs, usually addressed to the escheator of Ireland, ordering the seizure of Irish lands of several individuals for whom no resultant IPM survives. In the early fourteenth century there are *dce* writs but no inquisitions for some of the leading magnates of Ireland: Edmund Butler, earl of Carrick (1321); John Hastings, lord of Abergavenny, whose son inherited the earldom of Pembroke and the liberty of Wexford (1325); and Richard de Burgh, earl of Ulster (1326).[51] Despite the difficult military situation in Ireland after the invasion of Edward Bruce (1315–18) and the contemporary famine,[52] IPMs must have been carried out for such men. Extensive IPMs were later returned for Butler's son, James, first earl of Ormond, and de Burgh's grandson.[53] There is indeed proof that an IPM for Edmund Butler was taken and returned into the Irish chancery in the petition of 1327 of his son to have prise of wines from royal towns in Ireland as of his inheritance, which had been omitted from the writ for delivering his estates. The endorsed response called for examination of the inquisition [taken upon a

47 Evidence from endorsements on the writs.

48 *IEMI*, nos 273–85.

49 R.F. Frame, 'Butler, James, first earl of Ormond (*c*.1305–1338), magnate', *ODNB*: www.oxforddnb.com/view/article/50021?docPos=3 (accessed 13 July 2015).

50 For which see J.A. Watt, 'The Anglo-Irish Colony Under Strain, 1327–99', *NHI* II, 352–96.

51 Respectively *CFR 1319–27*, 71, 326, 409; *CIPM* vi.357, 457 (Butler), 612 (Hastings). There appears to be no IPM for Richard de Burgh.

52 The classic accounts are R.F. Frame, 'The Bruces in Ireland, 1315–18', *Irish Historical Studies* (1973), 3–37, reprinted in *Ireland and Britain*, 71–98; idem, *English Lordship in Ireland, 1318–1361* (Oxford, 1982).

53 *IEMI*, nos 251–67 (de Burgh), 273–85 (Butler).

writ] of *dce* returned into chancery after the death of the petitioner's father, and either to make delivery or summon jurors.[54] Where jurors found that the subject of an IPM held nothing in chief, moreover, returns could still find their way to chancery and were not always discarded, as with the 1351 inquisition for Robert Cokerel taken at Trim (co. Meath).[55]

These examples provide evidence that some IPMs, wherever ordered, could or were expected to be returned into the Irish chancery, records of which reveal IPMs taken solely at the initiative of the Dublin government for tenants with lands only in the Lordship, with their return to Dublin for processing and filing. In October 1391, for instance, the justiciar inspected and exemplified a writ and resultant IPM for William Roche, lord of Tullow (co. Tipperary), by which the escheator was ordered to inquire into the lands that William held on the day he died and return the same into the chancery of Ireland.[56] Such examples mostly date from the late fourteenth and fifteenth centuries, when management of Irish escheats weighed more heavily on the Irish government as the extent of the Lordship shrank.

Administration of Irish IPMs: The Escheator

The IPM system in Ireland, unlike that in England, where various mechanisms were trialled in the thirteenth and fourteenth centuries,[57] was managed by the escheator, who generally had authority in the area covered by royal administration throughout the medieval period. The role was never static and was bound to the relative value over time to the English crown of feudal revenues in Ireland. Its importance waxed with the emphasis placed on escheats during the reigns of the first two Edwards, but later waned as fewer tenants-in-chief held estates in Ireland and several office holders failed to fulfil their commissions responsibly. Consequently, the escheator enjoyed broad responsibilities and the bulk of his duties mirrored those of his English counterparts. He acted on writs from chancery, Westminster and Dublin relating to the management of the feudal revenues of the crown and was the primary official responsible for presiding over IPM juries and returning their findings.[58] However, in Ireland ecclesiastical

[54] SC 8/171/8522, printed in *Documents on the Affairs of Ireland before the King's Council*, ed. G.O. Sayles (Dublin, 1979), 130–1, no. 159. For the writ, see *CCR 1327–30*, 84.

[55] *IEMI*, no. 299. See also C 47/10/18/19, where a jury returned that Roger Mortimer of Chirk, then languishing in the Tower, held nothing in Ireland in right of his late wife, Lucy le Wafre.

[56] *CIRCLE*, PR 15 Ric. II, §106. Other detailed inquisitions returned upon writs of *dce* can be found, for example, at *CIRCLE*, CR 2 Hen. VI, §5 (James Uriell); PR 5 Hen. VI, §30 (Janico Dartas); CR 14 Hen. VI, §6 (William Darcy); CR 19 Hen. VI, §1 (Christopher Preston).

[57] Carpenter, 'Introduction', 5, 8–11.

[58] For an overview see A.J. Otway-Ruthven, *A History of Medieval Ireland* (London, 1968),

lands also came under his jurisdiction. Temporalities of episcopal sees or monastic houses fell to him. The grant of the escheatry to Master William de Bagpuize in April 1257 was made with the keepership of all void archbishoprics, bishoprics, crosslands and priories in Ireland, and 'of other escheats reserved to the king's use in his grant to the Lord Edward of the land of Ireland ...'.[59] In 1270, the prior and convent of St Thomas the Martyr, Dublin made fine in £20 that the escheator might grant royal assent to the election of a new abbot, and then restore his temporalities if confirmed.[60] Even during the early fifteenth century, escheators managed temporal estates of vacant sees: in 1431 Thomas Haukeslowe was ordered to deliver his temporalities to the new bishop of Cork and Cloyne.[61]

Additionally, during the period under consideration, the escheator sat on the Irish council and was one of the king's chief ministers. Evidence for this is sparse but the honour persisted: in 1406 Henry Stanyhurst, deputy escheator, is named as a councillor.[62] This role conferred military and legal functions which took precedence over administrative tasks and brought the escheator to the fore in moments of transition and controversy. In 1272, for example, John of Sandford, with the bishop of Meath and the justiciar, was commanded to oversee the oath of fealty to Edward I.[63] In December 1294, de la Haye was commissioned with the treasurer and Robert Bagot to inquire concerning articles relating to the corrupt activities of William de Vescy, the justiciar.[64]

Reforms during Edward III's reign united the escheatorship with custody of markets and weights and measures. Also, from around this time onwards, escheators regularly, and to the consternation of the political community, were granted permission to execute their office by deputy, as by the petition of Thomas Bathe in 1439.[65] Sub-escheators at county and national level had probably always been required since the formalisation of the escheatry in the late thirteenth century, but the fifteenth century witnessed endemic absentee office holding.[66] Throughout much of the Middle Ages, the escheator received a static fee of £40

161–2. Abundant evidence will be found for these standard duties in *IEMI*, *CIPM* and the other Chancery roll calendars.

59 *CPR 1247–58*, 551 (23 April 1257). His fee was 20 marks per annum, although this was supplemented in July 1260 by a grant of a benefice worth 50 marks annually: *CPR 1258–66*, 85.

60 *CFR 1269–70*, no. 1584 (*c*.13 May 1270).

61 *CIRCLE*, PR 10 Hen. VI, §9.

62 *CIRCLE*, PR 7 Hen. IV, §126.

63 *CPR 1272–81*, 2.

64 *CPR 1292–1301*, 108. For de Vescy see Otway-Ruthven, *Medieval Ireland*, 150, 174, 209–12, 214.

65 E 28/62/35. The letter patent of appointment upon petition is *CPR 1436–41*, 302 (11 July 1439). Other petitions include that of John Aldelyme: E 28/3/23 (17 February 1392).

66 Hugh de Burgh acted as sub-escheator of Ireland in 1339–41, for example: *Irish Exchequer Payments 1270–1446* [hereafter *IEP*], ed. P. Connolly (Dublin, 1998), 396.

per annum with a 40*s* allowance for robes.[67] By 1439, however, Thomas Bathe was appointed to an office to which 'there is no fee or reward attached'.[68]

The escheator also frequently presided over *ad quod damnum* inquiries, taken following the introduction of mortmain licences in 1279. These had initially regulated the alienation of secular land to the Church, but in the fourteenth century came to have more general usage.[69] In this role, the escheator exercised some jurisdiction over the flow of patronage within Ireland and also the preservation and/or use of land for military purposes. In 1342, the escheator Roger Darcy returned the findings of an inquiry into whether the king might grant Thomas de Blakeburne in fee, at his petition, six carucates of wasteland previously destroyed by the Irish in the marches of Leinster.[70] Thomas offered to find a hobelar and caparisoned horse for the better security of these marches in war in return, he having fought continually in the king's service in the marches near Saggart (co. Dublin) for over a decade to personal cost.[71] The jurors found that such a grant would be to the king's use, but would prejudice royal tenants, both English and Irish, in the surrounding area who took their easements and pastured animals there. Striking a balance between the interests of royal (and other) tenants and the military realities on the ground increasingly became an important aspect of the escheator's role. The military experience of several escheators while in office served to sharpen their focus.

On 15 July 1290 the officials of the Dublin exchequer were ordered to associate themselves with some of the Irish council

> whenever required by the escheator [Walter de la Haye] to view and allow his expenses for his custody of castles, manors and heirs in the king's hand, of difficult marches, for attacks on rebels, and in going and staying with a great body of armed men in the said marches, castles, manors and lands, for money spent on munition and for horse and foot for the king's defence, and having regard to his robes and wages, as the king is unwilling that he should come to him in person, or send messengers so frequently to claim these allowances, at great risk and expense.[72]

This is perhaps the best contemporary summary of the complexity of the escheator's role. Unrest in Ireland, almost endemic, often necessitated aggression, military ability and in-depth cultural awareness beyond mere knowledge of the legal and practical niceties of land and inheritance law. Walter himself had only a month previously been empowered to 'treat with all Irishmen offending against

[67] For which see *IEP*, *passim*.
[68] E 28/62/35.
[69] *IEMI*, nos 286, 294, 303, 310–18, 326–7, 330, 342–3. For the system see P. Brand, 'The Mortmain Licensing System 1280–1307', in A.L. Jobson (ed.), *English Government in the Thirteenth Century* (Woodbridge, 2004), 87–96.
[70] *IEMI*, no. 287.
[71] For the local situation, see Á. Foley, *The Royal Manors of Medieval Co. Dublin: Crown and Community* (Dublin, 2013), 171–86.
[72] *CPR 1281–92*, 378.

the king's fealty', and here he would have negotiated with both the settler and native communities.[73]

Following the Bruce invasion of 1315–18, in which violence spread across Ireland, the military role of the escheator expanded. Payments in Irish exchequer issue rolls reveal a dual role in managing escheats and restraining the king's enemies. John Morice received £40 as a gift in 1335–37 as compensation for going to Connacht to seize certain lands for the king and in accompanying the deputy justiciar to subdue Irish felons in 1334–35.[74] Morice had suffered in his normal duties in Connacht and Munster two years previously, receiving 100 marks for 'robberies committed against him by Irish enemies and rebels of the king'.[75]

IPM Jurors and Their Evidence

Information supplied to the crown through IPMs was provided by sworn juries. Irish juries usually consisted of twelve local men who presented their evidence before the escheator or other royal officials, although larger groups were deemed necessary for IPMs relating to important lands of wealthy and powerful individuals. In 1288, 39 men returned their findings on the Cork lands, properties and services of Thomas de Clare, lord of Thomond.[76] As in England, juries were selected and empanelled by the sheriff of the county in which the inquisition was to be heard. One IPM gives insights into the selection process. On 3 July 1282, writs of *venire facias* were issued to the sheriffs of Cork, Limerick and Kerry, rehearsing the petition of Thomas fitz Maurice for restoration of his inheritance in the lands formerly of John fitz Thomas, and ordering them to summon before the justiciar or his deputy at Kilmallock (co. Limerick) 'all of the more discreet, law-worthy and trustworthy free tenants' of their bailiwicks.[77] Schedules attached to the returned inquisition list several dozen men, knights and free tenants in each county, from whom the jury would be selected, the Limerick and Kerry writs naming nine knights who should be empanelled. Those who eventually served are marked '*iur[atus]*'; other names are struck through, being exempted for reasons now lost to us, with the exception of the Limerick juror David Gos, who is described as 'infirm'. Yet more are either marked with a cross or just not annotated. The Kerry document also names two summoners, presumably the ultimate source of the annotations.

These documents are suggestive of a careful empanelment process, only 11

[73] *CPR 1281–92*, 360 (5 June 1290).

[74] *IEP*, 622. During this period he had also served in Ulster 'to subdue certain Irish felons and enemies of the king ... who had risen against the king in war': ibid., 378; *CIRCLE*, CR 9 Edw. III, §32.

[75] *IEP*, 346.

[76] *IEMI*, no. 60.

[77] *IEMI*, nos 41–3.

out of 49 jurors being selected in Cork.[78] Criteria for selection clearly included knightly status in this IPM, ten knights being selected on a jury of 32. Indeed, the relatively widespread presence of knightly jurors on IPMs is one of the most significant characteristics of IPMs from medieval Ireland. The authority and local standing of men like Robert Schorthals made him worth empanelling on the juries of the IPM for Gilbert de Clare, earl of Gloucester, in Kilkenny in 1314 and an *ad quod damnum* inquiry in 1307 adjudging the damage should the earl of Norfolk's merchants be permitted to use his port of New Ross.[79] Knight service played a major role in land tenure across Ireland, and knights' knowledge of the military situation on the ground and its effect on the worth of properties and tenure would be invaluable. The writ appointing John Ellerker as escheator in May 1336 ordered sheriffs to summon before him 'knights and others to make inquisitions'.[80] Juries were frequently led by men of knightly status, a contrast with fifteenth-century England, where 'men from the upper ranks of local society occur relatively rarely in the panels. Knights are almost unheard of; esquires very rare; and gentlemen only a little more common.'[81]

Nevertheless, the limited surviving corpus and the preponderance of greater landowners therein may skew evidence away from those individuals of more gentle and middling status who manned IPM juries of fourteenth- and fifteenth-century England. Many writs which launched inquisitions specify the kind of individual who should be called to sit on juries. In the second-earliest surviving IPM, for Adam of Andon (1244), the writ commands the justiciar to take the inquisition 'by the oath of trustworthy and loyal men of his bailiwick ...', while the inquisition of 1252 to establish whether the manor of Ballymadun (co. Dublin) was royal demesne or an escheat was to be taken 'by the oaths of the most trustworthy and law-worthy *free* men of Ireland'.[82] By 1410, a bill would urge that 'every of the iiij men of the Baronies put in these inquests shall be inheritable of C s. of lands or rent by year, or otherwise the best inheritors within the Baroni',[83] which set the standard, but perhaps indicates that lesser men had previously been involved. Generally, IPM jurors were men of some means, those 'substantial leaders of local communities – bailiffs, constables and churchwardens – who contributed also to county government and the implementation of national feudal law', of whom Michael Hicks has written for the fifteenth century.[84] Much evidence exists that

78 A similar jury panel survives for the inquisition into the right to the manor of Moylagh (co. Meath) in 1331: *IEMI*, nos 247–8. The annotation practices are similar.
79 *IEMI*, nos. 116, 187. I follow Matthew Holford here in arguing that IPM juries came from the same body of men used for other types of inquisition: M. Holford, '"Thrifty Men of the Country"? The Jurors and Their Role', *IPM Companion*, 215.
80 *CFR 1327–37*, 484, 506.
81 Holford, '"Thrifty Men of the Country"?', 208.
82 *IEMI*, nos 3, 12. My emphasis.
83 H.F. Berry, *Statutes and Ordinances, and Acts of the Parliament of Ireland* (Dublin, 1907), 525.
84 *IPM Companion*, 22. See, for example, *CIRCLE*, PR 5 Ric. II, §251 (IPMs for Geoffrey Tryvers); PR 15 Ric. II, §106 (William Roche of Tullow).

many jurors were free tenants of the lords on whose IPM juries they served. In the IPM for Thomas de Clare held at Bunratty (co. Clare) in September 1287, jurors Hugh Pirun and Henry Albus are listed among the free tenants, holding a villate and part-villate respectively for a small render and suit of court, while Severen fitz Ralph held a weir.[85] This example shows a phenomenon common to the Irish IPMs. They support Holford's recent assertion in respect of fifteenth-century England that 'the majority of jurors whose station can be ascertained with any confidence came from the more prosperous middling ranks of rural and urban society'. Moreover, they reinforce Holford's findings that, alongside status and age, locality to the lands in question was of paramount importance in jury selection.[86]

Furthermore, recent work on the most settled, Anglicised areas of Ireland reveals the official status and local administrative service of several individuals who sat on inquisition juries in counties Dublin and Louth and in the liberty of Trim (co. Meath). Áine Foley's study of the royal manors of county Dublin highlights key individuals who acted as jurors and manorial officials, chief amongst whom was Warin Oweyn, receiver and reeve of Newcastle Lyons in 1321,[87] who sat on an *ad quod damnum* jury in 1330 to determine whether the king might demise seven villates in the Leinster marches and to make a full extent thereof.[88] Reeves were chosen by members of the manor community and men such as Warin were patently well-informed and respected figures. In 1315 he had been responsible for picking 80 men from Newcastle Lyons and Esker to maintain a ward in Saggart to protect that area against the Irish of the Leinster mountains.[89] Brendan's Smith study of colonisation and change in county Louth and Michael Potterton's examination of the community of medieval Trim highlight similar individuals. These include Ralph Burgeys, coroner of Louth in 1306 and then the king's receiver and serjeant of the manor of Ardee, also a juror on the 1315 IPM for Benedict Pippard,[90] and John Wodeloc, sheriff of Meath in 1302, who sat on the IPM jury for Milo Talbot in 1291 and was still of sufficient standing locally and regionally to sit on the *ad quod damnum* jury determining how the bishops of Down held their lands in Ulster in 1313.[91] Although providing only two examples, such men may show that many jurors bordered on the upper echelons of local society and that, with full juror lists, scholars can now build even richer pictures of local society in medieval Ireland.

85 *IEMI*, no. 65.

86 Holford, '"Thrifty Men of the Country"?', 206, 214.

87 Foley, *Royal Manors*, 4, 83.

88 *IEMI*, no. 244. Also on this jury was Nicholas Callan of Saggart, provost of Saggart in 1324–5: Foley, *Royal Manors*, 84.

89 Foley, *Royal Manors*, 138.

90 B. Smith, *Colonisation and Conquest in Medieval Ireland. The English in Louth, 1170–1330* (Cambridge, 1999), 77, 135; *IEMI*, no. 191.

91 Michael Potterton, *Medieval Trim: History and Archaeology* (Dublin, 2005), 372; *IEMI*, nos 83, 191.

Emphasis on the free status of jurors excluded much of Irish society from acting on juries; English law in Ireland, and therefore not only the ability to sue and be sued but to act as a juryman, was largely denied to those of native birth.[92] Many individuals purchased English law, and there is evidence amongst lists of jurors that men of native birth and others of mixed heritage shared the rights and duties of their 'English' counterparts. Among jurors convened in 1324 to take an extent of the lands at Odagh (co. Kilkenny) were Thomas Ocoryn and Thomas Omalgarf.[93] These men, either Irish or of mixed heritage, perhaps provided local administrative experience in this lordship as leaders of those communities from which Gilbert Omalegan and Maurice Odougyn were chosen to be sergeant and external sergeant of the town of Odagh, respectively, their ethnicity not necessarily hindering service on important local juries. It is naturally dangerous to make assumptions about ethnic origin and legal status on name evidence alone. Foley has shown that there may have been a number of administrators in the royal manors of county Dublin, all of whom appear among lists of inquisition jurors in Ireland, with names of Gaelic origin such as Kissok, Beg, Heyne and Bretnagh, which may have been nicknames adopted by English settlers that eventually developed into surnames.[94]

Furthermore, ethnicity is a complex question in the historiography of the Lordship and is an issue with which historians continue to grapple.[95] IPM evidence may possibly enrich that debate. Much land and important lordships examined by IPM juries lay wholly or partly in the Irishry, outside the practical, if not nominal, jurisdiction of royal officials, and this was increasingly so as the fourteenth century progressed. Many individuals from native Irish communities lived under the rule of English lords and sometimes had recourse to English law. In communities where frontiers between rival authorities and ethnic communities merged, many more intermarried and engaged in aspects of acculturation while retaining English legal standing. An inquisition of 1299 into the potential licensing of a grant of royal lands by the castle in Roscommon notably records that two juries were summoned. One, representing the [English] town of Roscommon, included men with 'English' surnames like Fleming, Arnold and Durand and 'Irish' surnames like Macgillawder and Macsery, while the other comprised seven men from the Irish town of Roscommon, all of whom have apparently 'Irish' names, perhaps demonstrating the crown's need for expert local advice.[96]

Once empanelled, jurors were expected to answer a number of questions, as exemplified in the writ initiating the IPM for John de Walhope on 12 June 1295:

[92] For the status of the Gaelic Irish see G.J. Hand, *English Law in Ireland, 1290–1324* (Cambridge, 1967).

[93] *IEMI*, no. 234.

[94] Foley, *Royal Manors*, 75.

[95] Frame, *Ireland and Britain*, 9. See also idem, '"*Les Engleys Nees en Irelande*": The English Political Identity in Medieval Ireland', in ibid., 131–50; J.F. Lydon, *The English in Medieval Ireland* (Dublin, 1984).

[96] *IEMI*, no. 100.

'Order ... to inquire as to how much land he held of the king in chief, how much of others, by what service, the value of the land, the heir and his age', a form of words closely echoed in a writ ordering the IPM of Joan, widow of John fitz Eustace, of 1 April 1395.[97] In England, the usual assumption is that jurors' answers could not be authoritative, given their lack of legal knowledge of feudal tenure.[98] Given the tenurial relationship between many jurors and the deceased tenant-in-chief, they may perhaps have had both personal and, probably, local official documentary evidence to inform their findings, but loss of many manorial rentals and surveys from medieval Ireland obscures the workings behind the IPM survey. Although differing in minor detail from the return made by 24 Dublin jurors in October 1291, an apparently authoritative statement was given by a panel of Cork jurors of the value of Milo Talbot's manor of Malahide (co. Dublin) in October 1292, and of the dower falling to his widow, possibly suggesting an exchange of information between seigneurial officials, or intervention of those who stood to gain – in this case Geoffrey de Welle, to whom Edward I had granted the custody of Milo's heir.[99] Family evidence may also sometimes be inferred; jurors in the 1292 IPM for Robert Cruys of Naul returned that Reginald de Sancto Bosco held 176 acres of arable land and meadow, a mill and orchard garden worth 40*d* or a render of 400 eels, with his wife, Cruys's mother. Reginald himself was one of those jurors and he and his wife could have been the source of some information.[100]

Economy and Society

As well as their valuable insights into many strata of society, IPMs are 'the single best source for reconstructing both the institutional and economic geography of the country'.[101] IPM extents, detailed statements of lands, buildings, rents and services, inform us about land tenure and services due to the crown across much of Ireland. They also provide assessments of the value of property and descriptions of standing structures, and consequently allow historians to examine general and particular trends in medieval seigneurial economy, fluctuations in wealth and developments in rural and urban society. This survey will examine the information that extents provide on the nature of tenure, the research value of IPM data and effects of warfare on the decline of lordly income in later medieval Ireland.

Before embarking, however, several caveats must be made. Firstly, this is ground expertly trodden 30 years ago by Kevin Down. In his essay on colonial society and economy for the *New History of Ireland*, Down made use of many

97 *IEMI*, no. 92; *CIRCLE*, CR 23 Edw. I, §§1, 5; *CIRCLE*, CR 18 Ric. II, §7.
98 Carpenter, 'Introduction', 20.
99 *IEMI*, nos 83, 87.
100 *IEMI*, no. 86.
101 Campbell and Bartley, *Atlas*, 5.

original IPMs at TNA and a range of other documentation to provide rich details of landholding, society and the economy in medieval Ireland.[102] While there have since been many excellent local and regional studies emphasising a multidisciplinary approach,[103] his remains a standard work and his broad conclusions are largely accepted here. Secondly, as Down himself acknowledged, the surviving records, both IPMs and manorial records, are few.[104] TNA holds several dozen accounts of ministers of the Bigod lordships in thirteenth-century Carlow and de Burgh lordships in Ulster, Connacht, Kilkenny, Tipperary and Meath from the fourteenth century, while archival sources in Ireland, such as the Red Books of Kildare and Ormond, provide more localised evidence.[105] Nevertheless, there is little overlap with the IPMs by which to evaluate more fully the medieval Irish economy, presenting difficulties in counteracting authoritatively the trend identified by Christopher Dyer, among economic and social historians, to be wary of using IPM extents as historical evidence, partly due to their formulaic nature, suspicious valuations and extensive borrowing from previous extents.[106] In his essay, Down further observed that IPMs for Ireland 'are not very reliable as they tend to undervalue estates'. Lastly, the incomplete nature of the English conquest and settlement of Ireland, and considerable regional differences between the 'comparatively fertile, well settled, and peaceful counties of Leinster and the rough and troubled west', makes drawing conclusions tentative at best. The same goes for the time shift between the expansionist era of settlement in the thirteenth century and the later fourteenth century, afflicted by famine, the Black Death, incessant warfare and a Gaelic revival.[107]

Analysing data from extents relies as heavily now on the usability of the documentation as it did to the officials who compiled them, largely resting on their format, which, in Ireland as in England, changed over time. However, from an early date much thought was put into organising and displaying information. The 1283 IPM for Roger Mortimer of Wigmore, lord of Dunamase (co. Laois), is carefully laid out, opening with a heading giving the date, followed by a list

102 Down, 'Colonial Society and Economy', 439–91.

103 L. Doran, 'Lords of the River Valleys: Economic and Military Lordship in the Carlow Corridor, *c.*1200–1350: European Model in an Irish Context', in *Lordship in Medieval Ireland: Image and Reality*, ed. L. Doran and J. Lyttelton (Dublin, 2007), 99–129; Mark Hennessy, 'Manorial Agriculture and Settlement in Early Fourteenth-Century Tipperary', in *Surveying Ireland's Past: Multidisciplinary Essays in Honour of Anngret Simms*, ed. H.B. Clarke, J. Prunty and M. Hennessy (Dublin, 2004), 99–117; M. Murphy, 'The Profits of Lordship: Roger Bigod, Earl of Norfolk and the Lordship of Carlow, 1270–1306', in Doran and Lyttleton, *Lordship in Medieval Ireland*, 75–98. The model study is Murphy and Potterton, *Dublin Region*.

104 Down, 'Colonial Society and Economy', 439.

105 SC 6/1237–9; *The Red Book of the Earls of Kildare*, ed. G. Mac Niocaill (Dublin, 1964); *The Red Book of Ormond*, ed. N.B. White (Dublin, 1932).

106 C. Dyer, 'The Value of Fifteenth-Century Inquisitions *Post Mortem* for Social History', *IPM Companion*, 97–115.

107 Down, 'Colonial Society and Economy', 440.

of jurors, itemising with marginal headings the various lands and services of which he was seised in demesne as of his wife, Matilda de Braose – demesne arable, demesne meadow, pasture, cottars, betaghs (unfree Irish tenants), free tenants, knights' services, burgages, mills and wastelands. The value of individual assets is given, summarised under each heading before a final total is given at the foot of the membrane, after other lands in Roger's possession.[108] One trend in thirteenth-century Irish IPMs is that even extents of 'lesser' men begin to be systematically laid out,[109] continuing for many of the huge, often dispersed estates of men of higher rank in the fourteenth century.[110] These features suggest a borrowing from efficient estate administrations of the deceased tenant and a desire of government and family for clear, concise information, particularly on the state of castles and manorial buildings at that period, when summary extents were also introduced in which chancery could see at a glance figures for the extent, widow's dower and knights' fees and other services.[111]

This organisation shows clearly the diversity of the medieval seigneurial economy in Ireland. Many extents prioritise large tracts of demesne arable land, usually sown with wheat or oats, and often larger areas of meadow and pastureland which dominated the landscape.[112] They also reveal the range of buildings on estates dedicated to food production.[113] The 1314 IPM for Peter de Andon, for example, details a kitchen, bakehouse, grange, kiln, dovecote, cowshed and pigsty at Howardstown (co. Limerick),[114] features not atypical of many fourteenth-century extents. It is rarer to find dairies, with only two examples extant, in IPMs concerning Danesfort (co. Kilkenny) and Askeaton (co. Limerick).[115] Peter also held a watermill, a common feature of surviving Irish inquisition material, with over 50 'mills' mentioned, and a further 50 'watermills'.[116] Before the calamities of the fourteenth century, milling was clearly profitable in Ireland; four mills in Dungarvan (co. Waterford) were worth over £7 each in 1282,[117] and there is evidence of valuable suit of the lord's mill in lands of the earls of Norfolk and Ulster

108 *IEMI*, no. 54.

109 *IEMI*, no. 46 (William de Mohun, 1282).

110 See, for example, the 1287/8 IPMs for Thomas de Clare (*IEMI*, nos 61–6), Roger Bigod in 1307 (nos 135–40), William de Burgh in 1333 (nos 251–67) and James Butler in 1338 (nos 273–85). But see nos 195–219, the IPM for Thomas fitz Richard de Clare, which has far less sectional arrangement.

111 *IEMI*, nos 138–40, 218–19, 266–7, 284.

112 *IEMI*, nos 10, 26, 180, 221, 264, 275, 277, 278, 282, 332 (corn); 149, 150, 154 (oats and wheat). There are over 100 index entries for 'meadows' and 'pasture' in *IEMI*.

113 For an overview see N. Brady, 'Food Production in Medieval Ireland. Aspects of Arable Husbandry', in *Food in the Medieval Rural Environment*, ed. J. Klápšte and P. Sommer (Turnhout, 2011).

114 *IEMI*, no. 190. None of these buildings has any value beyond upkeep.

115 *IEMI*, nos 149, 210.

116 Indexed separately in *IEMI*.

117 *IEMI*, no. 40. For milling in fifteenth-century England see *supra* 000–000.

in the fourteenth century.[118] There is even an isolated reference to fulling in lands of Henry Barbedor in county Dublin in 1277.[119]

Thirteenth-century expansion of the colony brought some of the most profitable trappings of English manorial lordship to Ireland, along with trading opportunities. Orchards and gardens often appear, and in 1282 John fitz Thomas was noted as taking pannage of pigs and vert in the forests of the Decies at 40*s* per annum.[120] The earls of Ulster enjoyed the chase sufficiently to stock parks at Ballycrinnigan (co. Carlow) and Loughrea (co. Galway) with deer.[121] Thomas de Clare, moreover, held an annual fair at his manors of Youghal (co. Cork), Knockainy (co. Limerick) and Bunratty (co. Clare), and the spread of markets and fairs in Ireland is sometimes evidenced within the IPM corpus. It is naturally associated mostly with established towns or ports and often linked, as in Wexford in 1324, with the lord's right to take ale or wine from his tenants – the right of prise.[122]

From the beginning of English involvement in Ireland, and as English lordship proliferated, 'the land was divided into manors, all held ultimately of the lord of Ireland through the process of subinfeudation'.[123] The manor is overwhelmingly the most documented form of lordship found within the IPMs. Nevertheless, many lords with English lands did assert authority over Irish units of lordship, such as James Butler, earl of Ormond, several of whose free tenants held tuaths, small territorial units where Irish law ran, in the lordship of Nenagh (co. Tipperary).[124] Frequent references to tenant farmers to whom land had been demised highlight the dual system of cultivation operated on many manors, where the demesne, on which the main estate buildings – castle, hall, chief messuage – were located, was cultivated by estate officials and tenants, and large areas demised to tenants for a render which permitted them to cultivate mainly as they wished. Mark Hennessy has recently noted a considerable difference in the size of Irish manors: Moyaliff (co. Tipperary) covered 16,000 acres, while Synone was much smaller.[125] In fertile lands around Dublin, royal demesne manors were smaller still, Esker and Crumlin covering only 1,800 and 2,500 acres each.[126] The

118 *IEMI*, nos 135, 149, 151, 154, 155, 228, 258, 261, 262.

119 *IEMI*, no. 31.

120 *IEMI*, no. 40.

121 *IEMI*, nos 251, 262.

122 *IEMI*, no. 228.

123 Down, 'Colonial Society and Economy', 441, 455. An invaluable work for the manor in Ireland is Mary C. Lyons, 'Manorial Administration and the Manorial Economy of Ireland, *c.*1200–1377' (PhD thesis, Trinity College Dublin, 1984). There were extensive liberties outside the remit of English royal government, although these did fall within the IPM process on the death of the lord, e.g. William de Burgh, earl of Ulster in 1333. For liberties in Ireland, see B. Hartland, 'The Liberties of Ireland in the Reign of Edward I', in *Liberties and Identities in Later Medieval Britain*, ed. M.C. Prestwich (Woodbridge, 2008), 200–16.

124 *IEMI*, no. 278. For other tuaths see *IEMI*, nos 33, 38, 44, 65, 263, 264, 282.

125 Hennessy, 'Manorial Agriculture and Settlement', 99.

126 Foley, *Royal Manors*, 17.

spread of the manor in Ireland was inextricably linked with further conquest and expansion; much of Ulster and Connacht, for example, was never manorialised, and there is no doubt that the IPM corpus thereby obscures the complexity of tenurial systems in Ireland.

Feudal tenure by knight service persisted, undoubtedly promoted by the militarised condition of the Lordship. Several comital IPMs include summaries of a huge number of knights' fees held by free tenants or, as the fourteenth century progressed, commuted to cash payments 'when royal service runs'.[127] Serjeanty – tenure in return for military service – is also widely evidenced in IPMs. In 1253, for example, Geoffrey de Costentin held seven carucates by the service of finding an archer in wartime.[128] Services of native Irish tenants by serjeanty appear to have had a major role in lordship in those areas at the fringe of English royal power in Ulster and Connacht, where tenurial arrangements and lordly authority ebbed and flowed with the fortunes of war and shifting political alliances. William de Burgh's IPM of 1333 outlines that the kings of the Irish of Fir-na-Craibhe, Tirowen, Fermanagh, Airgialla (cos Armagh, Louth and Monaghan), Airthir, Iveagh (co. Down) and Uí Tuitre (co. Antrim) held their lands by services of sustaining the earl's *satellites* assigned to them whenever commanded in wartime. These services had once been worth £355 to the earl, but by the time of his death they were valueless, due to being overrun by the Irish of those regions.[129] Tenurial relationships were therefore no guarantee of loyalty.

The IPMs best demonstrate the variety of free tenure in Ireland below elite society, since virtually every inquisition details the names, lands, rents and services of free tenants of English lords in Ireland. Many owed (fortnightly) suit of court and royal service whenever scutage ran in Ireland. One example is the 1307 IPM for lands in Carlow of Roger Bigod, earl of Norfolk.[130] Edmund Butler, future earl of Carrick, held the barony of Tullow by £8 whenever royal service was proclaimed; others held the baronies of Idrone, Obargy and Oboy (Uí Buide) and various knights' fees by similar payments and service. In this same IPM, moreover, is evidence of 160 plots held in burgage. The burgesses of Carlow worked a communal oven, owed rent and prise of ale at 40*s*. Urban property holding and services are widely evidenced in the IPMs and are worthy of further investigation.[131]

Across Ireland, although principally in the south and midlands, many tenants held their lands at the lord's will. The IPMs document the holdings of gavillers (*gabelarii*), who rented their lands for set terms.[132] Gavillers at Mahoonagh (co.

[127] *IEMI*, nos 139, 209, 213, 217, 219, 265. For royal service, often levied at 20*s*, see nos 135–6, 141–55, 191–216, 251–67, 273–83; Down, 'Colonial Society and Economy', 442.

[128] *IEMI*, no. 14.

[129] *IEMI*, no. 265.

[130] *IEMI*, no. 135.

[131] See R.E. Glasscock, 'Land and People, *c*.1300', *NHI*, II, 200–39.

[132] *IEMI*, nos 62, 154–5, 157, 231, 256, 262, 264.

Limerick) in 1287, for example, held four carucates (480 acres) worth two marks. Their estates could often be sprawling and of little practical value outside of their works, although in 1333 the jurors found that 140 acres of William de Burgh's gavillers in county Galway had dropped to 53*s* 4*d* a year from a not inconsiderable £6 6*s* 8*d*.[133] This sector generally represented the peasantry among the English community. They often sit with the most populous manorial community reflected in the Irish IPMs, the cottars and betaghs. Although Edmund Curtis demonstrated that the majority of cottars at Lisronagh (co. Tipperary) in 1333 were English, elsewhere in Ireland cottars and, particularly, betaghs overwhelmingly meant unfree, Gaelic peasants.[134] As is richly demonstrated throughout the IPMs, the bonded peasantry in Ireland often held quite sizeable quantities of land by a combination of rent, renders in kind and customary labour services. In William de Burgh's cantred of Sil Anmchadha (Longford barony, co. Galway) in 1333, betaghs held five villates and other parcels of land within the lordship of the castle of Meelick by a render of four cows, four pigs and four crannocks of oats, an annual rent of £18 10*s* and harvesting and carting services of 120 plough beasts.[135] Betaghs sometimes apparently laboured under insecure tenure. At Lyn in 1253 betaghs held from year to year for four marks.[136] As the fourteenth century progressed, however, many betagh services were starkly devalued and apparently even lost as they were ceded to Gaelic Irish authorities through military conquest and attrition on the margins of society. The Meelick renders and rents discussed above were described as having been uncollectable, as the tenants were living under the power of the Irish of Uí Maine and the Ó Madadháin.

The IPMs and War

There are two major issues which feed into each other in discussions of land and society in medieval Ireland as viewed through the prism of the IPMs: the supposed unreliability of the financial information supplied by jurors; and the effects of warfare on land values. The former has caused most controversy in English historiography.[137] Kevin Down was similarly sceptical on the undervaluation he perceived in Irish extents, although he observed that the paucity of surviving material makes such value judgements problematic.[138] This pinpoints the almost insuperable obstacle to making firm conclusions about the accuracy and value of the Irish IPM material. The surviving records rarely allow direct comparisons

133 *IEMI*, no. 264.

134 Edmund Curtis, 'Rental of the Manor of Lisronagh, 1333, and Notes on "Betagh" Tenure in Medieval Ireland', *Proceedings of the Royal Irish Academy* 43 C (1935), 41–76.

135 *IEMI*, no. 264. For other customary works see *IEMI*, nos 60, 62–3, 136, 144, 269, 289.

136 *IEMI*, no. 16.

137 For syntheses see the articles by Dyer and Holford, *IPM Companion*, 97–115, 117–44.

138 Down, 'Colonial Society and Economy', 440.

to be made between the same estates at around the same time; regional studies may bring out much of value but cannot speak directly to this issue. For example, there are two IPMs and two manorial accounts for the manor of Lisronagh (co. Tipperary).[139] The earliest dates to 1242 and values the dower third in the manor to Egidia, widow of Richard de Burgh, at £26 16*s* 4*d*. The others are closer in date, being a rental of 1333, a receiver's account from 1351 and the IPM for Lionel of Clarence, earl of Ulster, of 1369. The latter extends the manors of Lisronagh, Terryglass, Tibberaghny and Múscraige Chuirc at £40 per annum with a service of 17½ knights' fees and one third when scutage runs. These summary figures provide no information on buildings, lands, properties or services and are of little practical comparative value, although they do point to a serious devaluation of estates in Ireland over time. The picture is clearer within the manorial documents. Here, a relatively vibrant manorial economy emerges with fewer signs of the devastation reported widely in the IPMs of the mid-fourteenth century. Both documents, compiled for Elizabeth de Burgh, lady of Clare in the same year as the IPMs for her son, William, where widespread devastation is reported, show buoyant per acre values for demesne land of 14*d* over an estate of 358 acres, and 12*d* for the demesne meadow, per acre rents of 14*d* for the sizeable (100-plus acres) estates of the manor's betaghs and some similarly valued demised estates to the manor's gavillers. In this instance there is little wonder that historians have preferred manorial over IPM evidence. Nevertheless, this does not necessarily imply inaccuracy or deliberate undervaluation by jurors.

There is good evidence, even in those manors for which the IPM is the best or only document to survive, that jurors may have had access to records such as these manorial accounts which informed their findings. The jurors empanelled for the IPM of William de Burgh in 1333 refer frequently to 'old' and 'new' valuations.[140] The level of detail in these accounts, references to renders that can still be collected (or not) despite the war conditions prevailing in certain lordships, most notably in Galway, and what appear to be precise calculations of new extents do not immediately suggest inaccuracy. This set of extents may be an exception and relates to the importance of the earldom to the crown and to the survival of English lordship in several parts of Ireland, though. Did the increase in nil or low valuations reflect accurately the new military position, or a political desire on the part of the local community to demonstrate the challenges they faced and the financial consequences for the crown? The jurors who reported on the conditions at Ballintober (co. Roscommon) returned that there was an old, stone-walled castle 'which is of great value in terms of keeping and saving the peace but which has lacked a sufficient keeper for some time', a clear statement of what they saw as the best remedy. To reinforce the point, the new valuation effectively reduced

139 For what follows see *IEMI*, nos 2, 335; Curtis, 'Rental of the Manor of Lisronagh', 41–5; SC 6/1238/14.

140 *IEMI*, nos 254, 256–67.

the old by over 80%.[141] Certainly, it is around the mid-fourteenth century that more serious allegations of misconduct begin to arise. A statute of 1360 rails against escheators who have provoked '*diversez damages et perdes … par fauses enquestes par leschetour de la dite terre*'.[142] It may be that, as Matt Holford has argued for fifteenth-century England, some escheators returned low valuations as they were easy to collect and personal profit could be increased.[143] However, given the earlier discussion in this paper on the identity of jurors,[144] it is plausible to suggest for Ireland, as Bruce Campbell did for early fourteenth-century England, that land values were 'unusually accurate, while the doubts over the accuracy of later IPMs possibly grow in direct proportion to the declining importance of the crown's feudal revenues'.[145] The relative buoyancy of land values across Ireland evidenced in the thirteenth-century IPMs and the apparent collapse in most areas outside of the eastern seaboard largely reflects the narrative in Irish historiography of crisis and shrinkage in the extent and the value of the Lordship. It is, of course, worth emphasising that the particular circumstances of individual estates, their terrain, their location within local power structures and the availability of documentation and men of standing and local knowledge probably have most influence on the value of Irish IPMs.

On 26 May 1321, twelve jurors convened before John de Dufford, escheator of Ireland, at Bunratty (co. Clare).[146] They found that the estates of Thomas fitz Richard de Clare, the recently deceased heir to the liberty of Thomond, all but lay in a state of ruin. While the castle remained in a good state of repair, the associated buildings did not, including the castle mill and ovens, and none of the profits and liberties of the county could be collected. Most of the lordship had lain waste for three years since the death of Richard de Clare; consequently, no Englishman or Irishman made a render and the 400 marks of profits and perquisites, heriots and rents were expended in the governance of the land. Here in bold brush strokes is a picture of English lordship in Ireland in the fourteenth century. IPMs are key witnesses to the ravages of the Scots during their invasion, whose effects were felt for several decades. The Ulster IPMs for William de Burgh in 1333, for example, document the wasting not only of the castle of Dunadry (co. Antrim) but of the surrounding area.[147] The Bruce invasion combined with famine and animal disease to bring wide areas of the Lordship close to its knees, for which reason it has often been seen as a watershed, bringing English lords to quit their lands, if gradually, and to farm out large areas of demesne. From the early fourteenth century the IPMs are saturated, as Kevin

141 *IEMI*, no. 263, p. 151.
142 Berry, *Statutes and Ordinances*, 422–3.
143 *IPM Companion*, 118
144 See pp. 36–38.
145 Campbell and Bartley, *Atlas*, 25.
146 *IEMI*, no. 202.
147 *IEMI*, no. 258.

Down perceptively noted, with jurors' statements that lands 'lie waste and uncultivated for lack of tenants'.[148]

The fluidity of patterns of settlement and military conquest and retreat throughout the first 200 years of the English Lordship of Ireland means that such portraits can mask earlier trends or divert attention from evidence which points, however tentatively, in other directions. The 1253 IPM for Geoffrey de Costentin, for example, shows that his lands at Kenkelly lay waste 'by the default of William de Dene and the war waged by the Irish',[149] while the 1282 IPM for John fitz Thomas pays witness to the total destruction by the Irish of his tuaths in Kildare and of broad swathes of territory in Cork, Limerick and Kerry.[150] Conversely, there are pockets of profitability to be found even in those areas closest to conflict. The new valuation of the cantreds of Tirawley (co. Mayo) in 1333 shows a drop of only around 13*s* from the previous valuation, while surrounding areas demonstrate severe devaluation.[151] This phenomenon is perhaps best evoked in the 1415 assignment of dower for Margaret, widow of John Darcy – the final IPM in the chancery series – which intimately details apparently profitable lands in counties Louth and Meath and reveals a thriving rural and urban economy.[152]

Inquisitions *post mortem* are far from the easiest source to get to grips with. Their use in the context of medieval Ireland is far more difficult still. The peculiar conditions of the Lordship, where royal authority was never total and could be assailed from all sections of the community of whatever ethnic or political background, made administering the feudal rights of the crown extremely challenging. The survival of so few of their number and of few other written accounts of landed estates, properties and services makes their interpretation fraught with difficulty. This should not prevent their much wider use by historians for studies of royal and seigneurial lordship, agriculture and trade. This view extends to fields beyond economic, social and political history. Place name studies can now be enriched with a broader base of variant spellings, while architectural specialists and experimental archaeologists can, in the description of buildings and roofs, building techniques and materials, find new evidence to aid their interpretations. IPMs are a rich source of information for the history of medieval Ireland and deserve broader attention.

148 Beth Hartland, 'Reasons for Leaving: The Effect of Conflict on English Landholding in Late Thirteenth-Century Leinster', *JMH* 32.1 (2006), 18–26; Down, 'Colonial Society and Economy', 459–61.

149 *IEMI*, no. 14.

150 *IEMI*, nos 38, 44.

151 *IEMI*, no. 263.

152 *IEMI*, nos 347–8.

4

The Court of the Honour of Clare, 1308–60: Feudal Incidents and Inquisitions

Jennifer Ward

Feudal relationships between lords and vassals in the honour court are often shrouded in obscurity, as few honour court rolls survive before the fourteenth century.[1] By then knight service by vassals in the royal army and as castleguard was in terminal decline, and the relationship between lord and vassal was primarily financial. Yet the tenurial relationship remained important. The vassal was still expected to perform homage and swear fealty to his lord and to attend the honour court. On succession to a fee, the lord had the right to exact relief from the heir; if the heir was under the age of 21, the lord had the right to his wardship and marriage. For heiresses the age of majority was 14 (if married) and 16 (if unmarried). The lord was also entitled to collect financial aids. These seigniorial rights were not finally abolished until after the Restoration of Charles II.

The principal lands of the honour of Clare lay in Norfolk, Suffolk and Essex, with outlying holdings in adjacent counties; the term honour here denotes the demesne manors and tenanted land held by the lord and centred on Clare, Suffolk. The honour of Clare was formed after the Norman Conquest when the lands of Wihtgar and Phin the Dane were granted by William the Conqueror to Richard son of Count Gilbert of Brionne, the founder of the Clare baronial family, after the rebellion of the earls of 1075 which Richard, as one of the justiciars of the realm in the king's absence, helped to suppress. The lands in Norfolk were added in the early twelfth century and in 1189, when the Clares gained half of the lands of Walter Giffard, earl of Buckingham. The honour always remained an important part of the Clare estates, although the Clares' power was greatly augmented in 1217 when they inherited the more extensive lands of the honour of Gloucester in west and south-west England and in south

[1] The rolls of Ramsey abbey's honour court of Broughton for 1255–60 have been published in *Court Rolls of the Abbey of Ramsey and of the Honor of Clare*, ed. W.O. Ault (New Haven and London, 1928), 1–71. For discussion of the honour court of Clare before 1314, see R. Mortimer, 'Land and Service: the Tenants of the Honour of Clare', *Anglo-Norman Studies* 8, ed. R.A. Brown (Woodbridge, 1986), 177–97; J. Ward, 'The Honour of Clare in Suffolk in the Early Middle Ages', *Proceedings of the Suffolk Institute of Archaeology* 30 (1964), 99–107; J. Ward, 'The Place of the Honour in Twelfth-Century Society: the Honour of Clare, 1066–1217', loc. cit. 35 (1983), 195–9.

Wales. As earls of Gloucester and Hertford, the Clare family were leaders of the English baronage in the thirteenth century. Gilbert, the last Clare earl of Gloucester, was killed at the battle of Bannockburn in 1314. His only son had been born and died two years earlier. After a three-year delay, his estates were divided among his three sisters, with the honour of Clare passing to Gilbert's youngest sister, Elizabeth de Burgh, married to Roger Damory. It was confiscated by the king in 1322 when Damory and Elizabeth joined the Marcher rebellion, but restored to Elizabeth on 2 November 1322. Damory had died during the rebellion. From then until her death in 1360, Elizabeth was Lady of the honour.[2]

The honour court at Clare was held from the time when Richard, son of Count Gilbert, established himself and his vassals on the honour under William I. It was held at his principal castle and administrative centre of Clare in Suffolk: the castle existed by 1090. His descendants adopted the surname of Clare in the early twelfth century. The detailed series of court rolls of the honour of Clare survive from 1308. Both freeholders and tenants holding land in return for knight service owed suit of court, and were expected to attend the court every three weeks; they had probably been expected to attend since the late eleventh century. The court met on Wednesday, under the presidency of the steward of the honour, with the court year running from Michaelmas to Michaelmas (29 September).[3] In the fourteenth century, the court was active. Most of the business was concerned with cases of debt, detinue, trespass and covenant where the damages amounted to less than forty shillings. The levying of entry fines on acquisitions of land was always a major item of business, especially among small freeholdings, testifying to a lively land market. Matters concerning feudal tenures were very much in a minority, whereas they had probably been an important item of business in the twelfth century. The court remained profitable: £46 6*s* 11*d* was due from fines, amercements and feudal dues in 1312–13.[4]

In addition to the court at Clare, forinsec courts of the honour were held at demesne manors in Norfolk, Suffolk and Essex by the bailiffs of fees; they were described as forinsec, or foreign, to distinguish them from the honour court at Clare. They dealt with honorial business and with the enforcement of decisions made at Clare. The bailiffs of fees were responsible for carrying out distraints and attachments, summoning juries and carrying out inquiries. The existence of the forinsec courts probably made enforcement easier. The bailiffs were usually responsible for business in a single county, and the continuing profitability of the

2 For the Clare family and Elizabeth de Burgh, see M. Altschul, *A Baronial Family in Medieval England: the Clares, 1217–1314* (Baltimore, 1965); F.A. Underhill, *For her Good Estate. The Life of Elizabeth de Burgh* (Basingstoke, 1999); lives of Elizabeth de Burgh, her parents and other members of the Clare family are included in *ODNB*.

3 The honour court roll of 1308–9 was published by Ault, *Court Rolls*, pp. 75–110. All the court and forinsec court records are in TNA.

4 SC 2/212/35. Amercements denote fines in the modern meaning of the term; fines denote money paid for agreements.

honour court was largely due to their work. It is rare to find a bailiff reporting that he had been unable to do anything.

In discussing the role of the lord in the honour court, a contrast emerges between the twelfth and fourteenth centuries. In the twelfth century, it is likely that the lord acted as president of the court and he certainly took action to enforce its decisions. He acted in close cooperation with his chief vassals, known as honorial barons, who were regarded as his counsellors and who held the offices of steward and constable on the honour. The situation was changing by the late twelfth century, and in the thirteenth century the Clare lord had far wider landed responsibilities, as had many of his chief vassals, and stewards were often professional administrators. As a result, the relationship between lord and vassal became much more impersonal.[5]

In the fourteenth century, there is no evidence that Earl Gilbert was ever present at the court, although he occasionally intervened in the proceedings, as when he ordered the postponement of the demand for the homage of Aymer de Valence, earl of Pembroke.[6] This was possibly due to Aymer's possession of extensive estates in England, Wales and Ireland, and his considerable involvement in political events between 1308 and 1314. Elizabeth de Burgh, in contrast, made more frequent interventions, although there is no evidence of her actually attending the court. She spent much of her time at Clare castle and nearby residences. Although she also held the Clare family lordships of Usk in Monmouthshire and Cranborne in Dorset, she always exercised vigorous lordship over the honour of Clare.[7] Soon after the accession of Edward III, she ordered the steward to get the bailiffs of fees of Norfolk, Suffolk and Essex to summon all suitors to the honour court in order to inquire into their service.[8] By then, her position was more secure than it had been earlier in the 1320s, and she was getting to grips with administering the honour. Other instances of her intervention are found. In 1334, she wrote to her steward, John de Hertford, ordering him to find out whether Thomas Passelewe held ½ or ¼ knight's fee in Gazeley, Suffolk; her bailiffs of fees had been distraining him to pay relief on ½ knight's fee, but he asserted that he held only ¼. John was to find out which was correct and in the meantime to postpone the demand for Thomas's relief and homage.[9] In 1341, a fine demanded from Ralph son of William of Pebmarsh, Essex, was postponed until the Lady was in Suffolk.[10] A year later, she wrote to John de Hertford from Usk about the findings of the inquisition into John le Botiller's ½ fee in Clare and the payment of his relief.[11]

5 J.C. Ward, 'Place of the Honour in Twelfth-Century Society', 195–9.

6 SC 2/212/35, m. 5.

7 As well as Clare castle, Elizabeth de Burgh had residences at Anglesey priory, Cambridgeshire, and Great Bardfield, Essex.

8 SC 2/212/43, m. 4d.

9 *Elizabeth de Burgh, Lady of Clare (1295–1360). Household and Other Records*, ed. J. Ward, Suffolk Records Society 57 (Woodbridge, 2014), 125; SC 2/212/49, m. 11.

10 SC 6/1110/7, m. 1.

11 SC 2/213/5, m. 16.

The effectiveness of the honour court depended very much on the steward. The fourteenth-century steward of the honour was a layman, ranking as a knight or esquire, who was well versed in the law. In addition to holding courts, he acted as one of the Lady's counsellors. John de Hertford ranked as an esquire, as did John Bataille, steward in the early 1350s, who held land in Manuden in Essex. Robert de Bures, steward under Earl Gilbert, and his son Andrew, steward in the 1340s, of Acton in Suffolk, were knights, and were heavily involved in Suffolk local government as well as the honour.[12] The steward was occasionally mentioned in proceedings. Robert de Cheddeworth, steward in the 1320s, provided testimony, and on one occasion issued a pardon. John Bataille was said also to have provided testimony at a forinsec court held at Walsingham, Norfolk.[13]

The creation of knights' fees can be traced back to the time when Richard son of Count Gilbert was granted the honour by William I. At that time, the honour comprised several large manors, most of which Richard kept in his own hands, and a large number of freemen and sokemen who held small areas of land. Many of the latter were granted to Richard's followers in return for their homage and military service. About one-third of the honour had been granted to vassals by the time of the Domesday Survey in 1086, and the process of subinfeudation continued until about 1135, the death of Henry I. By 1166, when Henry II ordered his tenants-in-chief to submit lists of their knights, Roger de Clare, earl of Hertford, listed in his *Carta* approximately 133 fees of the old enfeoffment, created before 1135, and 8¼ of the new, established between 1135 and 1166; 44 fees of the old enfeoffment were situated on the Clare lands in Surrey and 88 in Essex, Suffolk and Norfolk. Many of the fees of the old enfeoffment were built up gradually between about 1075 and 1135, and a clear distinction can be drawn between the honorial barons with several fees and the lesser military tenants with one or two or a fractional fee. Few fees were created by the Clares after 1135.[14]

Over time, the situation over military tenancies became much more complicated. A few of the major tenancies which were recorded in the *Carta* of 1166 were still in the hands of a single vassal in 1314 when Earl Gilbert's inquisition *post mortem* was drawn up, such as the 5½ fees held by Walter son of Humphrey in Essex and Suffolk, and the 3¾ fees held by William fitz Ralph, also in Essex and Suffolk.[15] Some, however had more than one holder in 1314, although the group of fees was recorded as a whole: by 1314, 14 fees in Essex, Middlesex, Norfolk, Suffolk and Surrey were in the hands of at least three men, namely Richard de Taleworth, Roger de Bachesworth and the heirs of Alan de Clare.[16] Inevitably, the number of tenants increased over time as a result of the failure of male heirs and inheritance by women; wherever there were coheiresses, the holding had to be

[12] E101/92/23, m. 1; Ward, *Elizabeth de Burgh*, 69–70.
[13] SC 2/212/40, m. 9, 10; SC 6/1110/26, m. 1.
[14] Ward, 'Place of the Honour', 191–5.
[15] *CIPM* v. 538 (at p. 347).
[16] Ibid. v.538–9 (at p. 348).

divided equally between them. Many vassals came to hold land of more than one lord, and this was already happening by 1086. Vassals created their own fees by alienating land to followers in return for their homage and service, and they did not need to seek the consent of their own lord in order to do this; long scales of tenure were created before the practice was ended by the statute of *Quia Emptores* of 1290. By 1314, the complex structure of fees resulted in very small holdings; thus Robert de Bures and John de Peyton held ½ fee in Great Waldingfield, and Robert de Brokhole and Walter de Gaysele ½ fee in Hundon, Suffolk, while John atte Tounesende, William Doune and John Rey held ½ fee in East and West Raynham, Norfolk.[17] There was no economic distinction between tenants holding a fractional fee and freeholders, and it was a major task for the honorial officials to keep track of fees and their holders. Roger de Gyney held four knights' fees in 1314 and his ancestors had counted as honorial barons in the twelfth century, but in 1340–41 a later Roger denied that he held of the Lady at all.[18]

The performance of homage and the swearing of the oath of fealty by the vassal to his lord epitomised the bond between them. By the fourteenth century, however, vassals were reluctant to perform homage, and the efforts of the honour court to compel them do not appear to have met with much success. It was comparatively rare for a tenant to perform homage when he entered on his lands, although he sometimes swore fealty.[19] Homage was generally postponed; Philip de Broughton who held ¼ fee in Norfolk paid a fine of 20*s* in 1310–11 and 1312–13 for respite of suit and homage.[20] Moreover, by the early fourteenth century, the major tenants usually paid an annual fine for respite of suit to the honour court, and on the whole the Clares had lost control of this group. The court roll for 1308–9 mentioned approximately half of the military tenants, and nineteen fined for respite of suit until the following Michaelmas; not all these were major tenants.[21] In 1341 fines for respite of suit from Essex and Norfolk included Ralph fitz William with 3¾ fees, Richard son of Simon with 12¼, Richard de Boyland with ½ fee, and the prior of Colne with ¼ fee.[22]

No reference is found in the honour court rolls to personal military service. This had been expected in the late eleventh and twelfth centuries, and the Clare lords usually performed their military service in person. Jocelin of Brakelond depicted Earl Roger and his men of Clare (*Clarenses*) rushing to rescue Henry II on the Welsh campaign of 1157. By the reign of Henry III the earl appeared

17 C 47/9/25.

18 *CIPM* v. 538 (at p. 346); SC 6/1110/8, m. 1.

19 E.g. Richard Guncelyn in 1322–3; SC 2/212/39, m. 2.

20 SC 2/212/34, m. 1; SC 2/212/35, m. 2.

21 Ault, *Court Rolls*, 75–110. For a full list of knights' fees in 1314–17, see J. Ward, 'The Estates of the Clare Family, 1066–1317', Ph.D. thesis, University of London (1962), 300–41. This was compiled from Earl Gilbert's inquisition *post mortem* of 1314, the assignment of dower to his widow in 1314, and the partition of his lands among his three sisters in 1317; *CIPM* v. 538 (pp. 325–54); C 134/42–4; *CCR 1313–18*, pp. 131–9; C 47/9/23–5.

22 SC2/213/5, m. 1.

for service with only his quota of knights which could be recruited from his household; 20 knights were demanded in 1218 and 1229, by which time the earl held the honour of Gloucester as well as the honour of Clare.[23] In view of the more costly equipment needed by the knight in the thirteenth century, many vassals probably welcomed the change. The *servitium debitum* (the number of knights which the Clares had to produce for the royal army) demanded by the Norman kings is unknown, but with 133 fees the Clares had probably enfeoffed more men than they needed to produce, and it is therefore likely that even in the twelfth century there were vassals who did not perform military service in person. There are a few references to castleguard, but this obligation was virtually obsolete by the fourteenth century. In 1314, Richard de Bachesworth and Richard de Taleworth owed £1 17*s* for finding a watchman at Clare castle.[24] It is probable that the Norfolk fees had originally owed castleguard to the royal castle at Norwich. In 1351–52, at the forinsec court of the honour at Walsingham, 10*s* were received from the tenants for *waytefe* for Michaelmas term, which was paid to the king for Norwich castle.[25]

The feudal incidents of aids, relief and wardship developed in the twelfth century and were essentially related to personal military service. The lord might wish to levy an aid from his tenants in order to organise his military service to the king. Relief would be levied from a male heir succeeding to a military tenancy who was fit to carry out his military service. If the heir was a minor (under the age of 21) he would not be able to perform the military service due and he, together with his land, would come into the lord's wardship to be trained as a knight while the lord made provision for his service. However, with the ending of personal military service for the majority of vassals in the thirteenth century, if not earlier, these became financial obligations, increasingly subject to regulation from outside the honour and particularly affected by the growth of royal power and justice; vassals, moreover, found royal service more advantageous than service as an honorial official. The honour was never an autonomous unit and as early as the reign of Henry I it was decided that if a legal case arose between the tenants of two different lords, as could easily happen in East Anglia with its multitude of small freeholdings and fractional fees, it had to be heard in the county court and not by the honour. Henry II's possessory assizes and final concords were attractive to vasssals, whether they were bringing a case against their lord or another vassal. The jurisdiction of the honour court was further limited during the thirteenth century.

How did these developments affect the levy of feudal incidents? The lord's right to levy aids was limited by Magna Carta, which gave the lord the right to levy aids for the knighting of his eldest son, the marriage of his eldest daughter once, and

[23] *The Chronicle of Jocelin of Brakelond*, ed. H.E. Butler (London, 1949), 70; I.J. Sanders, *Feudal Military Service in England* (Oxford, 1956), 67.

[24] C 134/42, m. 1.

[25] SC 6/1110/26, m. 1.

his own ransom. This was the practice in the fourteenth-century honour court, but some vassals may well have considered that such a demand was by then irrelevant. Elizabeth de Burgh levied a 'reasonable aid' for the knighting of her eldest son, William, heir of the earl of Ulster, and the marriage of her eldest daughter, Isabella, in 1327 at the rate of £2 per knight's fee. The assessment for Suffolk survives.[26] The account of the bailiff of fees for Norfolk in 1337–38 indicates that some vassals at least were avoiding payment; in the final reckoning, £41 10*s* 10*d* of the 'reasonable aid' could not be levied, a statement which was repeated in the following years.[27]

Problems also arose over the payment of relief. Magna Carta laid down that relief was to be levied at the rate of £5 per knight's fee on the heir's succession to the holding. In the early fourteenth century this was also proving difficult to collect. Partly this was because of the number of small fractional holdings; John son of Simon and nineteen other tenants held ½ fee in Little Sampford, Essex. Alexander son of Peter le Moy held one messuage and eight acres of arable land in Rushworth, Norfolk, for which he owed 3*s* 4*d* relief.[28] Some vassals were finding ways of evading the obligation . If the heir was enfeoffed before the father's death, relief did not have to be paid. Major tenants may have had difficulty in finding the cash, or simply have been unwilling to pay. Either reason may have applied in 1309 to Simon son of Richard, who held 12¼ fees in Essex and Norfolk: the sum was still being demanded nearly two years later. In 1337–38, relief was being demanded from his son, Richard son of Simon. The payment of £40 was postponed, and was to be paid over the next two years; in 1340–41, payment of £30 was further postponed 'because it could not yet be levied'.[29]

As far as wardship was concerned, the Clare lords in the thirteenth and fourteenth centuries were losing out not only to their vassals' ability to find ways of avoiding seigniorial demands, but also to the king's right to prerogative wardship. Increasingly, vassals arranged for their estates to be held jointly by husband and wife. On the husband's death, when the wife took over the land, the lord could not exercise wardship over the under-age heir's lands as long as his mother survived, although he retained the right to the heir's marriage. From the thirteenth century, feudal settlements were mostly made by chirograph before the royal justices, but examples of collusive enfeoffments are found in the honour court rolls. This was the method chosen by the major tenant, Walter son of Humphrey, who paid £2 10*s* to have licence to enfeoff anyone he liked of his manor of Borley, Essex, so that the feoffee (trustee) could then re-enfeoff Walter and his wife of the manor, to hold to them and their heirs.[30] On Walter's death, his wife continued to hold

[26] *EHD 1189–1327*, 318; *Feudal Aids* vi, 555 7. William succeeded to the earldom of Ulster in 1330 when he was eighteen years old; Isabella married Sir Henry de Ferrers of Groby.

[27] SC 6/1110/4, m. 1; SC 6/1110/8, m. 1; SC 6/1110/15, m. 1.

[28] *EHD 1189–1327*, 317; Ault, *Court Rolls*, 99; *Feudal Aids* ii, 147; SC 2/212/36, m. 9.

[29] Ault, *Court Rolls*, 87, 91–2; SC 2/212/34, m. 2d; SC 6/1110/4, m. 1; SC 6/1110/8, m. 1.

[30] Ault, *Court Rolls*, 93. Walter held 5½ knights' fees in Essex and Suffolk.

the lands until her death, when the heir would succeed. If the heir had been still a minor at that point, the lord would have enjoyed the rights of wardship.

Similar arrangements were made on smallholdings. In 1355, Henry Cosyn enfeoffed John, the vicar of Chaureth church, of one messuage and eight acres of arable land of the Lady's fee in Broxted, Essex. John re-enfeoffed Henry for life, with the proviso that after his death the holding was to pass to Henry's son Richard; a fine of 9*s* was paid for this. Five years later, Simon atte Water enfeoffed Gilbert Poleyn of one messuage and 28 acres of arable land of the Lady's fee in Ickburgh, Norfolk, and Gilbert enfeoffed Simon's two daughters who were his heirs; a fine of 13*s* 4*d* was paid.[31]

Prerogative wardship benefited the king at the expense of the lord. If a tenant held of several lords and also held land by knight service of the king, all his lands, together with the custody of the heir and his marriage, passed to the king. (When the tenant held land of several lords but not of the king, each lord had custody of the land of his own fee; the wardship of the person of the heir and his marriage passed to the lord of the oldest tenancy, according to the statute of Westminster II of 1285.) As early as 1130, the Clares lost at least one wardship to Henry I; the marriage of the widow of Geoffrey de Favarches of Walsingham, Norfolk and the wardship of her son were in the king's hands. Prerogative wardship was exercised by the Angevin kings and regulated in Magna Carta.[32] During the thirteenth century, some of the Clares' most valuable wardships passed to the king. The number of prerogative wardships was constantly increasing as a result of marriage and inheritance. Their number can be calculated approximately from the inquisition *post mortem* of Earl Richard de Clare of 1262.[33] The figures are for all the earl's fees in England, both for the honour of Gloucester and the honour of Clare. Calculating to the nearest whole number, the inquisition lists 384 fees, of which 116 were held by tenants-in-chief of the crown and owed only relief to the earl. Earl Richard still had rights of wardship, marriage and relief from 268 fees: a very substantial number.

Wardships were essentially occasional windfalls for the lord, and the honour court was closely involved in their administration, and followed royal procedure. By the early fourteenth century inquisitions *post mortem* were drawn up. On the death of a tenant, his lands were taken into the lord's hands; this occurred even if the heir was of age. A jury was summoned to inquire into the lands held by the tenant on the day he died, the services due and the name and age of the next heir. If the heir was of age, he appeared before the honour court to perform homage and fealty and to pay relief, or postpone them as the case might be; he then received his lands. In the event of a minority, arrangements were made for the wardship and a proof of age was taken when the heir reached the age of 21. The

31 SC 2/213/12, m. 6d; SC2/213/15, m. 4.

32 *Magnum Rotulum Scaccarii de Anno 31 Henrici I*, ed. J. Hunter (London, 1833), 94; *EHD 1189–1327*, 317, 320.

33 C 132/27/5; SC 11/610; *CCR 1261–4*, 284–93.

widow produced security that she would not remarry without the lord's consent, and dower was allocated.

The honour court rolls fully illustrate the various steps in the procedure. For instance, it was ordered in 1323 to take into the Lady's hands all the lands of the late Robet Belet in Beechamwell and Wereham, Norfolk because his heir was a minor. Similarly, the late Walter Olyver's lands in Ash, Cotton and Burstall in Suffolk, held as ¼ fee, were taken into the Lady's hands in August. In September a note was added that Benedict Olyver came and did homage and fealty to the Lady.[34]

Jury findings were reported succinctly in the honorial court rolls. The death of Adam de Lyons of Weston Longville, Norfolk was reported in November 1318, when the order was given to take his lands into the lord's hands, and a jury was summoned. The following June, the jury reported that Adam held one fee in demesne and ½ fee subinfeudated. He had enfeoffed his son Arnold and his wife, Alice, of his demesne lands by a fine levied in the king's court, namely one knight's fee, and Arnold paid relief on ½ fee (£2 10*s*) and 6*s* 8*d* for entry.[35] In May 1323, a jury was summoned to give information about the lands and heir of the late William de Badele, and Robert de Badele was ordered to attend the court in order to pay his relief. At the next court in June, he was summoned to the court on 20 July to pay five marks towards his relief; the rest of the money and his homage and fealty were postponed until August, when he was to produce his charters and other evidence to show how his lands were held. He did homage and fealty to the Lady in August 1324.[36]

As in the royal system, juries were also used for proofs of age, which could be taken at Clare or at a forensic court in Norfolk. A jury at Walsingham in 1323 reported that John, son and heir of Philip de Broughton, had reached the age of 21 on 2 December 1322, and had received the manor of Sharrington as his inheritance. He held Sharrington and also land in Bale and Gunthorpe as ¼ fee, and had sworn fealty.[37]

Arrangements for widows likewise followed royal practice. When William Walgor's lands were taken into the Lady's hands in 1323, his heir was a minor. William's wife, Isabella, was ordered to appear before the court to give security that she would not remarry without licence. She apparently died soon after her husband.[38] Dower could be acquired only as a result of obtaining the Lady's writ; Elena, widow of Philip de Broughton, paid £1 to have her dower without this

[34] SC 2/212/39, m. 6, 7, 12, 14. Robert Belet held 1¼ and $^1/_{16}$ fees in nine Norfolk villages in 1314.

[35] SC 2/212/36, m. 3d, 9. Adam's holdings in 1314 lay at Weston Longville and three other Norfolk villages.

[36] SC 2/212/39, m. 8, 9; SC2/212/40, m. 2. In 1314, William held 4½ fees in ten places in Suffolk.

[37] SC 2/214/4, m. 2.

[38] SC 2/212/39, m. 7d, 11d.

writ.[39] The widow was entitled to one-third of her husband's land as dower. It is likely that some widows entered their husbands' lands before the allocation of dower; in 1309, the order was issued to distrain Amicia, widow of Richard son of Simon, for entry on the manor of Great Dunmow, Essex.[40]

Some at least of the heirs who came into wardship were brought up in the Lady's household. The wardrobe and household account of 1331–32 recorded expenditure of £1 16*s* 2*d* on 22 pairs of shoes, linen, nails, hooks, candlesticks and other small items bought for Roger Damory, Robert Sturmy and Robert de Wyveton, who were in the Lady's wardship.[41] The honour court rolls recorded details of some of the wards' lands, which often consisted of smallholdings. Some were kept in the Lady's hands, but some were used for patronage in reward of servants or officials, and some were leased. Marriages could be sold. Thus in 1355 Geoffrey Marham, who served as a bailiff of fees for Norfolk, was granted a cottage and one acre of arable land together with the marriage of Ralph, son and heir of Walter de Gaysele, for no rent, because Geoffrey was in the Lady's service.[42] Apparent relatives were sometimes granted custody; in 1355, one cottage and one acre of arable land in Griston, Norfolk were granted to Geoffrey Clement because of the minority of John, son and heir of Thomas Clement, aged six years; Geoffrey was to hold this until John came of age in return for a rent of 12*d* a year, and he was also granted John's marriage.[43] Rents of grain are found; in 1351–52, 25 acres of arable land in Buckenham, Norfolk, once held by Robert de Bokenham, were let to two men for a rent of four quarters and 5½ bushels of barley.[44]

The honour court in the first half of the fourteenth century faced pressures from the exercise of royal rights, the popularity of common law and the royal courts, the sheer complexity of honorial tenures and the changing interests and outlook of sub-tenants. Yet the court remained active, due to vigorous lordship and the bureaucratic administration of the honour. Feudal ties remained a social reality, despite having lost their original military significance. The lord or lady was still perceived as the head of the honour, making the most of the feudal incidents which he or she still retained.

39 SC 2/212/35, m. 5.

40 Ault, *Court Rolls*, 109.

41 E 101/ 91/27, m. 4; Ward, *Elizabeth de Burgh*, 129.

42 SC 2/213/12, m. 8. The place-name is missing.

43 Ibid. m. 7, 8.

44 SC 6/1110/26, m. 2.

5

Landscape, Farming and Society in an English Region: The Inquisitions *Post Mortem* for the West Midlands, 1250–1509

Christopher Dyer

Defining local differences in farming, land management and rural society is a great achievement of the historians working on the early modern period, and in particular Joan Thirsk.[1] They were helped by the comments of the early modern antiquaries and topographers, who described the countryside in such terms as champion, woodland and wold, which we still find appropriate. The systematic and scientific study of land use and farming systems arises from the thousands of probate inventories, which covered the whole country using fairly standard formulae from the mid-sixteenth into the eighteenth centuries. These documents listed for each holding the acreages of crops and the numbers of all types of livestock, and historians could note the patterns of similarity and difference.

Historians of the later Middle Ages can carry out a similar exercise for the agricultural economy of lords' demesnes by using manorial accounts compiled by reeves and bailiffs, but their geographical spread is rather restricted.[2] They appear in abundance between about 1280 and 1380, and they become very scarce after about 1420. How can the extents attached to IPMs supplement the accounts in defining local varieties of land use and farming methods? They inform us about lay estates, whereas many of the accounts were made for church landlords, and consequently the extents cover some regions where accounts are scarce.[3] Detailed extents were compiled over a long period, from the mid-thirteenth century into the sixteenth, so they are capable of reflecting long-term changes. They rarely say much about crops and animals, but they tell us more than the accounts about the various uses of land, and very occasionally they contain information about specific fields, pastures and woods. As with any source, they gain in value when they are combined with other documents.

[1] *AHEW* iv, *1500–1640*; J. Thirsk, *Agricultural Regions and Agrarian History in England, 1500–1750* (Basingstoke, 1987). I am grateful to Andrew Watkins for letting me use his transcript of the Coleshill (Warwickshire) IPM extent ahead of publication, Andy Isham for the map and Graham Smyth for allowing me to quote figures from his PhD thesis.

[2] Campbell, *ESA*.

[3] Campbell & Bartley, *Atlas*, 4–6.

This paper begins with questions about local variations in the use and organisation of land, and the social structure associated with different landscapes, based mainly on the IPMs of c.1250–1350. It then asks how land management changed through the 250 years covered by the extents attached to the inquisitions. It concentrates on the three West Midland counties of Gloucestershire, Warwickshire and Worcestershire, most of which lay within the diocese of Worcester, and which can be regarded as a coherent topographical unit coinciding roughly with the valley of the River Severn and its tributaries.[4] High ground is encountered to the west, on the Malvern Hills, to the north, around the Birmingham plateau, and its eastern boundary meets the Edge Hill and the hills of north-west Oxfordshire. Each county, and the region as a whole, is formed of contrasting *pays*, that is, sections of countryside with distinct landscapes and societies. Wooded and pastoral country, at its most extreme in the Forest of Dean in western Gloucestershire, runs through the west and north of Worcestershire (including the royal forests of Horwood, Malvern and Feckenham), to join with the Arden of Warwickshire. The Vale in Gloucestershire, which lies along the Severn, especially on its southern and eastern banks between Bristol and Gloucester and on to Tewkesbury, shares some similarities with the woodlands in its dispersed settlements, irregular fields and 'old enclosures'. The Vale on the Severn edge tended to be marshy and had to be defended from marine flooding. On both sides of the Warwickshire Avon, on the northern edge of Gloucestershire and in the vale of Evesham, a champion country of nucleated villages and open fields dominated, and in south and east Warwickshire was called the Feldon. The wold country of south and east Gloucestershire, though mostly at a higher altitude than the champion, had similarly compact villages and large common fields, though there were wooded areas, notably around the Stroud valley in the centre, and, of course, some large hill pastures.[5]

The map (Map 5.1) depicts the *pays* of the Forest (that is, Dean), woodland, Vale, Arden, champion, Feldon and wold. It does not attempt to identify the smaller sub-regions, such as the wetlands in the Severn estuary, or the wooded wolds around Stroud, or the part of the Cotswolds which dips gently into the Thames valley around Lechlade and Fairford. This is not because these smaller *pays* are unimportant, but instead reflects the limited size and sometimes thin distribution of the inquisitions. There are usually not sufficient extents from these areas to make large enough statistical totals for comparative purposes.

[4] R.H. Hilton, *A Medieval Society. The West Midlands at the End of the Thirteenth Century*, 2nd edn (Cambridge, 1983), 7–22.

[5] *The Domesday Geography of Midland England*, ed. H.C. Darby and I.B. Terrett (Cambridge, 1954), pp. 50–3; D. Hooke, *The Anglo-Saxon Landscape: the Kingdom of the Hwicce* (Manchester, 1985), 190–247; J.A. Yelling, 'Livestock Numbers and Agricultural Development, 1540–1750: a Study of East Worcestershire', in *Field and Forest. An Historical Geography of Warwickshire and Worcestershire*, ed. T.R. Slater and P.J. Jarvis (Norwich, 1982), 281–2; C. Dyer, 'Rural Settlement in Medieval Warwickshire', *Transactions of the Birmingham and Warwickshire Archaeological Society* 100 (1996), 117–32.

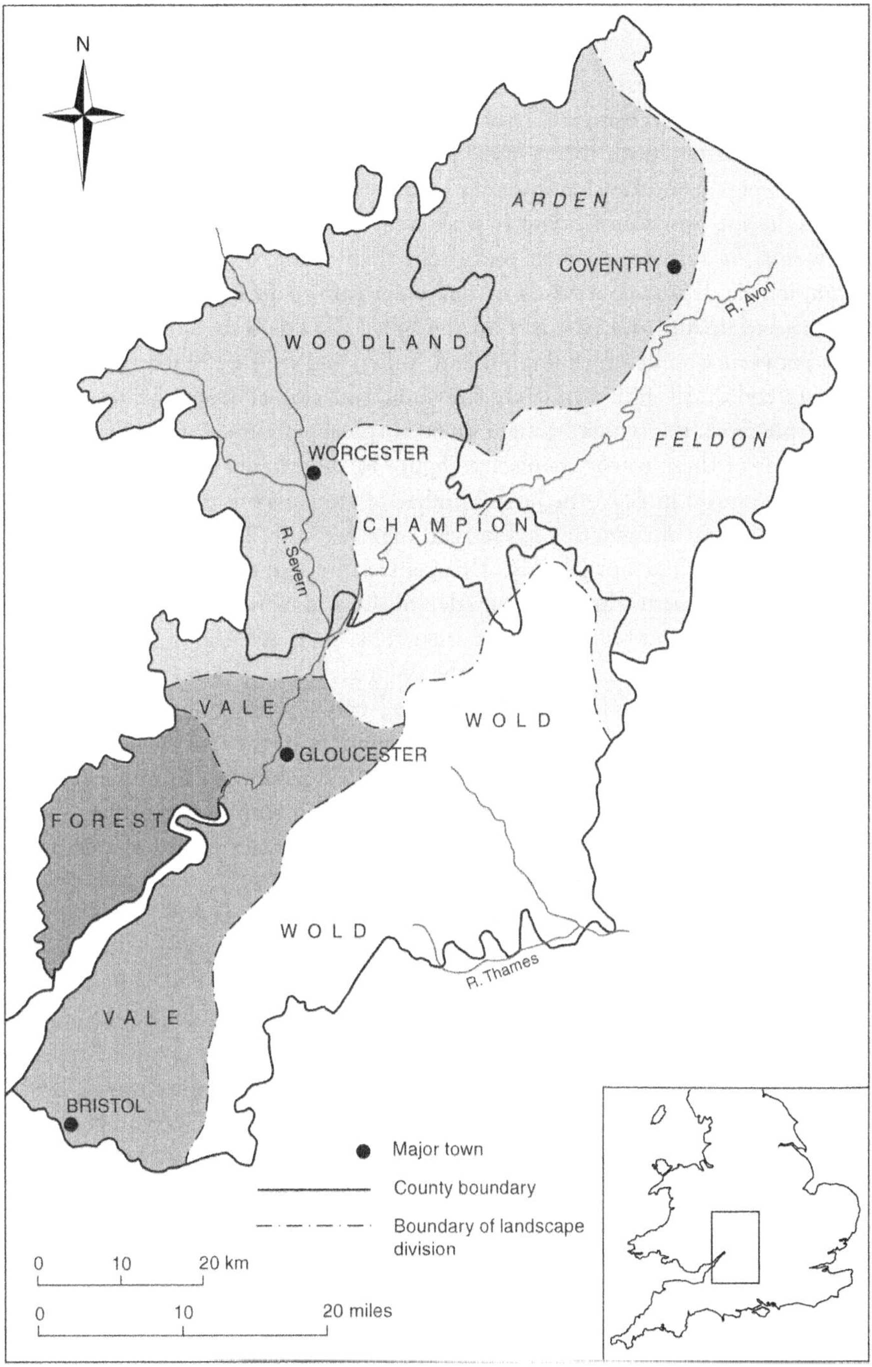

Map 5.1 The three West Midland counties (in 1931–74), with boundaries of the main types of historic landscape.

Analysing the inquisitions, as other researchers have found, requires a broad-brush approach.[6]

The people of these *pays* were not pursuing an isolated existence dependent on their own resources. They complemented one another in a complex web of exchanges, both direct and indirect. In the thirteenth and fourteenth centuries pigs from the champion and wolds were driven to feed on mast and acorns in the woodlands. Sheep were sent from the champion country to the wolds for summer pasture, and spent their winters in the more sheltered champion landscape. Cartloads of hay were carried from the river valleys to distant settlements and pastures on the hills.[7] Towns were sited on the frontiers between woodland, champion and wolds, and in their markets champion farmers could sell grain, and buy firewood and timber from the woodlands, or people from the wolds brought their surpluses of sheep, wool and barley. A number of these towns themselves figure in the extents attached to inquisitions. One notes in 1273 the large number of almost 76 burgages at Chipping Campden, many of them divided in half, together with 21 messuages, implying well over a hundred households. This centre of commerce owed its existence to its location near to the northern edge of the wolds in Gloucestershire. Busy trade is implied by a high level of market tolls, such as £4 in 1296 at Henley-in-Arden on a major road joining the Warwickshire Feldon to the Arden, and the substantial quantities of rents and court profits of £15 7*s* 2*d* from Chipping Sodbury on the south-western boundary of the Cotswolds in 1307.[8] Interregional trade helped to provide a livelihood for hundreds of townspeople, who handled enough commodities, and provided a sufficient number of services, to allow lords (according to the extents) to extract plenty of cash from their seigneurial boroughs.

Exchanges through such practices as transhumance, carriage of hay, and trade in the market-places are recorded in the reeves' manorial accounts. The extents occasionally provide evidence for complementary connections, for example when, in the inquisition of the estates of Guy Beauchamp, earl of Warwick in 1315, Tanworth-in-Arden in Warwickshire was called a hamlet belonging to Brailes in the champion country 20 miles (32km) to the south-east. Brailes was, and had been for centuries, a manor practising mixed agriculture with much arable, while Tanworth served as its woodland appendage, providing pasture, firewood and timber.[9] In 1367 an extent for Temple Guiting in the Cotswolds values an area

[6] Campbell & Bartley, *Atlas*, pp. 7–11.

[7] C. Dyer, *Lords and Peasants in a Changing Society. The Estates of the Bishopric of Worcester, 680–1540* (Cambridge, 1980), 136; C. Dyer, 'Sheepcotes: Evidence for Medieval Sheepfarming', *Medieval Archaeology*, 34 (1995), 136–64.

[8] *Abstracts of Inquisitiones Post Mortem for Gloucestershire*, part 4, *1236–1300*, ed. S.J. Madge, British Record Society 30 (1903) [henceforth *IPM Glos 4*], 63–9; C133/76/4; *Abstracts of Inquisitiones Post Mortem for Gloucestershire*, part 5, *1302–58*, ed. E.A. Fry, British Record Society 40 (1910) [henceforth *IPM Glos* 5], 81–5.

[9] C134/49/35; *VCH Warw*. v (1949), 168, 174.

of upland 'summer pasture' at 40*s*, referring to the transhumance which brought sheep, sometimes from a distance, onto the hills.[10] At nearby Longborough, also in Gloucestershire, in 1275 the earl of Cornwall's extent reveals that this hilltop manor included an unusually large area of meadow amounting to 61¼ acres. This land was so essential for producing hay for feeding livestock in the winter that each acre was worth 20*d*, and in all it was equal in value to the much larger area of arable land at 4*d* per acre. The meadow belonged to an outlying hamlet of Frogmore, which consisted of four peasant holdings as well as grassland.[11] True to its name, the hamlet lay in the broad and damp valley of the river Evenlode, where lush grass grew. The extents did not need to spell out distant connections, but a noted feature of the organisation of landed estates was the distribution of manors over different types of countryside, facilitating transhumance, or the transport of seed corn or fodder to be practised as part of the estates' seasonal routine. If crops did badly in one manor, climatic or soil differences might enable higher levels of production on another. Estates demonstrating this prudent dispersal include that of Fulk Lucy in Warwickshire, who in 1302 held both Shrewley in the Arden and Charlecote in the Feldon.[12] The Gurneys, from their centre at the castle of Beverston in Gloucestershire, combined two Cotswold manors with Over in the Vale and Aylburton near the Forest of Dean.[13]

Extents usually state the area and value of arable and meadow and indicate the presence of pasture and wood. Occasionally a more detailed description of the fields is given, usually when a widow is being assigned her dower, and the jury had to be more precise about the division of land. At Farmcote in the Gloucestershire Cotswolds in 1418 the lord of the manor was cultivating strips of land scattered over the furlongs of an open-field system divided between a North Field and South Field. Two-field systems did not necessarily follow a two-course rotation, so it is helpful to be told that the land could be sown in 'every other year', suggesting a conventional cropping regime.[14] More briefly, in October 1315 a two-field system appears in the extent of the earl of Warwick's manor of Lighthorne in the Warwickshire Feldon, where the arable was said to lie 'in both fields'.[15]

In the woodlands the manor of Pendock in Worcestershire was divided in 1322, and Cecily, widow of John Pendock, received as a one-third share of the demesne strips or selions scattered over eleven pieces of land, four of them called fields, but also in a croft and in a garth (yard or garden). Among these fields and enclosures, forming a much more complex arrangement than the two fields encountered in the wold and champion, there is evidence of relatively

10 *Abstracts of Inquisitiones Post Mortem for Gloucestershire*, part 6, *1359–1419*, ed. E. Stokes, British Record Society 47 (1914) [henceforth *IPM Glos* 6], 44–5.

11 *IPM Glos* 4, 102–3.

12 C133/106/16.

13 *IPM Glos* 4, pp. 40–2 (1269); 129–32 (1286).

14 *CIPM* xxi, pp. 45–6.

15 C134/51/69.

recent origin in such names as Newland and 'Old' (meaning former woodland).[16] In 1423 an unusually detailed description of Elizabeth Lady Clinton's manor of Birmingham names fourteen 'closes', a number of which were called fields, each containing between 4 and 13 acres.[17] This arrangement was characteristic of the north Warwickshire woodlands, where the closes were well suited for keeping cattle. Birmingham was, however, a special case, because the town's market handled large numbers of cattle, and in particular those beasts brought to the Midlands from distant pastures in Wales.[18] The lords of the manor or their lessees could have profited from keeping and feeding these animals while they awaited sale, and may have fattened some of them to gain a price advantage. These commercial opportunities must explain why the jury compiling the extent valued the land in the closes at such high figures: between 5*d* and 12*d* per acre, mostly at or near the higher figure. High land values also prevailed in the Gloucestershire Vale, in the manors around Berkeley which figure in the 1439 Beauchamp inquisition. The juries gave a detailed list of assets, including tenant holdings, employing the terminology of enclosure: the land lay in crofts, curtilages, gardens, parcels and plots, with occasional reference to land surrounded by hedges and ditches. Selions and fields were also mentioned, so this was a mixed, partially enclosed landscape.[19] Similar complexities are found in the 1374 extent for Ela de Bradeston's share of a manor at Stinchcombe, located on the edge between the hilly and woody wolds near Dursley and the vale of Berkeley. At first sight the arable land seems to lie in two fields, *Northfeld* and *Westfeld*, each with 27½ acres consisting of parcels in named furlongs, closely resembling Farmcote and Lighthorne, but land is also held in severalty, in crofts. A description of 21½ acres in *Aldewyk* suggests a third field. Field names like *Litelrudyng* show that there was a history of clearing woodland for cultivation, and indeed woods survived in the form of four groves.[20]

The extents contribute to a composite picture of local differences and connections between places when they are combined with other sources, such as the surveys of manors on large church estates (with which the West Midlands is well supplied), transfers of land by charters or final concords, or the manorial accounts already mentioned. The jurors who gave the information for the majority of extents took for granted the landscape in which manors lay, regarding such commonplaces of daily life as irrelevant to the main purposes of the inquisition, which were to value the assets and to establish the succession of a new landholder.

16 *The Inquisitiones Post Mortem for the County of Worcester*, part 2, *1300–1326*, ed. J.W. Willis Bund, Worcestershire Historical Society 21 (1909) [henceforth *IPM Worcs* 2]; C. Dyer, 'Dispersed Settlements in Medieval England. A Case Study of Pendock, Worcestershire', *Medieval Archaeology* 34 (1990), 97–121.

17 *CIPM* xxii.344 (at pp. 314–15).

18 R.A. Holt, *The Early History of the Town of Birmingham 1166–1600*, Dugdale Society Occasional Paper 30 (1985), 10–11.

19 *CIPM* xxv.287 (at pp. 234–42).

20 *IPM Glos* 6, 84–5.

This reminds us that, while noting vivid insights into the landscape and farming, we should be aware of the gaps and deficiencies which make the extents attached to the IPMs very imperfect sources. The obvious problem is that they are confined to recording the property of lay lords, which in the West Midlands in particular leaves some districts, such as south-east Worcestershire and eastern Gloucestershire, with few inquisitions, as so much of the land was held by monasteries, the bishop of Worcester and the archbishop of York. At least the IPMs have the virtue of enabling us to observe parts of the region where church land was less prevalent, especially in the northern woodlands.

Another obvious problem in using the extents stems from their recording of the lord's assets, such as demesne land, and not the fields and pastures of the whole community. They value the income that lords gained from the tenants, and this can be compared with the demesne values. In Worcestershire between 1273 and 1320 the median figure for the value of demesne assets was 30% of the value of the whole manor, suggesting that by a substantial margin most of the productive land was held by tenants. Acreages can be estimated for some manors, and they confirm this proportion. At Naunton Beauchamp in 1296 the lord's arable demesne amounted to 140 acres, while the customary tenants were working at least 375 acres and (including the free tenants) the tenants' share was probably well over 400 acres, three times the size of the demesne[21] The extents do not usually describe the agricultural land in the hands of peasants. That does not mean that we are entirely ignorant of the peasants' occupation of the landscape, as no demesne was an island. Lords and their tenants shared assets, and often held land together in open fields, or both put animals to graze on the same pasture, so a description of a demesne is at least a pointer to the state of the land in the hands of the peasants.

The greatest obstacle to gaining useful information from the extents is their failure to treat all types of land evenly. A typical extent makes some attempt to assess the arable area by means of carucates (ploughlands), virgates (yardlands), bovates (oxgangs) or acres. This information lacks precision, as a carucate varied in size between 60 and 120 acres, and a virgate could be as small as 20 acres or as large as 50 acres. A bovate rated about half of a virgate, but was rarely used in the West Midlands as it lay outside the former Danelaw. Acres were not always standardised, as we read of 'great acres' and other suggestions of local customary measures. Nonetheless, the size of the arable is indicated, however imprecisely, and meadow land is assigned an acreage, but pasture and wood is often given a round monetary value of 6*s* 8*d*, 20*s* or 40*s*. A frequent troubling entry states that pasture or wood lay in common and therefore was worth nothing, which must mean that the value was difficult to calculate because the lord did not have exclusive use. A value is sometimes given, like the 40*s* for summer pasture at

[21] *The Inquisitiones Post Mortem for the County of Worcester*, part 1, *1242–1299*, ed. J.W. Willis Bund, Worcestershire Historical Society 20 (1894) [henceforth *IPM Worcs* 1], 61–2.

Table 5.1 Land use by values, aggregated from a sample of manors, Gloucestershire, 1256–1311

	Arable	Meadow	Pasture	Wood	Other	Total
Wold (19 manors)	£67	£32	£9	£6	—	£114
%	59	28	8	5	—	100
Vale (17 manors)	£88	£61	£15	£8	—	£172
%	51	35	9	5	—	100

Sources: *IPM Glos* 4; *IPM Glos* 5

Temple Guiting, and the common of Chipping Campden in 1273 was said to accommodate a thousand sheep and was worth 20*s*, an improbably low sum of money.[22] It is possible to allow for this problem by aggregating and analysing the values, because these are given for all types of land.

This has been done for a sample of Gloucestershire manors (Table 5.1) but the result is rather inconclusive – the percentages representing the values of different types of land use for the Vale and wold manors resemble one another, and clearly pasture and wood are under-represented in both. Meadow was evidently more plentiful in the Vale than on the wolds. The importance of meadow is enhanced because its value per acre was very high, at four times or eight times that of arable, as an acre was usually worth 12*d* to 30*d*. Our frustration at such unbalanced information is allayed somewhat when a few extents give acreages. For example, a group of inquisitions for Forest of Dean manors for 1256–86 record acres of pasture amounting to 8% of the total, and wood at 19%, but these figures still understate the assets of the manors, as they were concerned to value the 'several', that is, enclosed grazing and woodland, and leave as uncertain the amount of land over which the lords had rights along with the commoners. At least these Dean surveys point to the special character of the district, in which lords held a considerable quantity of enclosed non-arable land. In the other parts of the region it was presumably thought unnecessary to itemise the pasture and wood because access to these resources was attached by custom to the ploughlands and yardlands. This under-rating of pasture means that the extents do not reflect fully the lords' sources of landed income, as they often derived large profits from their pastures, especially from flocks of sheep.

Leaving aside these criticisms of the extents, although accurate judgements of the relative importance of arable and grazing land cannot be made, some insights can come from the quantity of arable. Most demesnes contained between 50 and 300 acres, which meant that they maintained one, two or three plough teams of oxen. Very large demesnes can be encountered in the sub-region where the south-eastern Cotswolds sloped gently down into the upper Thames valley, notably 832½ acres at Kempsford in 1258, 610 acres at Fairford in 1307, and 518 acres

22 *IPM Glos* 6, 44–5; *IPM Glos* 4, 64.

in 1275 at Lechlade.[23] To the west, and higher up on the wolds, 400- to 500-acre demesnes are found at such manors as Beverston and Dyrham, but also in the western vale at Siston. Nearer to Gloucester, also in the Vale, the demesne of Badgeworth in 1327 was said to have 700 acres of arable.[24] In the Warwickshire Feldon a 596-acre arable demesne is recorded at Brailes in 1315, and 420¾ acres at Kineton in 1325.[25] The areas of demesne arable appear to have diminished after 1350. Very large quantities of arable in the fifteenth century are recorded in 1420, at Beckford (12 carucates) and Ashton-under-Hill (10 carucates) below Bredon Hill on the Worcestershire–Gloucestershire border, but there must be some uncertainty about the size of the carucate. More precise is the figure of 525 acres of arable found at Burton Dassett in the Warwickshire Feldon in 1443.[26] In the woodlands at all periods arable demesnes rarely exceeded 300 acres, and in north-west Worcestershire a number of small manors each cultivated demesne of less than 50 acres.

To set these figures into a landscape, we can visualise the experience of a traveller of *c.*1300 riding in the Thames valley between Lechlade and Fairford in July, when ripening corn occupied a considerable part of the vista, well attested by the arable acreages in the extents. The relatively flat land was also occupied by the fallow, which had carried a crop in the previous year. By July this had been given its extra summer ploughing. Towards the river to the rider's left, newly mown meadow occupied a very large area, also a feature of the extents. On the traveller's right were the downs, on slightly higher ground and full of grazing sheep. All of these different types of land were being exploited by both lords and peasants. Woods, perhaps trees in general, were scarce. As John Leland remarked after making the same journey two centuries later, 'all by low ground, in manner in a level ... very barren of wood'.[27]

When Leland travelled from Bromsgrove in north Worcestershire to Birmingham in Warwickshire he found 'good plenty of wood and pasture and meetly good corn'.[28] His route was traversing land recorded in a number of inquisitions from the previous century and earlier which depict a land producing some corn (probably in patches of open field), but there was much enclosed land. Trees grew in small woods, but also in parkland and hedgerows, and in the summer the trees in leaf dominated the observer's impression of the countryside. Here, as in the south Gloucestershire example, other sources, such as manorial court rolls of the fourteenth and fifteenth centuries, show that peasants gained their living in the same landscape as their lords. In north-east Worcestershire in

23 *IPM Glos* 4, 21, 102; *IPM Glos* 5, 78.
24 *IPM Glos* 4, 40, 59–60, 130; *IPM Glos* 5, 120, 210.
25 C134/49/34; C134/97/4.
26 *CIPM* xxi.645 (at p. 212); xxvi.109 (at pp. 62–3.).
27 *Leland's Itinerary in England and Wales*, ed. L. Toulmin Smith (London, 1906), I, 26; *VCH Glos* vii, 95–6.
28 *Leland's Itinerary* ii, 95–6.

Bromsgrove, King's Norton and Northfield, and in Edgbaston and Birmingham in Warwickshire, the peasants grew corn, grazed cattle and profited in various ways from the woods and trees.[29]

The value given to demesne land was presumably based on how much revenue a lord could expect to make in a year either from direct management of the demesne land or by renting it out. The value per annum of each acre tended to be higher in champion districts when compared with the woodlands. In Warwickshire in 1272–1325 arable was rarely valued as low as 2*d* or above 4*d*, though exceptionally it could attain 6*d* or even 8*d*. In the Arden the median value was 3*d*, and less than a third was rated at 4*d* or above. Arable acres in the Feldon had a median value of 4*d*. In Gloucestershire, arable land values on the wolds fell below those in the Vale. In a sample collected between 1256 and 1311 areas of arable on the wold were assessed at 4*d* or more in 37% of cases, compared to 60% in the Vale.

Land was valued unequally, depending on the *pays*, on church estates as well as on the lay estates in the IPMs. On the bishop of Worcester's manorial demesnes in the Cotswolds and woodlands, in c.1290 arable was valued at 3*d* per acre, and in the champion at 6*d* to 7*d*.[30] Land values on church and lay manors alike derived from a complex combination of environmental and market forces. The soil was more fertile and productive in the Vale and the Feldon, compared with the woodlands and wolds, and the climate favoured arable crops. In the river valleys, especially near the Severn, grain and legumes were more marketable, and could be transported to larger towns and even (from the port of Bristol) carried overseas.[31]

Lordship and the structure of manors clearly differed from one *pays* to another. Some large manors, mainly in the woodlands, were depicted in extents in the period around 1300 as possessing relatively small demesnes but many tenants – the demesnes of Martley and Suckley in Worcestershire were worth below 10% of the value of the whole manor.[32] The well-off knightly family of the Oddingseles held Solihull in the Arden of Warwickshire, and when it was surveyed in 1295 it had an arable demesne of 30 acres worth 10*s*, with tenant rents, mostly paid by freeholders, amounting to £42.[33] The tenant share of the

[29] The inquisitions include *IPM Worcs* 1, pp. 16–17, 36 ; *IPM Worcs* 2, p. 113 ; *CIPM* xxii.344, 491(at pp. 314–15, 435); for the peasants, C. Dyer, 'Lords in a Landscape: the Berkeley Family and Northfield (Worcestershire)', *The Fifteenth Century* 14 (2015), 13–37; A. Baker, 'A Study of North-Eastern King's Norton: Ancient Settlement in a Woodland Manor', *Transactions of the Birmingham and Warwickshire Archaeological Society* 102 (2003), 131–59; *The Court Rolls of the Manor of Bromsgrove and King's Norton 1494–1504*, ed. A.C. Baber, Worcestershire Historical Society (1963); George Demidowicz and Stephen Price, *King's Norton. A History* (Chichester, 2009), 22–9, 39, 44–6, 51–3.

[30] Dyer, *Lords and Peasants*, 68; Campbell & Bartley, *Atlas*, 178–9 also suggest lower arable values in the woodlands and wolds.

[31] R.H. Hilton, *The English Peasantry in the Later Middle Ages* (Oxford, 1975), 89.

[32] *IPM Worcs* 1, 20; *IPM Worcs* 2, 53.

[33] C133/73/2. For a map showing a high ratio of rents compared with demesne values, see Campbell & Bartley, *Atlas*, Map 14.9.

manorial land must have totalled at least 2,000 acres, and the primary function of the manorial administration was the collection of rents. It was once supposed that these numerous free tenants had moved into the woodlands in a great movement of internal colonisation in the twelfth and thirteenth centuries, but the type of manor which had small demesnes and many tenants is found in the Domesday surveys of the woodland manors (in Warwickshire at such places as Great Alne and Sutton Coldfield; at Rowington in 1086 there was no demesne at all).[34] They seem to represent a type of pre-Conquest estate management that survived into later centuries, and the colonising movement after 1100 was adding to the number of woodland tenants rather than initiating extensive settlements.

Another eccentric type of manorial structure lacked any tenants at all, and again they are encountered most often in the woodlands, including five manors (in the period 1273–1326) in north Worcestershire. Another eight small manors in that county had an unusually high proportion of their values, of 45% or above, deriving from the demesne. These unconventional manors tended to have lords who can be classified as gentry.[35] In the Cotswolds tenantless manors can only rarely be found, and invariably the tenants' rents were valued more highly than was the demesne. This is just one indication of the prevalence of orthodox manors and the greater degree of seigneurial control on the wolds, though to some extent this was a characteristic of all parts of Gloucestershire, except in the Forest of Dean, where manors tended to have irregular structures.

The best statistical guide to the power of lords comes from the relative importance of free and unfree tenure. Many extents do not give a list of tenants or even an indication of their number, but they often estimate the rent income for the manor, and usually divide that sum of money between free and unfree (or customary) tenants. The sample of manors in Worcestershire (especially in the champion area) is not very large, but it is still possible to note that in a majority of champion manors free rents account for below 33% of the manorial revenues deriving from tenants, while on two-thirds of the woodland manors free rents were in excess of the 33% figure. The lords of small manors in north Worcestershire often received no rents from customary tenants, but only from free tenants, as in the case of the manors of Eymore, Hanley Child and Hanley William.[36]

The differences between woodland and champion are very clearly demonstrated by the figures from Warwickshire for a sample of 39 manors in the decades around 1300 (Table 5.2), when about a quarter of rents in the Feldon came from free tenants, but more than two-thirds of the rents in the Arden.

[34] *Domesday Book*, ed. A Farley, Record Commission (1783), fos 238b, 239a, 242a.

[35] E.A. Kosminsky, *Studies in the Agrarian History of England in the Thirteenth Century*, ed. R. Kisch (Oxford, 1966), 262–82; R. Britnell, 'Minor Landlords in England and Medieval Agrarian Capitalism', *Past and Present* 89 (1980), 3–22; P. Coss, *The Foundations of Gentry Life. The Multons of Frampton and their World 1270–1370* (Oxford, 2010), 75–8, 100–6.

[36] *IPM Worcs* 1, 50–1.

Table 5.2 Total values (of rents and services) of free and unfree (customary) tenants, Warwickshire, 1272–1325

	Free	Unfree	Total
Feldon (18 manors)	£45	£138	£183
%	24	76	100
Arden (21 manors)	£187	£84	£271
%	69	31	100

Sources: TNA, C 113; C133; C134.

Table 5.3 Total values (of rents and services) of free and unfree (customary) tenants, Gloucestershire, 1256–1311

	Free	Unfree	Total
Wold (17 manors)	£22	£139	£161
%	13	87	100
Vale (17 manors)	£67	£247	£314
%	21	79	100

Sources: See Table 5.1.

The higher proportion of free tenants in the woodlands is also apparent in the Warwickshire Hundred Rolls in 1279–80, and from a later date in the surveys of the estates of Coventry priory, with a pronounced majority of free tenants on woodland manors in the vicinity of the city of Coventry.[37]

In Gloucestershire (Table 5.3) the difference between manors on the wolds and in the Vale is not so well defined, though free tenure was relatively scarce on the Cotswolds. Again, surveys of a church estate of the same period – that of Gloucester abbey in 1265–67 – gives evidence of tenant numbers rather than the total rents, but a similar pattern emerges, with 25% of tenants being freeholders on the wolds, compared with 29% in the Vale. In the champion manors north of the Cotwolds the figure for free tenants fell to 16%.[38] A major conclusion that emerges from Tables 5.2 and 5.3 is the peculiar character of Gloucestershire society: the whole county had a tradition of strong lordship, with a large number of slaves at the time of Domesday Book, as well as unfree tenants, accounting for three-quarters or four-fifths of the total in the thirteenth and fourteenth centuries.[39]

Another indication of lords' ability to extract revenues from the rest of society comes from the amount demanded annually in rents and services, especially from

[37] Hilton, *English Peasantry*, 126–8; D. Greenblatt, ' The Suburban Manors of Coventry, 1279–1411', PhD thesis, Cornell University (1967), pp. 20–31.

[38] G. Smyth, 'The Estate of Gloucester Abbey, 1086–1348', PhD thesis, Birmingham University (2004), p. 176.

[39] H.C. Darby, *Domesday England* (Cambridge, 1977), 76–7, 338.

the customary tenants. The levels of exactions are most easily analysed using the value of rents, services and customs paid by the villeins or *nativi* or *rustici* per yardland or virgate, because that is how they were described by the jurors giving information for the inquisition extents. In the Arden or the woodlands of north Worcestershire the value of rents and services rarely rose above 10*s* per yardland. In the Feldon and champion districts they could fall as low as 7*s* or 8*s*, but more often stood between 10*s* and 20*s*. Some low rents are found in the Cotswolds, and few exceeded 15*s* per yardland. Rents were calculated by the acre rather than for yardlands in Dean and its immediate surroundings, but yardlands could be valued at 5*s* 6*d* and 9*s* 6*d* in manors on the western side of the Severn adjacent to the Forest. In comparison with the mediocre payments in the woodlands and wolds, the rents owed in that part of the Vale near to the Severn stand out. From the manor of Over just north of Bristol to Haresfield to the south of Gloucester annual payments at rates of 28*s*, 32*s*, 36*s* and 40*s* per yardland must have been among the highest in England. The view that these rents were not really so high because the yardlands of the Vale could be very large, as much as 40 or 50 acres each, has some validity but, even if calculated per acre, the rents are still in the region of 8*d* to 11*d*. Large yardlands prevailed also in the Cotswolds, making their rents as low as 2*d* per acre.

What caused these pronounced variations in rents and services? As is the case with values per acre of demesne land (see above), the combination of the physical environment and the market made some land more productive and its crops more profitable. Peasants, like their lords, had to grow corn on land of variable quality, and they could not be expected realistically to pay high rents for land that was difficult to work and did not readily produce high yields. Lords and peasants alike wished to sell their surplus of crops, but this might have been difficult if they lived and farmed in remote hilly or woodland locations. The geography of the Vale offered many advantages, and the lords of Vale manors could expect to receive large sums of money from tenants gaining good returns. The records produced for the Berkeley family for the Vale of Berkeley manors show them in the late thirteenth century creating forms of leasehold, with high rents, on the assumption that there was a strong demand for the land.[40]

The power of lords has to be built into any model of the rural economy, and this undoubtedly had an effect on the levels and types of rent. In the extents for the decades around 1300, taking all the counties together, 24 out of a total of 92 stated that tenants' obligations included three days of work on the lord's demesne. These records of heavy labour services are not notably concentrated in one type of landscape. In Gloucestershire they are distributed evenly between wold and Vale; in Worcestershire seven occur in woodland manors and four in the champion, but the sample is biased in favour of the woodlands. Only one Warwickshire manor has three-day weekwork: Brailes in the Feldon. There is, however, a clear

[40] B. Wells-Furby, *The Berkeley Estate 1281–1417. Its Economy and Development*, Bristol and Gloucestershire Archaeological Society (2012), 100–18.

Table 5.4 Size of tenant holdings from IPM extents, around 1300

	Small	¼ yl	½ yl	1 yl	1 yl+	Total
Gloucestershire wold	139	11	36	236	0	422
%	33	3	8	56	0	100
Gloucestershire Vale	170	26	72	61	5	334
%	51	8	22	18	1	100
Gloucestershire champion	25	7	2	53	1	88
%	28	8	2	60	1	100
Warwickshire Feldon	46	5	52	36	6	145
%	32	3	36	25	4	100
Worcestershire champion	112	8	87	18	5	230
%	48	4	38	8	2	100
Worcestershire woodland	117	60	153	65	9	404
%	29	15	38	16	2	100

Notes: yl = yardland or virgate. For the size of these units in acres see text.
Sources: See Tables 5.1 and 5.2; *IPM Worcs* 1; *IPM Worcs* 2.

link between heavy weekwork and the estates of major lords. They include the earls of Gloucester, Norfolk and Warwick, and representatives of such baronial families as Berkeley, Corbett, Giffard and Gurney. A similar prominence of the upper ranks of the aristocracy is found among those lords demanding tallage (an annual charge in cash, paid by unfree tenants) in excess of 40*s* per manor. Again, the earls appear on the list of lords receiving substantial sums of tallage, and a Corbett and the Somerys. The tenants of these last two prominent baronial families were subject to the strong hand of lordship even in the woodlands of north Worcestershire, where seigneurial power was often relatively weak.

The extents attached to IPMs tell us a good deal about the relationship between lords and tenants, because their aim was to calculate manorial values, but they can indirectly reveal dimensions of the economy of the peasantry. Many extents give the size of tenant holdings in terms of the standard unit, the yardland or fractions of that unit, or occasionally in acres (Table 5.4).

On the basis of a comparison across England, the tenants of full yardlands appear by c.1300 as a relatively well-off minority.[41] The yardland amounted to about 30 acres of arable in most of the West Midland region but, as we have just noted, yardlands could be considerably larger in Gloucestershire. A noted feature of parts of Gloucestershire was the survival into the thirteenth and fourteenth centuries of the yardland as the holding of a high proportion of tenants, even a majority in many villages. In the Cotswolds 56% of holdings recorded in the extents were full yardlands and the equivalent figure in the champion country to

[41] P.R. Schofield, *Peasant and Community in Medieval England 1200–1500* (Basingstoke, 2003), 22–8, 132–3.

the north of the hills was 60%. Statistics compiled for the Gloucester abbey estate reveal similar figures.[42] This perpetuation of full yardlands suggests a lack of pressure – from population growth, for example – to split these large holdings, or more likely the tenants knew that holdings of 15 or 20 acres were not productive enough to sustain a family securely, so they did not press for them to be divided between heirs. Lords would have been concerned that divided holdings could not pay the rents and perform the labour services.

In other parts of the West Midland region full yardlands accounted for a minority, and half and quarter yardlands represented about 40% or even (in the Worcestershire woodlands) more than a half of holdings. Those with smallholdings would have earned wages to supplement the produce of their few acres, and normally they accounted for about a third of the tenant holdings. They were more numerous in the champion country in Worcestershire, and rose above a half in the Gloucestershire Vale. The smallholders and the fractional yardlands, not just in the Vale but in the champion and woodland districts to the north and east, must reflect a dense and rising population, with peasants exploiting resources intensively enough to enable a family to live on modest holdings. Smallholders could find employment because peasants as well as the larger landholders needed extra labour. This pressure of numbers is apparent in the distribution of taxpayers in the lay subsidies of 1327 and 1332, which reached the high levels above 100 per 10 square miles in parts of the Vale, champion and Feldon.[43] The extents attached to the IPMs suggest the commercial development of the region when they include market towns (and some aspirant towns with busy markets): Bewdley, Dudley, Dymmock, Fairford, Kidderminster, Kineton, Lechlade, Newent, Newport-on-Severn, Tewkesbury and Thornbury as well as those already mentioned (see p. 000), and the towns founded on church estates. The majority of rural rents were paid in cash, of course, which tenants obtained by selling either produce from the land or the labour of themselves and their families. Many of the labour services that had been demanded in earlier generations had been commuted for money, hence the relatively small number of manors with records of heavy weekwork.[44]

The extents also record industries which generated employment for smallholders, often in the woodlands where fuel and raw materials could be readily obtained. Droitwich, an urban centre of salt making, required many cart loads of wood from the surrounding countryside, and Dudley, also in Worcestershire, had iron forges and a coal mine. In the Forest of Dean part-time peasant workers could find employment in iron and coal mines, and in forges. Likewise in other wooded areas craft activity was based on the local supplies of fuel and raw materials, such as the pottery kilns of Hanley Castle in Worcestershire.[45] Fulling mills

42 Smyth, 'Gloucester Abbey', 117.

43 Campbell & Bartley, *Atlas*, Map 18.10.

44 Hilton, *English Peasantry*, 128–9, 142–6.

45 Droitwich: *IPM Worcs* 1, 8, 13, 25, 59; J.D. Hurst, 'Fuel Supply and the Medieval Salt Industry in Droitwich', *Transactions of the Worcestershire Archaeological Society*, 3rd ser. 19

in north Worcestershire and south Gloucestershire show the early development of rural cloth making, and fishing on a large scale at the confluence of the Wye and Severn sustained a community of smallholders at Tidenham in 1306.[46]

To sum up this overview of the IPM extents for the West Midland region, mainly from the first tranche of documents in the late thirteenth and early fourteenth centuries, the variety of land use is not immediately obvious because of the uneven treatment of arable, meadow, pasture and wood by the compilers of the documents. Only occasionally are the differences revealed between the open fields of the champion and wolds and the more irregular fields and enclosures of the woodlands and the Vale. Contemporaries were clearly conscious of differences, however, judging from the many links and connections which were made in order to redress imbalances in resources. Large arable demesnes are found in the areas of open fields in the wolds and champion, though they also occur in the Vale. Land values, both estimates of the demesne and the values of rents and services owed by tenants, show that the Vale enjoyed many advantages, and the lowest returns on arable land could be expected from the Cotswolds. Gloucestershire estates, and especially in the wolds, stand out for the dominance of the conventional manor, and indeed the strength of lordship in general. Irregular manors, both those with very small demesnes, and those where demesnes accounted for a high proportion of value, are most often found in the woodlands. Free tenure featured prominently in the Arden of Warwickshire, reinforcing the impression of the less developed structure of manors in that *pays*. The peasant holdings retained their large size, a full yardland, most often in the wolds, and the subdivision of tenant land and proliferation of smallholders, especially in the Vale, points to a more intense economic environment. Lordship had an independent influence, as is shown by the imposition of heavy labour services and substantial tallage payments on the estates of the higher aristocracy, even in the woodlands where lordship tended to be less oppressive. The large church estates confirm most of these findings. Their manors varied between woodland, champion and wold in such matters as field systems, land values, free tenure and the size of tenant holdings. Like the earls and barons, they could impose lordly power.

Long-term change

The great advantage of the IPMs is the sense that they give of change over more than two centuries. The surveys compiled by the administrators of church estates

(2004), r 111–32; Dudley: *IPM Worcs* 1, 35; Dean: *IPM Glos* 4, 35–6, 39, 93, 144–5; *IPM Glos* 5, 168; Hanley Castle: *IPM Worcs* 1, 56, but for a better version, *Records of Hanley Castle, Worcestershire, c.1147–1547*, ed. J.P. Toomey, Worcestershire Historical Society, new ser. 18 (2001), 143–55.

46 Fulling mills: *IPM Worcs* 1, 34, 43; *IPM Worcs* 2, 7; *IPM Glos* 4, 86, 138, 179, 199; fishing: *IPM Glos* 5, 63–72.

and the Hundred Rolls of 1279–80 resemble still photographs, providing a sharp and revealing image of a single moment in time. The IPM extents, like a cine-film, allow us to observe moving images. Unfortunately the movie camera does not take pictures from the perspective we would prefer, and they are fuzzy and out of focus.

The extents of the period 1418–47 are more abbreviated, and lack detail and precision as compared with those of the previous centuries, but they reveal some changes. Land values were falling: in Gloucestershire the arable in the wolds had a median value of 3*d* per acre around 1300, but the figure sank to 2*d* in the early fifteenth century. In the Vale the median remained at 4*d*. In the Arden of Warwickshire the median value of an acre had fallen from 3*d* to 2*d*. Tenant yardlands in the Feldon, which had been said to be worth between 8*s* and 20*s* in 1272–1325, corresponding presumably to their annual rent, had been reduced to the range of 3*s* 4*d* to 13*s* 4*d* in 1418–47. The comparable figures in the Arden took the value of the yardland from 5*s*–16s before 1325 to 5*s*–6*s* 8*d* after 1418. Such steep falls in land values were not universal. In the 1439 inquisition of Richard Beauchamp, earl of Warwick for the Vale of Berkeley manors such as Ham sums as high as 40*s* per yardland are found, comparable with those prevailing around 1300.[47] Throughout the region acres of pasture, which were often valued below arable, at a penny or two, were occasionally assessed in the fifteenth century at 6*d*, 8*d* or even 12*d*, presumably because they had been enclosed and improved in some way.

These values have to be seen in the context of the economy of the manor, as they were recorded in order to calculate the lord's revenues. The cumulative effect of the decline in values of both demesne and tenant land was to reduce the income that the lord gained from each manor. The earl of Warwick's manor of Lighthorne in the Feldon was said to be worth £39 12*s* 0*d* in August 1315, and after a revaluation this rose to £51 16*s* 5½*d* in the following October. In 1439 the total had shrunk to £25. Tanworth on the same estate, in the Arden, diminished from just below £34 and £35 in successive 1315 valuations, to £12 15s 0d in 1439.[48] Documents coming from the lords' archives give different figures, and these discrepancies have been debated, but no one can doubt that manorial revenues experienced a downward trajectory, which affected all *pays*.[49] This should not lead us to make very negative judgements of economic and social change. Reduced manorial profits posed problems for the earls of Warwick, but tenants may well have found some benefit from a lowering of rents. The large manors belonging to great magnates deserve some attention, but the IPM extents bring to our notice the small manors, often held by the gentry. A good number of large

[47] *CIPM* xxv.287 (at p. 237).

[48] C134/49/32, 35; C134/51/69, 72; *CIPM* xxv.283 (at pp. 218–19). Some of the 1439 figures were derived from earlier extents: M. Holford, '"Notoriously Unreliable": the Valuations and Extents', *IPM Companion*, 117–44, especially p. 133.

[49] Ross and Pugh, 'Materials', 187–8.

manors, with values in excess of £15, appear in the Warwickshire Feldon and the Gloucestershire wolds. Small manors, worth £5 or less, are found everywhere, but especially in the Vale and the Worcestershire woodlands. These often differ from the magnate manors not just in their small size but in their structure. As was the case around 1300, the demesne could be quite prominent, so that (from a sample of 15 manors in the Worcestershire woodlands) in four of the small manors the demesne was valued more highly than the tenants' rents, and in another three the value of the demesne accounted for more than 40% of the total. The large manors were well-established institutions, which changed only gradually, but some of the small manors seem more subject to change and could be quite dynamic, as gentry families built up new accumulations of land.[50]

According to the extents, many manors in the fifteenth century, like their predecessors around 1300, derived 20% or 30% of their value from their demesnes, but other sources show that demesnes were no longer being managed directly by the lords' officials, but were rented out to farmers. In 1428 on the estate of John de Berkeley based on Beverston in Gloucestershire, it is stated explicitly that the demesne was farmed, and the values, such as 2*d*–6*d* per acre for the arable, represented leasehold rents.[51] 'Service rents' mentioned in extents of the 1440s may also refer to the payments made by demesne farmers. The proportion of a lord's assets in the hands of tenants was increasing, and there were other important changes in the proportion of the manorial values which traditionally derived from tenant rents. The former division between free and unfree (or customary) tenure is not clearly apparent after 1418, as the old vocabulary of villein, native, bond and customary is only sparingly employed. Sometimes a total for free rent is provided, but the other rents are not given any descriptive label. In Gloucestershire, a strongly manorialised county, a distinction is sometimes drawn between 'tenants at will' and free rents, 'at will' being one form of customary tenure. Labour services were not mentioned, and tallage is hinted at only once, in 1439 at Brailes in Warwickshire.[52] In this respect the extents differed from the documents produced by the lords' own administration, which are full of references to customary tenure, and 'naifs by blood' and a few labour services survived into the middle of the fifteenth century. The manorial documents and the extents also differ in the information that they provide about the peasant economy, as there are only occasional references in the extents to the size of holdings, whereas rentals and court rolls show individuals accumulating an increased acreage of land. Some IPM extents separate the messuages, cottages and tofts from the land, and itemise 'six cottages' and 40 acres of arable land held at will by the tenants of the cottages, which in the manorial documents are usually connected together, as for

[50] C. Carpenter, *Locality and Polity: a Study of Warwickshire Landed Society 1401–1499* (Cambridge, 1992), 132–7; eadem, 'The Lesser Landowners and the Inquisitions Post Mortem', *IPM Companion*, 47–78, especially p. 60.

[51] *CIPM* xxiii.109 (at pp. 57–9).

[52] *CIPM* xxv.283 (at p. 218).

example 'a messuage, a toft and two yardlands'. These discrepancies between sources do not mean that we should be unduly critical of the extents. The jurors and the officials who advised them were well informed, and evidently in their eyes the distinction between free and customary tenure, and the connection between messuages and landholdings, had diminished in importance.

The extents refer to the commercial world, but do not allow measurement of changes in urban centres or trade. Properties in the larger towns, such as Bristol and Coventry, were valued in extents, and the smaller towns sometimes formed part of a lord's assets. Rugby in Warwickshire in 1423 was by no means impoverished, judging from the value of £7 put on its market, with £2 for its fair. In the same year Birmingham's market was said to have brought its lord a modest £2, and struggling Brailes, once *en route* to becoming a town, had its market valued at £1.[53] Industries make an occasional appearance, as in the period before 1350, notably coal mines in the forest of Dean and fulling mills in the Cotswolds, but other sources can tell us more.

Turning to the agrarian economy and the use of land, a remarkable feature of extents made after 1323 in the Vale and in both the woodland and champion parts of Warwickshire and Worcestershire was the evidence for three-course rotations, meaning that about two-thirds of the arable on individual demesnes was said to be cropped each year, whereas on the wolds a half was under crops, as the traditional two-course cultivation tended to prevail.[54] The managers of lowland manors were apparently taking more crops from a limited area of land, though we do not know if this was a response to the growing demand for corn in the thirteenth century, or to the economic troubles of the early fourteenth. The change from two- to three-course rotation might be compared with the parcellation of tenant holdings into smaller units (see pp. 72–3), both representing a more intensive use of land.

The compilation of the earliest extents coincided with the last phase of assarting, the clearance of new land, which is mentioned in IPM extents relating to manors in the Forest of Feckenham (Worcestershire) in the 1250s and 1260s; assarts also figure in manors of the Forest of Dean, in west Gloucestershire and Badgeworth near Gloucester in 1327.[55] The 1292 extent for Middleton in the Arden values 118 acres of new land.[56] The enclosure of waste provided one route to the profitable improvement of pasture, taking it out of use as common. This may explain the appearance in the extent of Bordesley (Warwickshire) in 1272 of a close worth £5. Parks were being created in the woodlands in the thirteenth century, and the extents assign a value to them of £2, £3, £5 and even £10 on the basis of their timber and underwood, but the sum also reflects income derived

53 *CIPM* xxii.106, 344 (at pp. 136, 314); xxv.283 (at p. 218).

54 Campbell & Bartley, *Atlas*, 130–2, 135–6.

55 *IPM Worcs* 1, 4, 6; *IPM Glos* 4, 53, 59, 231; *IPM Glos* 5, 42, 45–6, 172–3, 210.

56 *IPM Worcs* 1, 41–2 (this Warwickshire document was included in a volume of Worcestershire IPMs in error).

from their use as pastures. One Worcestershire extent (for Weoley in 1273) spelled out that the park could be regarded as a valuable asset if it was grazed, but if it was full of deer it was worth nothing.[57]

Assarting slowed down in the early fourteenth century, except perhaps in Dean, but even here in 1347 the clearance of new land seemed to promise no great benefits. At Abenhall, on the edge of the forest, the dovecot and two mills were in ruins, and 60 acres of new assart were estimated to yield only enough to pay a rent of 1*s* 2¼*d* (that is, about a farthing per acre).[58] Land was falling out of cultivation in Gloucestershire from the 1320s onwards. Extents, some of them for wold manors, describe land as sterile, hilly, stony and sandy. Some of this unprofitable land was valued at 1*d* per acre. This coincides with a concentration of gloomy testimony to the low quality of wold land in the *Nonae Inquisitiones* of 1341, which also record the migration of tenants from some small settlements.[59] In 1325 the Warwickshire Feldon manor of Fulbrook had four of its 20 holdings vacant, and we know from a subsequent survey of 1392 and an IPM extent of 1436 that the village experienced terminal decline.[60]

A loss of tenants and the abandonment of houses, leading to land losing value and falling out of use, began in the early fourteenth century but gathered pace and affected more places after the epidemics of the mid- and late fourteenth century. At Tidenham in 1432 (on the west bank of the Severn) it was said that 100 acres had been 'in the lord's hands', that is, untenanted 'after the death of tenants', which may refer to earlier plagues.[61] In the Vale at both Leigh and Lassington in 1420 ten sites of houses were called tofts, accounting for about a third of the once-occupied holdings. In a similar way a third of the dwellings at Dunton in Curdworth in the woodlands of Warwickshire in 1444 were described as tofts. In the champion country in 1430, on the northern border of Gloucestershire at Weston-on-Avon and Pebworth tofts accounted for 45% and 29% of the formerly inhabited tenant housing.[62] This decline of rural habitation was thus found in every type of *pays*, but the point must be made that the IPMs of 1485–1509 serve as a silent witness to the abandonment of villages in the champion. Manors like Compton Murdak, Kingston and Wormington were described without any reference to tenants or the former existence of settlements, and the land consisted in large measure of pastures, which we know from earlier evidence were the sites of villages and their open fields.[63] Large pastures are recorded in all types of landscape in the fifteenth century. A pasture called Oldgore in Calmsden on

[57] C113/2/6 ; *IPM Worcs* 1, p. 17; Campbell & Bartley, *Atlas*, 155.

[58] *IPM Glos* 5, p. 315.

[59] *Nonarum Inquisitiones in Curia Scaccarii*, Record Commission (1807), 407–15.

[60] C. Dyer, 'A Landscape for Pleasure: Fulbrook, Warwickshire, and John Duke of Bedford in the Fifteenth Century', *Warwickshire History* 15 (2014), 239–50.

[61] *CIPM* xxiv (at p. 88).

[62] *CIPM* xxi.597 (p. 184); xxvi.402 (p. 230); xxiii.385 (p. 202).

[63] C. Dyer, 'The Value of Fifteenth-Century Inquisitions Post Mortem for Economic and Social History', *IPM Companion*, 97–115, esp. pp. 112–13.

the Cotswolds contained 600 acres, while 1,000 acres of pasture is found in the Warwickshire Arden in 1506, at Lapworth and Bushwood, and another 452 acres in Lapworth at Broom Hall and Kingswood, all in the hands of George Catesby esquire. He also held 450 acres of pasture at Wellesbourne in the Feldon.[64]

In many aspects of the rural economy and society the IPM extents are corroborating, supplementing and amplifying knowledge gained from other sources. In some areas, such as rural industry or peasant tenures, they make only a small contribution. In the study of land use, however, they provide systematic statistical evidence that cannot be obtained from the manorial and estate records. These show changes over time, which varied from one *pays* to another. Of course warnings must be given about accepting the figures at face value. It has already been shown that pastures and woods tended to be omitted from the extents if they were shared in common, which makes arable and meadow seem overwhelmingly predominant in the thirteenth and fourteenth centuries. While this distorts the value of the extents when compared with other sources, such as manorial documents or landscape surveys, they become more meaningful if they are compared with other inquisitions through time.

The Gloucestershire figures in Table 5.5 analyse the acreages of land use in the wold and Vale at four sample periods, roughly 40 years apart. The differences between *pays* in 1256–1311 are not very great.. There is no suggestion of major changes after the crises of famine and plague in 1315–17 and 1348–50, with arable hovering around 80% of all land analysed in 1349–75. A really striking shift is apparent by 1418–47, when arable totals dip and the proportion of pasture rises, together with wood to some degree. The changes in the wold manors were much more pronounced. Moving to the fourth sample from around 1500, during the fifteenth century the wolds seem to slip back, with arable increasing and pasture falling – though still very different from the fourteenth-century figures. We cannot be sure of this late fifteenth-century reversal because the sample size is rather small. Land use in the Vale continued to move in the direction established before 1418, with yet more pasture being recorded, and a further reduction in arable.

For Warwickshire we have three samples (Table 5.6). Comparison between the extents of around 1300 and those of the early fifteenth century suggests that major changes had not occurred over the intervening decades. We have to wait until the end of the fifteenth century to observe a dramatic drop in the percentage of arable, and a leap in the amount of recorded pasture. The experience of Arden and Feldon clearly diverged, with arable accounting for a minority of the recorded acreage in the Arden, and the Feldon's pastoral percentage, in spite of the conversion of some arable fields into leys and permanent grazing, registering well below that in the Arden.

In Worcestershire (Table 5.7), where the samples for the late fifteenth century are too small to be usable, comparison between the figures around 1300 and those

64 *CIPM* xxvi.199. (at p. 114); *IPM Henry VII*, iii, p. 57.

Table 5.5 Gloucestershire: land use by regions from IPM extents (acres)

	Arable	Meadow	Pasture	Wood	Other	Total
1256–1311						
Wold	2655	311	143	178	—	3287
%	81	9	4	6	—	100
Vale	3284	337	188	99	—	3908
%	84	9	5	2	—	100
1349–75						
Wold	3809	306	117	55	—	4287
%	89	7	3	1	—	100
Vale	4055	707	282	92	—	5136
%	79	14	5	2	—	100
1418–47						
Wold	1544	157	1503	303	—	3507
%	44	4	43	9	—	100
Vale	5158	895	1501	520	—	8074
%	64	11	19	6	—	100
1485–1509						
Wold	960	117	316	6	—	1399
%	69	8	23	0	—	100
Vale	2910	588	1802	177	—	5477
%	53	14	29	4	—	100

Sources: See Table 5.1; also *IPM Glos* 6; *CIPM*, xxi–xxvi; *CIPM Henry VII*, i–iii

from the early fifteenth century shows that the woodlands were moving towards a smaller arable area and larger amount of pasture, in a fashion paralleled in the Gloucestershire Vale.

An alternative source of statistical evidence comes from the Feet of Fines, which also run from the thirteenth century to the sixteenth, recording conveyances from one land owner to another in fictitious law suits that provided evidence of title. They describe parcels of land, often much smaller than a manor, with figures for arable, meadow, pasture and wood. The Warwickshire Feet of Fines, like the IPM extents, show in 1300 a large percentage of arable in both Arden and Feldon in c.1300, and no great change in the fourteenth century, though the Arden had a lower proportion (71–85%) of arable, as compared with 94–96% in the Feldon. The dramatic increase in the pasture for Arden came in the middle years of the fifteenth century, after which arable in the Arden fell below 50% and pasture accounted for between 38% and 48%, depending on the precise date of the samples analysed. This is much in line with the IPM extents, which suggest that the main change came after the sample of 1418–47.[65] The

[65] C. Dyer, *Warwickshire Farming 1349–c.1520*, Dugdale Society Occasional Paper 27 (1981),10; C. Dyer, 'Documentary Evidence: Problems and Enquiries', *The Countryside of Medieval England*, ed. G. Astill and A. Grant (Oxford, 1988), 18; A. Watkins, 'Cattle Grazing in the Forest of Arden in the later Middle Ages', *AgHR* 37 (1989), 21; *AHEW*, iii, *1348–1500*,

Table 5.6 Warwickshire: land use by regions from IPM extents (acres)

	Arable	Meadow	Pasture	Wood	Other	Total
1272–1326						
Feldon	4223	258	157	41	—	4679
%	90	6	3	1	—	100
Arden	3153	312	30	9	—	3504
%	90	9	1	0	—	100
1418–47						
Feldon	4495	386	323	100	—	5304
%	85	7	6	2	—	100
Arden	6635	739	535	608	500*	9017
%	73	8	6	7	6	100
1485–1509						
Feldon	2813	390	1668	72	—	4943
%	57	8	34	1	—	100
Arden	2196	339	2435	568	—	5538
%	40	6	44	10	—	100

Notes: * heath, waste
Sources: See Table 2; *CIPM*, xxi–xxvi; *CIPM Henry VII*, i–iii

Table 5.7 Worcestershire: land use by regions from IPM extents (acres)

	Arable	Meadow	Pasture	Wood	Other	Total
1273–1320						
Champion	1953	117	3	—	—	2073
%	94	6	0	—	—	100
Woodland	2767	192	85	6	0	3050
%	91	6	3	—	—	100
1418–47						
Champion	4156	211	170	75	—	4612
%	90	4	4	2	—	100
Woodland	2583	320	817	96	12	3828
%	68	8	21	3	0	100

Sources: *IPM Worcs* 1; *IPM Worcs* 2; *CIPM*, xxi–xxvi

figures for Gloucestershire (Table 5.8) demonstrate a very high proportion of arable around 1300, as if the compilers of the fines, like their counterparts writing the IPM extents, concentrated on the ploughlands and yardlands They assumed that rights in meadow, pasture and wood were attached to these units, and these did not need to be separately specified. After the Black Death the arable percentage dipped a little in both wold and Vale, whereas the IPM extents show little change. Pasture was expanding significantly in the fines in the early fifteenth

ed. E. Miller (Cambridge, 1991), p. 78. Similar patterns, with regional comparisons, are in M. Yates, 'The Description of Land found in the Inquisitions *Post Mortem* and Feet of Fines: a Comparative Study of Berkshire', *IPM Companion*, 145–54.

Table 5.8 Gloucestershire: land use by regions from the Feet of Fines (acres)

	Arable	Meadow	Pasture	Wood	Other	Total
1290–1308						
Wold	4060	160	93	77	—	4390
%	92	4	2	2	—	100
Vale	4093	107	35	104	—	4339
%	94	3	1	2	—	100
1349–75						
Wold	1685	158	4	121	—	1968
%	86	8	0	6	—	100
Vale	4165	406	119	202	—	4892
	85	8	3	4	—	100
1418–47						
Wold	5946	605	1543	377	0	8471
%	70	7	18	5	0	100
Vale	3167	425	602	159	0	4353
%	73	10	14	3	0	100
1484–1509						
Wold	8396	1320	4412	1251	0	15379
%	55	8	29	8	0	100
Vale	9286	1546	3661	534	250*	15277
	61	10	24	3	2	100

Notes: * furze, heath, marsh.
Sources: *Abstracts of Feet of Fines Relating to Gloucestershire 1199–1299*, ed. C. R. Elrington, Bristol and Gloucestershire Archaeological Society Record Series 16 (2003); *Abstracts of Feet of Fines Relating to Gloucestershire 1300–1359*, ed. C. R. Elrington, Bristol and Gloucestershire Archaeological Society Record Series 20 (2006); *Abstracts of Feet of Fines Relating to Gloucestershire 1360–1508*, ed. C. R. Elrington, Bristol and Gloucestershire Archaeological Society Record Series 27 (2013).

century, though less dramatically than in the extents, and then in 1484–1509 both show a marked drop in arable, though in the Fines the wolds had rather more pasture than the Vale, while the opposite was true according to the extents. Nonetheless, applying the broad brush as we must do, the two sources are telling much the same story.

The movements over time could be attributed to changes in the administration of the inquisitions, perhaps because jurors were encouraged to reduce their focus on arable land when they valued a manor. However, the Feet of Fines were produced by a different administrative process, but arrived at a similar result. Nor can bureaucratic practices explain the clear variations among the *pays*. Certainly the jurors lacked objective mathematical precision in their judgements, but their extents reflected their perception of changes in the land and its worth. Arable cultivation in the long run after 1350 became less profitable, and lords and their tenants became more appreciative of the benefits of pastoral farming, which required lower labour costs, and satisfied a growing demand for such products as beef cattle. Arable land was being converted into pasture, which is reflected in the decline in the amount of grain and legumes being harvested from demesnes and collected in tithe. In fifteenth-century Worcestershire the cultivators of the woodlands reduced their output of arable crops on a larger scale than did their equivalents in the champion country.[66] More pasture and wood became 'several' (separate), being fenced off and brought under the control of the lords or major tenants. The management of the demesne land was coming into the hands of farmers, and the desire for profits among these leasehold tenants provided an extra motive to convert land to pasture and to fence it.

The differences between the uses of land in the *pays* in the period 1350–1509 reflect variations in soils, climate and access to markets. Producers in the woodlands in the north of the region were prone to convert to pasture because their soils were less fertile and they were well placed to supply the carnivorous urban populations of Coventry and Worcester. The nature of the countryside and its organisation also made it easier in some cases to make changes. In the woodlands and the Vale much land was enclosed before 1350, and it was easier to increase the area in enclosures and to convert the 'several' land to grazing. Sometimes parcels of extensive common heath, moor and pasture could be taken into private hands, though this could stir controversy. Conversion to pasture in the champion, Feldon and wolds required agreement among members of the village community to leave some areas uncultivated (as leys) and to take parcels of land out of the open fields to be fenced and hedged. Wholesale enclosure and conversion to pasture plunged the community into trauma, and could result in the termination of a village's existence. That helps to explain the different pace of change between open-field countries and woodlands or areas of 'old enclosure'. The different chronologies of innovation in the three counties ought to be a subject for future investigation: the relatively early advance of pasture (before 1450) in Gloucestershire and the Worcestershire woodlands cannot be easily explained, nor can the more drastic effects of changes when they came to Warwickshire in the late fifteenth century.

[66] C. Dyer, 'Peasant Farming in Late Medieval England: Evidence from the Tithe Estimations by Worcester Cathedral Priory', in *Essays in Honour of Bruce M.S. Campbell*, ed. M. Kowaleski, J. Langdon and P.R. Schofield (Turnhout, 2015), pp. 83–109.

6

Beyond the Dots: Mapping Meaning in the Later Medieval Landscape

STEPHEN MILESON[1]

Historians are increasingly interested how past people used and understood their material surroundings, including the way in which ordinary inhabitants shaped their sense of identity in relation to the places where they lived. The aim of this paper is to highlight the value of inquisitions *post mortem* (IPMs) for the study of peasant perceptions of landscape in the period between 1200 and 1500. IPMs not only help us to reconstruct the character of the environment at a local level, they also include many peasant bynames as well as field-names and other minor place-names, which shed light on contemporary practices and attitudes in relation to specific territories. Because they were coined by ordinary inhabitants, bynames and field-names offer a rare glimpse of the experiences and outlook of peasants rather than of lords or clergy. The analytical value of these names is all the greater when they are mapped at a large scale – in other words that of the village, parish and hundred – rather than in the kind of small-scale distribution maps familiar from the work of economic historians who have used IPMs to study medieval farming.[2] Insights will be taken from the South Oxfordshire Project, an intensive study of the fourteen parishes of Ewelme hundred in south Oxfordshire, as well as from a broader survey of the IPMs, mainly from the most recent and detailed calendars.

The Research Context

Concern with people's sensory and cognitive engagement with their environment in the past has grown in recent decades, thanks to related developments in several disciplines. In the medieval field, the concepts of 'space' and 'place' have become

[1] I would like to thank John Baker, Stuart Brookes, Chris Dyer and Chris Wickham for helpful comments on draft versions of the text. Simon Draper of VCH Oxfordshire kindly supplied transcriptions of material from Canterbury Cathedral Archive. The illustrations were prepared by Stuart Brookes and Alessio Palmisano.

[2] For example, *A Medieval Capital and its Grain Supply: Agrarian Production and Distribution in the London Region c.1300*, ed. B.M.S. Campbell, J.A. Galloway, D. Keene and M. Murphy (London, 1993); Campbell & Bartley, *Atlas*.

fashionable amongst literary scholars, art historians, place-name specialists and archaeologists as well as social historians.[3] One area in which such concepts have been fruitfully applied is the study of buildings. There have been important investigations into the way that houses, churches and religious precincts were used to shape or reinforce behaviour and attitudes, notably amongst those tracing the development of gender norms.[4] Beyond the confines of buildings, attention has been paid to the creation and use of public spaces in cities and towns.[5]

Research on medieval rural settlements has felt some of the influence of this 'spatial turn', but the impact has so far been limited. Most of the landscape history work of medievalists continues to focus on landscape as structure rather than landscape as meaning. The result, according to one recent survey, is that addressing 'perception and performance or practice' is 'a prospect that still lies largely ahead'.[6] Nevertheless, the existing strengths of medieval settlement studies provide considerable opportunities for those interested in perceptions. Thanks to many years of work on landscape development, peasant communities and material culture, medievalists have the chance to create interpretations based on close knowledge of particular places as well as awareness of larger trends. There is no need to settle for the abstraction and speculation which have characterised some discussions of 'space' in other fields. On the contrary, the strong potential of locally focused explorations of meaning is suggested by the handful of accounts of later medieval English settlements which have looked closely at the relationship between spatial arrangements and mentalities.[7]

[3] *People and Space in the Middle Ages, 300–1300*, ed. W. Davies, G. Halsall, A. Langlands and A. Reynolds (Turnhout, 2006); *Rural Space in the Middle Ages and Early Modern Age: The Spatial Turn in Premodern Studies*, ed. A. Classen (Berlin, 2012); *Locating the Middle Ages. The Spaces and Places of Medieval Culture*, ed. J. Weiss and S. Salih (London, 2012); *Sense of Place in Anglo-Saxon England*, ed. R. Jones and S. Semple (Donington, 2012).

[4] *The Medieval Household in Christian Europe, c.850–c.1550*, ed. C. Beattie, A. Maslakovic and S. Rees Jones (Turnhout, 2003); C.P. Graves, *The Form and Fabric of Belief: An Archaeology of Lay Experience of Religion in Medieval Norfolk and Devon*, British Archaeological Reports British Series 311 (2000); R. Gilchrist, *Gender and Material Culture: The Archaeology of Religious Women* (London, 1994); *Ritual and Space in the Middle Ages*, ed. F. Andrews (Donington, 2011).

[5] For example, C. Symes, 'Out in the Open, in Arras: Sightlines, Soundscapes, and the Shaping of a Medieval Public Sphere', in *Cities, Texts and Social Networks, 400–1500. Experiences and Perceptions of Medieval Urban Space*, ed. C. Goodson, A.E. Lester and C. Symes (Farnham, 2010), 279–302.

[6] C. Dyer and P. Everson, 'The Development of the Study of Medieval Settlements, 1880–2010', in *Medieval Rural Settlement: Britain and Ireland, AD 800–1600*, ed. N. Christie and P. Stamper (Oxford, 2012), 11–30, at 28.

[7] D. Austin and J. Thomas, 'The "Proper Study" of Medieval Archaeology: A Case Study', in *From the Baltic to the Black Sea. Studies in Medieval Archaeology*, ed. D. Austin and L. Alcock (London, 1990), 43–78; S.V. Smith, 'Houses and Communities: Archaeological Evidence for Variation in the Medieval Peasant Experience', in *Deserted Villages Revisited*, ed. C. Dyer and R. Jones (Hatfield, 2010), 64–84; *A History of Wharram Percy and its Neighbours*, ed. S. Wrathmell, York University Archaeological Publications 15 (2012), 327–56 (contributions by Dyer, Wrathmell and others).

The South Oxfordshire Project is a concerted attempt to build on existing studies of medieval perceptions by developing a methodology for interdisciplinary work at a regional scale. The study, funded by the Leverhulme Trust, aims to uncover broad patterns by comparing and contrasting the dwelling practices, interactions and attachments of inhabitants of the south Oxfordshire clay vale and the wood-pasture of the Chiltern Hills over the long period from 500 to 1650. This short chapter is not the place to explain the methodology adopted in the project as a whole, but it should be emphasised that much of the study's strength derives from the combination of historical, archaeological and onomastic evidence and approaches.[8] The pages that follow pick out just one strand of evidence, that which can be obtained from documentary sources such as the IPMs, especially peasant bynames and field-names.

The IPMs provide important raw material for any investigation of peasant perceptions in the later Middle Ages. IPM extents almost always convey a general impression of rural settlements and their agricultural resources.[9] Some extents go beyond this and actually name certain features of the village. Assignments of dower in particular often supply numerous field-names and describe and locate buildings (especially manorial ones), roads, paths, gates, hedges, open-field furlongs, pits, ponds, streams and much else besides.[10] All IPM descriptions relied on oral depositions from villagers, chiefly the more substantial men usually chosen as jurors.[11] This reliance is occasionally made clear, as in a group of early fifteenth-century Essex assignments which state that they were made in the presence of the farmer and tenants.[12] Sometimes the IPM descriptions take us very obviously into contemporary ways of seeing the landscape, for instance where they include field-names with supernatural associations. Usually they are more prosaic and meaning has to be teased out painstakingly, as is the case with the information supplied about the fabric of villages and their residential arrangements.

[8] For an introduction to the project see S. Mileson, 'The South Oxfordshire Project: Perceptions of Landscape, Settlement and Society, c.500–1650', *Landscape History* 33:2 (2012), 83–98.

[9] For example, *CIPM* xxii.170 (pp. 182–3: Yoxall, Staffs., 1423), 178 (pp. 187–9: King's Sutton and Halse, Northants, 1423), 495 (pp. 437–8: Shilling and Wickhambreaux, Kent, 1425).

[10] *CIPM* xxi.151 (pp. 45–6: Farmcote, Glos., 1418), 964 (pp. 352–4: Dodford, Northants., 1422); xxii.159 (pp. 175–6: Ingoldisthorp, in Snettisham, Norf., 1423), 236 (p. 244: Arundel, Sussex, 1423).

[11] M. Holford, '"Thrifty Men of the Country"? The Jurors and their Role', *IPM Companion*, 201–21.

[12] *CIPM* xxv.134 (pp. 94–5: assignments at Woolston and Margaretting, 1437). In 1436 a perambulation of the boundaries of a detached part of the prior of Canterbury's manor of Newington in the Chilterns was explicitly based on the information given by named local men: Canterbury Cathedral Archive, DCc-Register/B, f. 364v.

People in the Village

IPMs and similar documents can tell us a great deal about the layout of rural settlements, which has implications for the way they were experienced and understood. Most obviously, extents remind us of the way later medieval households were physically separated from each other by the enclosures around their homesteads. There are many IPM references to curtilages (enclosed areas surrounding houses),[13] and sometimes distinctive perimeters supplied the names of tenements, as in Cuxham (Oxon.), where one was called *Asshe Heys* (1449, meaning 'ash hedges') and another *Brandheys* (1509, 'burnt hedges').[14] Archaeology confirms this separateness: in lowland areas house plots were surrounded by banks and ditches which, in combination with a sunken village street, partly screened off the houses within.[15] Entry was secured through gates, sometimes reached by crossing small bridges spanning ditches or streams. Presumably separation served to emphasise the identification of the resident household as a distinct unit. It also made it easier to regulate comings and goings, which helped to preserve good repute and to secure valuables from theft.

Of course, households collaborated with each other on a regular basis, and they shared more public areas and facilities such as the village street, springs and streams, commons and open fields, as well as the church and, intermittently, the hall of the manor house (where the manor court usually met). Amongst the IPM documents, proofs of age are a particularly useful reminder of shared experiences in the form of plausible, though sometimes invented, stories of memorable happenings which coincided with the births of heirs.[16] One clear thread of jurors' tales is the central social importance of the church as a public space. Not only did the church bring people together for regular services, it also provided a venue for doing business or socialising.[17] At Dixton (Glos.) in January 1402, for example, a group of men met in the church to resolve certain disputes while, by coincidence, a baptism was going on.[18] The church bells, which created a common timetable for the day, might be used by parishioners as a kind of public announcement system, as in Watford (Northants.), where one inhabitant rang the bells discordantly (*pulsavit campanas contrarie*) to sound the alarm when a house fire broke out.[19]

[13] For example, *CIPM* xx.488, pp. 152, 181, 227.

[14] P.D.A. Harvey, *A Medieval Oxfordshire Village: Cuxham 1240 to 1400* (Oxford, 1965), 28, 162–3.

[15] G. Astill, 'Rural Settlement: The Toft and Croft', in *The Countryside of Medieval England*, ed. G.G. Astill and A. Grant (Oxford, 1988), 36–61, at 53.

[16] J. Bedell, 'Memory and Proof of Age in England 1272–1327', *Past & Present* 162 (1999), 3–27, at 10–12. For birth, death, hunting and the start of a pilgrimage to Santiago de Compostella in Ewelme in 1343: *CIPM* xii.88 (pp. 68–9).

[17] See, more generally, R.N. Swanson, *Church and Society in Late Medieval England* (Oxford, 1989), 257–8; D. Dymond, 'God's Disputed Acre', *Journal of Ecclesiastical History* 50:3 (1999), 464–97; ch. 12 below.

[18] *CIPM* xxi.370 (p. 112).

[19] Ibid. xxv.475 (p. 392).

How people interacted, where they did so and when was influenced by a range of factors, including status, age, sex and the character of the settlement itself.[20] Perhaps rather unexpectedly, part of this variegated picture can be recovered from peasant bynames, the predecessors of hereditary surnames (which emerged gradually amongst the peasantry mostly between the thirteenth and fifteenth centuries).[21] Bynames, which appear in IPMs as well as other sources, can be divided into several types, principally those which identified individuals in terms of family relationships, occupation, personal characteristics (nicknames) or place of abode or origin.[22] Of these, the last category is most helpful, especially since it includes topographical bynames, which identified individuals in terms of where they lived within the settlement. These names are especially useful in the thirteenth and early fourteenth centuries, before the increasing heredity of names and more frequent migration broke down the link between name and place. IPM extents of this period are a useful source of bynames from particular settlements, such Rycote in Great Haseley (Oxon.), where the tenants were listed in 1302.[23] The early extents were not published in the calendars, but a considerable number appear in editions (of varying quality) published by county societies.[24] In some cases IPMs augment the names supplied by manorial documents or the hundred rolls, in others they are the only source.

Topographical bynames can be used to show something of the way identities were shaped in relation to the environment. In these names we can detect how inhabitants' daily conversations would have generated a shared sense of place. Bynames such as *de Cruce* ('of the cross'), *Buvebrok* ('above the brook'), *de la Ford* ('of the ford') and *de la Cumbe* ('of the combe'), all used in Ewelme in 1279,[25] reflect an intimately known geography in which people were linked to locations, each of which would have had its own associations. The constituent parts of this mental geography varied from settlement to settlement. Some features commemorated in bynames were unusual and may have distinguished a village in the minds of inhabitants and those living in surrounding settlements: at Britwell (Oxon.) the byname *de Castello* ('of the castle') described those living next to the earthwork of

20 B.A. Hanawalt, *The Ties that Bound: Peasant Families in Medieval England* (Oxford, 1986); R.M. Smith, 'Kin and Neighbours in a Thirteenth-Century Suffolk Community', *Journal of Family History* 4 (1979), 219–56; C. Dyer, 'The Late Medieval Village of Wharram Percy: Living and Consuming', in Wrathmell, *Wharram Percy and its Neighbours*, 327–40.

21 G. Redmonds, T. King and D. Hey, *Surnames, DNA, and Family History* (Oxford, 2011), 41–58.

22 There can be no wholly satisfactory categorisation of these names, but a helpful schema is provided by C. Clark, 'Onomastics', in *The Cambridge History of the English Language*, Vol. 2: *1066–1476*, ed. N.F. Blake (Cambridge, 1992), 542–606, at 567.

23 C 133/104/ 11.

24 For example, *Abstracts of the Inquisitiones Post Mortem relating to Nottinghamshire*, ii, *Henry III, Edward I and Edward II, 1242 to 1321*, ed. J. Standish, Thoroton Society Record Series 4 (1914).

25 *Rotuli Hundredorum Temp. Hen. III & Edw. I*, ed. W. Illingworth and J. Caley, 2 vols, Record Commission (London, 1812–18), ii, 759–60.

a Stephanic siege castle.[26] Broader patterns include differences between areas of greater and lesser nucleation. In Ewelme hundred, for example, in the late thirteenth and early fourteenth centuries names suggesting clustered settlement (such as *atte Strete, Tunesende, Bovetoun*) were found in the vale but not in the Chilterns, presumably because houses in the Chilterns were so scattered. Such patterns help us appreciate not just the contrasting layout of settlements, but the implications of layout for the way inhabitants identified each other and how they thought about their group life. In the one area they shared a perception of the collection of homesteads as a single entity, in the other they did not.

The associations and memories attached to particular elements in a settlement must have been very varied. Some would have been shared and public, others individual, idiosyncratic, perhaps secret. An orchard would have meant one thing to its owner, another to the lovers who secretly met there: as one sixteenth-century deponent in a church court case put it, 'if the orchard could speak it would say somewhat'.[27] One aspect which we can recover is that status played a part in the identification of people with places. Bynames can help to identify what seem to have been areas of distinctive social character within settlements. Leading free tenants often had toponymic bynames, which were taken from settlement names rather than features within the village. This presumably reflected their status and range of social contacts. But some free tenants did have topographical bynames, and these most often related to a limited number of features. In Oxfordshire as a whole in 1279 the most common topographical identifiers for free tenants appear to have been the mill, spring, green and churchyard or cross.[28] These were valuable resources, materially and socially, and they were also located outside the main row of homesteads. Other names common amongst free tenants were *Bovetoun, Est, West* and *atte Hyde* (the last implying a land unit which originated as an Anglo-Saxon hide farm). All of these likewise indicate houses on the fringes of, or beyond, the main built-up area of the settlement.

Where records are good, the way people of different status were grouped around the village can be recovered in detail. In early fourteenth-century Cuxham, for example, most of the villeins lived in a row on the south side of the street, near the manor house and church, and a clutch of cottagers lived on the colder north side, around a bend out of sight of the church. The leading free family and easily the wealthiest inhabitants, who were called *atte Grene*, had a house by the funnel-shaped green in the north-west (Map 6.1).[29] Nearby, the larger village of Chalgrove included three semi-detached ends, the entrances to which were secured by gates (presumably to control the movement

[26] William de Castello was mentioned c.1200: Canterbury Cathedral Archive, DCc-ChAnt-M-355, m. 2d. For the castle: *VCH Oxon*. viii, 45.

[27] *Oxford Church Courts: Depositions 1570–1574*, ed. J. Howard-Drake (Oxford, 1993), 33.

[28] R. McKinley, *The Surnames of Oxfordshire*, English Surnames Series 3 (Oxford, 1977), 42.

[29] Harvey, *Cuxham*, 27, 120, 172–3.

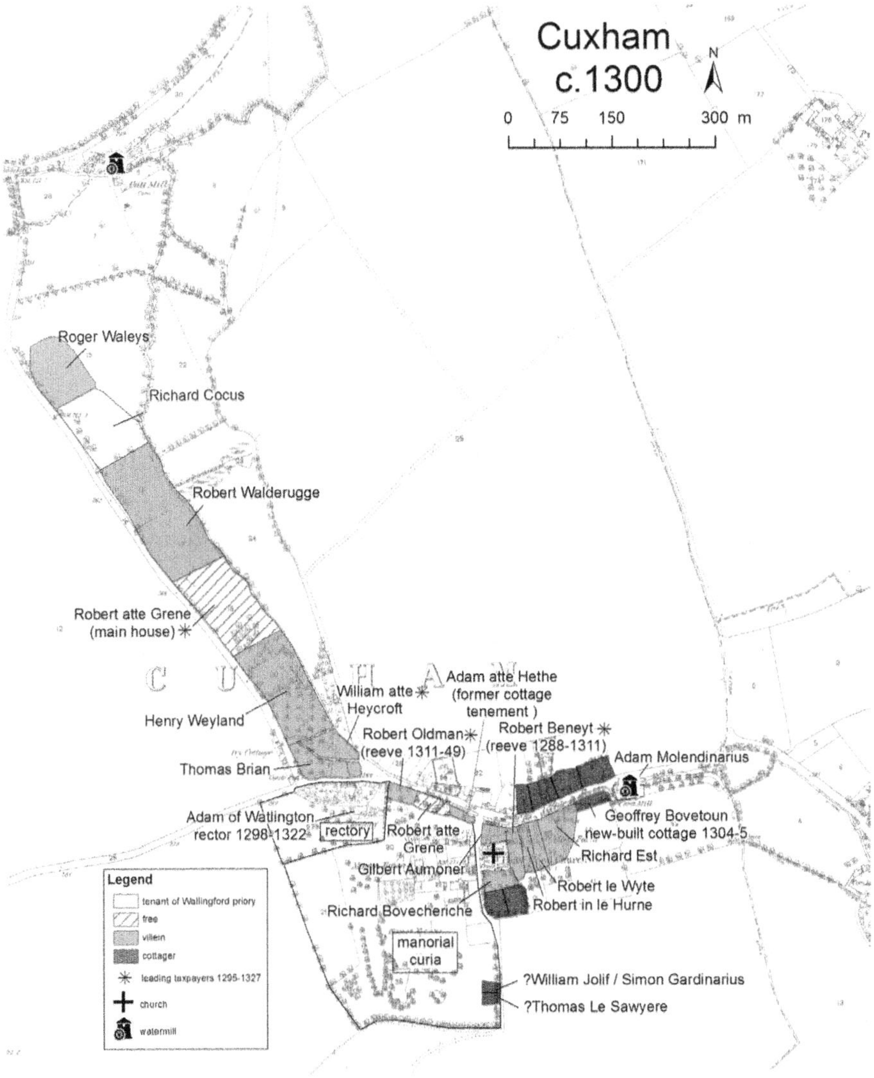

Map 6.1 The village of Cuxham (Oxon.) c.1300, after Harvey (1965). Copyright: Stuart Brookes and Alessio Palmisano.

of animals).[30] In 1295 the most peripheral end was called *Bourende* ('end of the (*ge*)*burs*', or 'dependent peasants'), a name which spells out its origins as an area of lowly social status. Everywhere, of course, settlement and social structure was dynamic. In Cuxham the arrangements of c.1300 probably had early origins, but they were partly the result of recent changes: the block of houses near the

[30] Magdalen College Archive, 122/5 (court order of 1442).

church was almost certainly one of the first established elements and the group of cottage holdings to the north earlier than the individual plots cut out of the demesne curia, but the villein holdings in the north-western arm of the settlement had probably been converted from cottage holdings in the 1290s.[31] In Chalgrove it is unclear how long the distinctive character of *Bourende* lasted, but in the fifteenth century the other two ends had a greater number of larger holdings of a yardland or more.[32]

Differences in wealth and status in the thirteenth- and early fourteenth-century village should not be exaggerated, but they were significant and from this kind of evidence it seems that they were reflected in spatial arrangements.[33] Smith has shown, through detailed study of later thirteenth-century court rolls of Redgrave (Suffolk) – a manor of hamlets and farmsteads rather than a large village – that some of the strongest social bonds were between people living close to each other, especially within the same hamlet. So, not surprisingly, propinquity of residence influenced relationships, but there was also a class dimension. Those with the densest documented localised social networks were the middling villagers, while the poorest and richest had more diffuse relations.[34] These findings are likely to have applied elsewhere (though not necessarily everywhere), and the Oxfordshire evidence indicates that residential arrangements would have reinforced the class divergence. The richer freemen (and sometimes villeins) lived outside the main group of houses; the middling folk tended to live in a row, and at least some of the cottagers lived in their own neighbourhood, though the closeness of this neighbourhood may have been weakened by cottagers' greater tendency to migrate, to work as labourers at a distance from home and to form small households from which children moved out early.[35] Social changes after the Black Death may have had a solvent effect on neighbourhood links as housing density was thinned out, settlement plans altered and middling and better-off tenants sought to emphasise the standing of their individual households by building bigger houses and creating larger house plots.

People in the Landscape

Thanks to IPMs and other documents such as court rolls, rentals and deeds, the search for medieval inhabitants' experiences does not have to stop at the end of the village street. By using field-names from these sources we can follow

31 B.K. Roberts, *The Making of the English Village: A Study in Historical Geography* (Harlow, 1987), 52; Harvey, *Cuxham*, 120–2.

32 Magdalen College Archive, 141/42 (1452–53); 142/28 (c.1503).

33 For a balanced assessment of the village hierarchy see Z. Razi, 'The Toronto School's Reconstitution of Medieval Peasant Society: A Critical View', *Past & Present* 85 (1979), 141–57, at 155–6.

34 Smith, 'Kin and Neighbours', 228–47.

35 Ibid. 248.

inhabitants past the 'duck stream' in Ewelme (*Dukesborne*, early thirteenth century) or the 'pillory barn' in Great Haseley (*Peloribarne*, 1492–93), out into the fields, pastures and woods.[36] Field-names reveal much about peasant perceptions. They represent, after all, a subjective and collective choice: any feature or area could be described in numerous different ways, so the name which was most commonly used (or most commonly written down) during a certain period says something about those doing the naming. Field-names require careful handling, of course, and there are many potential pitfalls for the unwary. The most obvious difficulty is deciding on the meaning of a name. It is not always possible to determine a single, certain meaning, though it is easier to reach a likely interpretation where a name is investigated topographically as well as etymologically, in other words in a known landscape. The first recorded appearance of a name cannot be taken as marking its origin. Few names are recorded before 1200, but this does not mean field-names did not exist earlier. It is also difficult to decide when a name changed. Patterns of change can be more plausibly recovered where documentation is very dense and covers a long period, but even then there is the possibility of uncovering the first surviving record of an alternative name rather than a new one. There may be many layers of unrecorded naming, influenced perhaps by age, sex and status, but if they did exist we know nothing about them. Such caveats could be continued, but for now it is more useful to indicate the potential.

Field-names provide a vicarious experience of the peasant landscape which is hard to find elsewhere. Time and again they show a great sensitivity to soil and terrain, acting as a kind of guide to good farming practice for those constantly engaged in agricultural work. As the IPMs show, individual furlongs might be named after their sandy, stony or heavy character, or by reference to the colour of the soil as an indicator of its properties.[37] In south Oxfordshire there are many names denoting clay and marsh in the vale and chalk and heath in the Chilterns. Some areas of open field were marked out as particular problem patches, including the *slo* ('slough' or 'mire') in thirteenth-century Benson, which was described as a *voleslowe* ('foul slough') in the 1480s.[38] Amongst the names were signposts to resources useful for dealing with difficult soils, including the *marlyngput* ('marling pit') in Chalgrove (1336).[39] Besides this sense of the texture and qualities of the land, field-names convey an insider's knowledge of topography, including the

[36] For these two features: *The Langley Cartulary*, ed. P.R. Coss, Dugdale Society 32 (1980), 5, 8; M. Gelling, *The Place-Names of Oxfordshire*, 2 vols, English Place Name Society 23–4 (Cambridge, 1953–4), i, 130.

[37] Some examples: *CIPM* xxi.677 (p. 230: Kirkby in Ashfield, Derbys., including *Redewonge*, *Unthankwonge*; xxii.235 (p. 243: Swaffham Bulbeck, Cambs.); xxiv.131 (p. 116: South Moreton, Berks.). See also Magdalen College Archive, 141/40 (Chalgrove); Harvey, *Cuxham*, 155 (*Sterfurlong*, Cuxham, 1282–92: OE *stūr*, unfriendly, heavy, stiff; Fig. 3).

[38] E210/9539; Exeter College Archive, unlisted deed.

[39] Magdalen College Archive, 141/40. Cf. *CIPM* xxiv.276 (p. 215: a furlong of pasture called *le Marled Rudyng*, Cressage, Shrops., 1432).

Figure 6.1 View of *Symmesdene* (centre) cutting down through the high ground south of Cuxham. Possibly this shallow, sinuous valley (OE *denu*) was named after the Symms family, mentioned in 1445. Photo: Stephen Mileson.

sinuous valleys (*Hecchelesdene* and *Symmesdene*, 1447–48) on top of Cuxham's hills which are only visible to those who leave the village and tramp out into the fields (Figure 6.1 and Map 6.2).[40]

For those moving about the landscape it was important to have visual reference points. In open country isolated trees provided useful markers and meeting places; in hedges or woods, trees with a distinctive appearance stood out, such as willows, maples or 'white' beeches.[41] Many marks were made on the land to signify ownership, including stakes or stones used to define individual strips of arable or meadow.[42] Crossroads and boundaries were marked by freestanding crosses of wood, stone or iron (see the *Bryghtwell' Crosse* in Map 6.2), or by signs of the cross etched into tree trunks.[43] Field-names sometimes incorporated personal names, conveying ownership or some other association between person

[40] For the names: Harvey, *Cuxham*, 155, 156–7.
[41] *CIPM* xxiv.131, 276; S. Mileson and S. Brookes, 'A Multi-Phase Anglo-Saxon Site in Ewelme', *Oxoniensia* 79 (2014), 1–29, at 5. For 'white' beeches in the Chilterns: Canterbury Cathedral Archive, DCc-Register/B, f. 364v; Magdalen College Archive, 142/8 (Nuffield, 1524).
[42] *CIPM* xxiv.276 (p. 215: oak stakes).
[43] Ibid.; *CIPM* xxiii.679 (p. 355); Canterbury Cathedral Archive, DCc-MA/31, f. 147 (*le iron crosse*, 1489, Britwell Prior, Oxon.). See also A. Winchester, *Discovering Parish Boundaries* (Princes Risborough, 2000),46–54.

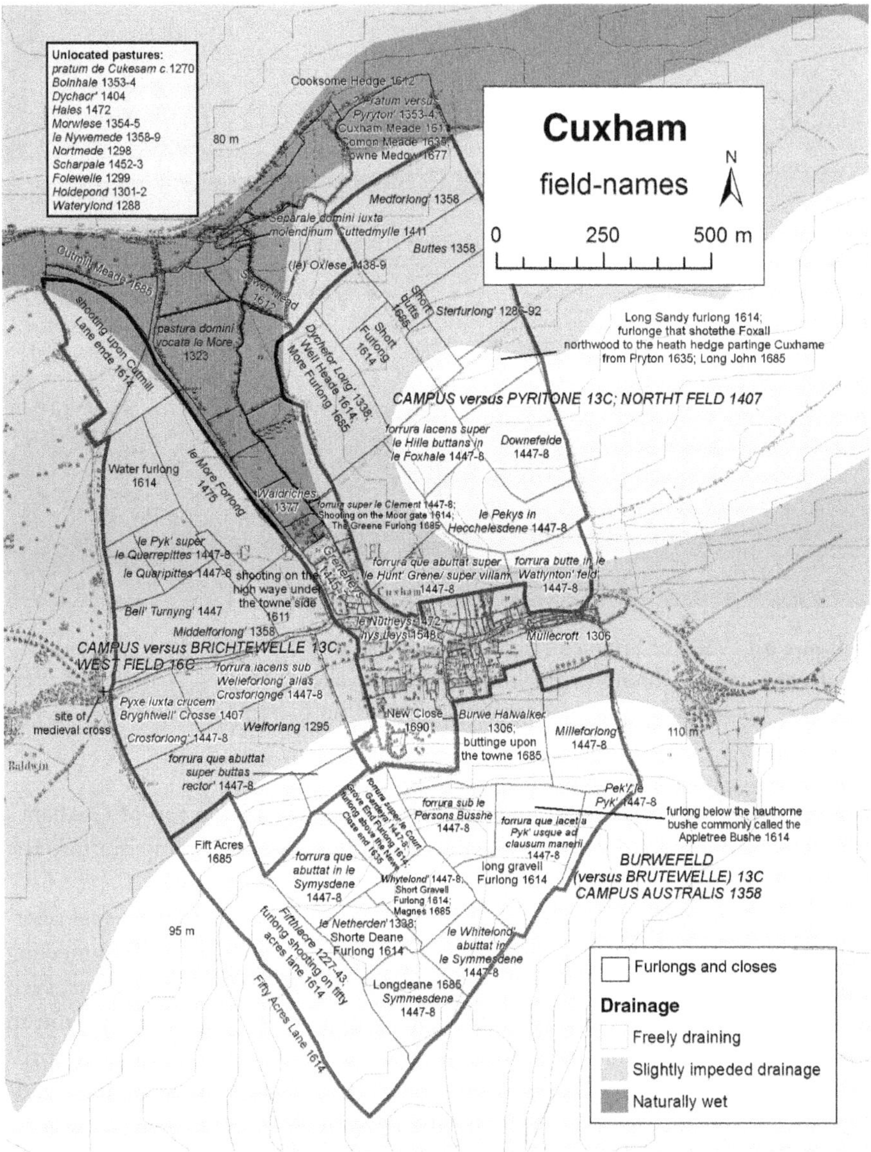

Map 6.2 Medieval and early modern field-names in Cuxham. Copyright: Stuart Brookes and Alessio Palmisano.

and place. Some of these can be linked to known families or even individuals, such as *Bell' Turnyng* or *the Turnyng of Bell' the Fermo'* in Cuxham (1447), presumably named after John Bell(e), farmer of the demesne from 1434 to 1440 (Map 6.2).[44] Roads and tracks were mentally sorted into types which signified

[44] Harvey, *Cuxham*, 158; Merton College Archive, 5889 (farmers' accounts).

different scales of movement, from the port ways leading to towns and roads between villages down to the very local routes such as church ways, mill ways, green ways, blind lanes and common paths through the fields. Certain sites had more mysterious and otherworldly associations, such as *La Holiwelle* ('holy well') mentioned in Brightwell Baldwin (Oxon.) in 1248, and the *Pukkespytte* ('goblin pit') in Newington (Oxon.) c.1470–80.[45]

The social memory encapsulated in names was important for practical reasons, but it was also a form of discourse through which relations were shaped. Collective identity was fostered by common activities in the landscape, but also by the stories which became attached to these activities and the sites where they took place. Inhabitants took possession of their villages by marking and naming their key social features such as springs and greens, where crosses were often erected. They might also develop their own name for the settlement itself. By the thirteenth century Ewelme's name (*Auuilma/e*, 1086, OE *ǣwelm*, 'spring, source of a river', or 'powerful spring')[46] was sometimes changed in popular parlance to *Newelme* or *the newelme*.[47] This may have been partly through Middle English mis-division (*atten Ewelme* becoming *atte Newelme*), but it seems also to have become a way of making sense of the place-name by reference to what was a prominent stand of elm trees by the manor house and village pond, first mentioned in the sixteenth century but probably existing much earlier.[48] In the entwining of repeated actions (meeting at the pool) and naming, inhabitants took over public spaces for themselves – as the people who shaped the story of a place. The same thing happened out in the fields and especially at the edge of the manor or parish, where there was a special need to mark and know the limits of the village territory. Early modernists have shown the importance of the ritual of the rogationtide procession around the parish boundaries as a way of promoting social cohesion and passing on knowledge of territory and rights from one generation to the next.[49] Such processions, which were well established in the late Middle Ages, involved seeing and touching boundary markers and often bumping boys' heads against them as an aid to remembrance. In 1524 a lane near Hayden Farm in the Chiltern parish of

[45] *The Feet of Fines for Oxfordshire, 1195–1291*, ed. H.E. Salter, Oxfordshire Record Society 12 (1930), 152; Gelling, *The Place-Names of Oxfordshire*, i, 133.

[46] Gelling, *The Place-Names of Oxfordshire*, i, 127; V. Watts, *The Cambridge Dictionary of English Place-Names* (Cambridge, 2004), 220.

[47] H.A. Napier, *Historical Notices of the Parishes of Swyncombe and Ewelme in the County of Oxford* (Oxford, 1858), 17 (*Newelme*, c.1223–61); *CPR 1321–4*, 258, 308 (*the newelme*, 1323); *1436–41*, 82 (*newelme*, 1437).

[48] The antiquary John Leland seems to have picked up on the popular etymology: 'I think that Ewelme tooke name of a great poole afore the maner place and elms grouing about it' (L. Toulmin Smith, *The Itinerary of John Leland in or about the Years 1535–1543*, 5 vols (London, 1906–10), i, 112).

[49] N. Whyte, *Inhabiting the Landscape: Place, Custom and Memory, 1500–1800* (Macclesfield, 2009); A. Wood, *The Memory of the People: Custom and Popular Senses of the Past in Early Modern England* (Cambridge, 2013), 200–15.

Nuffield (Oxon.) was described as a way used 'to go a prosession ... on the rogation dayes'.[50]

Research on south Oxfordshire has uncovered a number of names which suggest the development of shared popular histories of the landscape. Some might seem to imply a vague sense of the past which lacks precise time depth, of the kind which might support the idea of a cyclical peasant culture with little conception of change:[51] *le Ruene*, 1430 ('the ruin') in Benson's open fields;[52] *Buristede*, late thirteenth century (*burh*, 'place' or 'fortification place') in Ewelme's, at or near the site of a multiphase Anglo-Saxon site (Map 6.3);[53] and *Aldebir(e)*, 1235 ('the old *burh*', 'old fortification') in the woods on the boundary between Nettlebed and Swyncombe, almost certainly the substantial and still extant earthworks of a large ?Roman fort at Digberry.[54] To this category one might add many of the supernatural names – the holy wells and goblin pits.

Other names suggest a closer attempt to characterise a place (whether correctly or not), based on greater information: *Yeldenbrigge*, 1300 ('the ?guildsmen's bridge') near the Benson–Warborough boundary, possibly recalling an association liable to the payment of dues;[55] and perhaps *Birineshulle*, c.1220 (?Birinus's hill) in Chalgrove, which may commemorate Birinus, bishop of Dorchester (d. 649), the local saint.[56] Complexity may have developed over time as stories accrued additional layers. In Ewelme the boundary of the 'home parish' near the '*burh* place' was marked c.1200 by a stone called the *Durlvestane*, which was rendered as *Derlestane* or *Dernestane* (OE *derne-stān*, hidden stone?) in the late thirteenth century.[57] By 1604, and presumably before the Reformation, this was the site of the *Dunstone Crosse*,[58] named possibly after St Dunstan, archbishop of Canterbury (d. 988) (Map 6.3). In this second category of more specific associations – or perhaps just of documented names which happen to be more specific – we might put some of the lords attached to landscape features during or soon after their lifetimes. Late-medieval south Oxfordshire was Chaucer country and the indomitable Alice Chaucer (1404–75), whose influence reached down to the village level,[59] seems to have been particularly remembered: in 1489 there

[50] Magdalen College Archive, 142/8.

[51] For the dangers of such a view: J. Fentress and C. Wickham, *Social Memory* (Oxford, 1992), 98–100.

[52] Magdalen College Archive, Chalgrove 23B.

[53] E326/8308; Mileson and Brookes, 'A Multi-Phase Anglo-Saxon Site in Ewelme', 26.

[54] *CCR 1234–7*, 106; Oxfordshire HER, MOX6455.

[55] Gelling, *The Place-Names of Oxfordshire*, i, 118–19.

[56] Magdalen College Archive, Chalgrove 29B. Cf. *Berynescley*, Benson, 1458: ibid. Chalgrove 232.

[57] *Langley Cartulary*, 5; E326/8308; E326/8281; E326/8333.

[58] Exeter College Archive, Benson terrier (1604).

[59] In 1468 'My old lady of Suffolk' oversaw the arbitration by two members of the gentry of a minor dispute over land in Easington and Golder (Pyrton parish): Magdalen College Archive, Golder 24B.

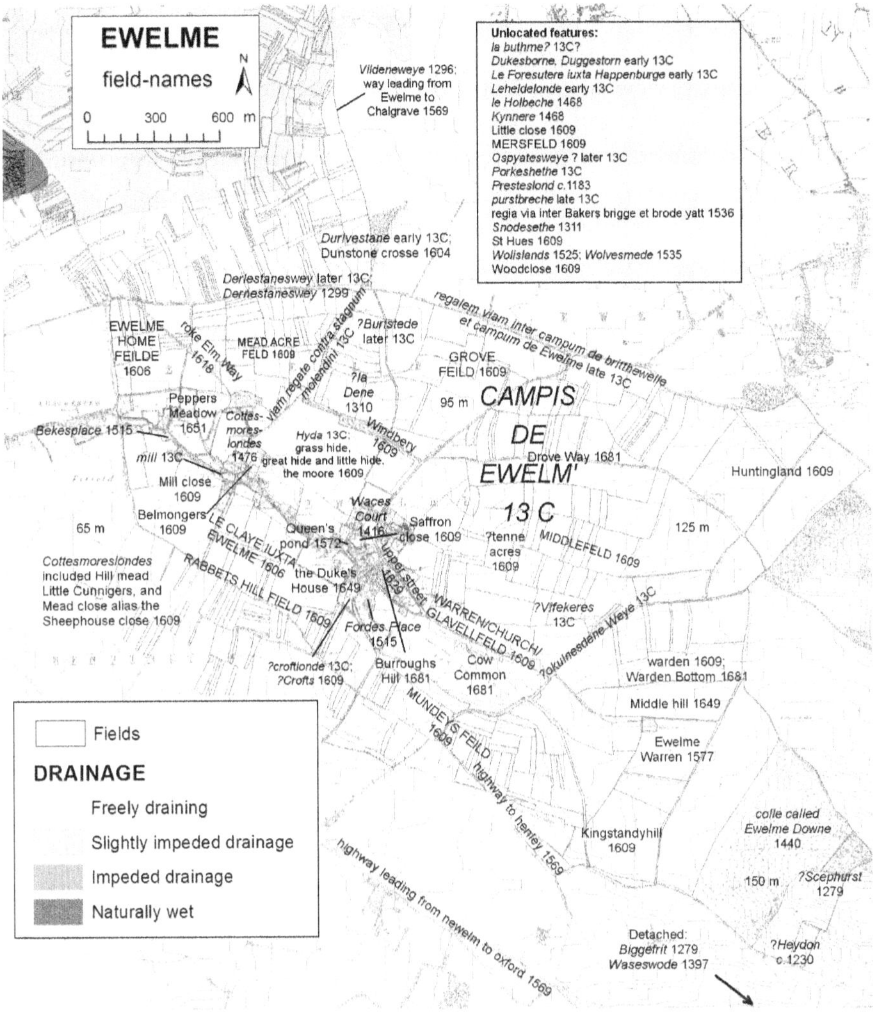

Map 6.3 Medieval and early modern field-names in Ewelme. The spring-fed pond was called *the Queen's pond* in 1572. Copyright: Stuart Brookes and Alessio Palmisano.

was a *Damealys lane* (or *way*) in Newington,[60] and in the early sixteenth century a croft in Roke (Benson) was called *Dame Alys*.[61]

These kinds of names drew on local topography and experience, but they also incorporated broader knowledge conveyed by learned culture. Some of

60 Canterbury Cathedral Archive, DCc-MA/31, ff. 150v, 152v. Mentioned also in the 1520s: SC 12/14/11.

61 Merton College Archive, Misc 312. Apparently it was still so-named in 1606: LR2/224, f. 28.

the interplay of ideas was probably stimulated by the sermons and teaching of the parish clergy. The supernatural qualities (and dangers) of barrows, pits and wells, for example, were an idea developed by ecclesiastical writers from the later Anglo-Saxon period.[62] Other ideas may have developed from broader reception of literary works. It is at least possible that the later-medieval sprouting of 'Icknield Way' names in certain counties was partly due to the popularity of the 'Four Highways' story which first appeared in Henry of Huntingdon's *Historia Anglorum* (c.1131).[63] A desire to link local lore to outside knowledge might also be detected in some of the names ascribed to what were supposed (often correctly) to be Roman roads. The *Greteakmanstrete* and *Litilakmanstrete* (1490) in Newington, for instance, were nowhere near the course of Akeman Street through Oxfordshire, but naming them in this way may have helped make sense of them, or make them seem more important.[64] In a similar way, the clustering of supernatural names in certain areas may have been due to the continuation or recurrence of more widely shared stories as well as the presence of suitable topographical features. Forest areas appear to have had a high number of these names, as befitted their place in romance literature.[65] At Cressage (Shrops.) in the Long Forest, there was an extraordinary collection of such names, including three oaks called *lez Cursed Okes*, another oak called *le grete* [Cu]*rsed Oke*, a *Knavescastell*, *le Lesewebarowe*, *le Stublebarowe*, *le Thornybarowe* and *le Medewebarowe*, all mentioned in an IPM of 1432.[66] The 'cursed oak' may have been derived from the Old English place-name, *Cristesache* (1086), which meant '(place at) Christ's oak'.[67]

Writing would have played an important role in memorialisation. Some historical figures may have been remembered, at least early on, through oral tradition, possibly including Brihtric, a tenth-century lessee in Brightwell Baldwin who appears to have been commemorated in the field-name *Breytriggescrofte* (1423).[68] So too perhaps the names of routeways such as the 'fielden ways' mentioned in late Anglo-Saxon charters (see the *Vildeneweye* in Map 6.3). But the written word was, of course, an aid to and a shaper of memory. The manor court

[62] S. Semple, *Perceptions of the Prehistoric in Anglo-Saxon England: Religion, Ritual, and Rulership in the Landscape* (Oxford, 2013), 143–92.

[63] S. Harrison, 'The Icknield Way: Some Queries', *Archaeological Journal* 160 (2003), 1–22, at 1–3, 7–9. The name is documented several times in late-medieval south Oxfordshire (*contra* Harrison, 7–8).

[64] Canterbury Cathedral Archive, DCc-MA/31, f. 118; P. Booth, 'Roman Oxfordshire', in *An Historical Atlas of Oxfordshire*, ed. K. Tiller and G. Darkes, Oxfordshire Record Society 67 (2010), 16–17.

[65] For an example from the IPMs: *CIPM* xxii.236 (p. 244: barrows and other features in Arundel chase).

[66] *CIPM* xxiv.276 (pp. 214–16). Gelling suggested that the 'barowe' names here derive from OE *bearu*, meaning grove (*The Place-Names of Shropshire*, ii (EPNS 70), 144), but *beorg* (hill, mound) is also possible and may make more sense in the context: A.H. Smith, *English Place-Name Elements*, 2 vols, EPNS 25–26 (Cambridge, 1956), i, 29.

[67] Watts, *Cambridge Dictionary of English Place-Names*, 167–8.

[68] *Langley Cartulary*, 11; information from Simon Draper, VCH Oxfordshire.

was the place where names would be recorded, adapted and transmitted. As population turnover increased from the fourteenth century, documents such as court rolls and deeds would have become more and more important tools in passing on names. After all, in many villages few (if any) of the families present in the late thirteenth century would have remained in the fifteenth. Writing could be part of a process of selectively drawing on the past to promote the particular interests in the present. This occurred in 1436 when 70-year-old John Champyon cited a 'sermon' of Thomas Sympul, a former resident of Watlington, in support of the right of tenants there to gather firewood in nearby Maidensgrove (Oxon.).[69] Documentation also served to petrify old names in the landscape as convenient shorthand for lands and tenements which frequently changed ownership. In terms of continuity, it is notable that in south Oxfordshire there was a much higher rate of field-name survival from the later Middle Ages to the seventeenth century in manors owned by bureaucratic lords (such as Oxford colleges) than in those owned by minor gentry. In all probability this was true earlier as well, though it is hard to prove. If it was the case, there must have been implications for inhabitants' sense of connection with their surroundings.

Such a brief survey cannot be comprehensive, but it may open up the possibilities of using IPMs and related sources to reconstitute something of ordinary rural inhabitants' perceptions in the later Middle Ages. As in any historical enquiry into meaning, there are difficulties of disentangling representation and experience, especially given the mediation of scribes and the written word. But through IPM depositions and field-names significant things can be found out about the relationship between the mental and material worlds of the small-scale farmers who underpinned medieval society. By investigating perceptions in detail at the level of the village and parish it is possible to match experiences to the fabric of street and field which shaped everyday patterns of activity. Knowing about local stories and contributing to their creation and development would have helped families and individuals to make sense of their lives and also claim a stake in land and resources. The greatest public role went to the middling and upper level of male villagers who held land in the open fields and who would have been at the forefront of rogation processions and in investing in crosses and other furniture. These individuals, especially those from the longer-resident families, probably played a greater part in establishing and perpetuating documented field-names than cottagers with just a single acre in the fields or no landholdings apart from their croft. Poorer villagers shared in the same world and walked the same streets, but the location of their homes and the nature of their working lives probably made their experiences and attachments somewhat different.

[69] Canterbury Cathedral Archive, DCc-Register/B, f. 364v.

7

Fairs and Markets in the Inquisitions *Post Mortem*

MATTHEW HOLFORD

'Too unreliable to be of any value', or 'the single most useful source' for analysing many aspects of medieval agrarian history? The reliability of the extents and valuations in the inquisitions *post mortem* has indeed been hotly debated.[1] And while many historians have been dismissive, the need for a more nuanced assessment is increasingly recognized. Bruce Campbell's pioneering researches for the period 1300–48, in particular, showed that large-scale analysis of the extents over a broad chronological and geographical framework, using geospatial and other visualizations, can be very revealing. The precision and reliability of the IPMs may vary from one period to another: Campbell found that the years of exchequer reform between approximately 1322 and 1340 were characterized by particularly detailed extents. The IPMs may also vary from area to area: local administrative, geographical or social conditions may mean that some escheators recorded some items in more detail than was true elsewhere. Some types of information may also, typically, be more reliable than others: valuations, in particular, are apt to underestimate.[2]

A sound, accurate assessment of the late medieval extents and valuations requires not only comparison with other sources, such as accounts, but for Campbell's methods to be extended to other periods. The digitization and georeferencing of the IPMs from 1399–1447 now enables comparable approaches to be applied to documents from the first half of the fifteenth century. This paper offers a small contribution to this project by exploring records of fairs and markets in the inquisitions. It focuses on the period 1399–1447, for which the calendared texts contain full details of valuations and extents. All references to markets and fairs in this period were identified from keyword searches of the digitized text and checked against the published subject indexes.

Markets and fairs present an approachable topic because so much on the subject has been collected in an authoritative and comprehensive secondary source, the *Gazetteer of Markets and Fairs in England and Wales to 1516* compiled

[1] For a review see M. Holford, '"Notoriously Unreliable"?: the Valuations and Extents', in *IPM Companion*. A shorter version of the present article previously appeared as a blog entry for *Mapping the Medieval Countryside*: http://www.inquisitionspostmortem.ac.uk/blog/cipm-xxiii538-markets-and-fairs-in-the-ipms/.

[2] Campbell and Bartley, *Atlas*, 18–29, 99, and *passim*.

by Samantha Letters and others and maintained by the Centre for Metropolitan History.[3] Furthermore, although IPM extents were not included in the early volumes of *Calendars*, the existence of markets and fairs was noted and indexed from *CIPM* iii (1912) onwards, allowing us to explore data from c.1291 onwards. (These calendars must be used with caution, however, as neither the calendaring nor the indexing of markets and fairs was carried out with complete accuracy or comprehensiveness.)[4] It is, lastly, a significant topic because the history of many fairs and markets in the fifteenth century is obscure. Historians have long been struck by the contrast between the 'proliferation' or 'multiplicity' of markets in the period before the mid-fourteenth century and the much smaller number recorded in the sixteenth century. Clearly, many markets suffered greatly in the fifteenth century from declining trade, but much more remains to be discovered about the chronology and causes of decline: there have been few attempts to pursue Alan Everitt's plausible suggestion that 'the history of England's vanished market towns would be as interesting a study as its lost villages'.[5] IPMs can help us reconstruct this history, although, as is often the case, they must be used with caution.

Markets and Fairs: A Short Introduction

Markets and fairs were places where formal and regulated trading took place. A market was usually weekly, on a set day, typically dominated by local and retail trade; a fair was annual, on a set feast day and often on the vigil and morrow of that day, characterized by regional and wholesale trade.[6] An unquantifiable but undoubtedly large amount of trading took place privately, outside of such formal environments.[7] But markets and fairs offered advantages to both buyers and

[3] Samantha Letters, *Online Gazetteer of Markets and Fairs in England and Wales to 1516*, http://www.history.ac.uk/cmh/gaz/gazweb2.html (henceforward *Gazetteer*; accessed June 2015); print version, S. Letters et al, *Gazetteer of Markets and Fairs in England and Wales to 1516*, List and Index Society Special Series 32–33 (2003). Information on fairs and markets is drawn from the online text unless otherwise noted.

[4] E.g. C 136/104/34, m. 15 (Roger Mortimer), referring to market and fair at Little Walsingham, Norf.: the calendar in *CIPM* xvii.1190 mentions the fair, but not the market, and the fair does not appear in the subject index; C 135/95/7 m. 4, extent of two parts of the manor of Wantage (Berks.) referring to fairs on the feasts of the Translation of Thomas Martyr and of St Faith, and a Saturday market, none mentioned in the calendar (*CIPM* ix.177). Markets and fairs are indexed as subjects in *CIPM* 2nd ser. iii (two entries) but appear in *CIPM* 2nd ser. i–ii under the relevant places, not as separate subject entries.

[5] *AHEW* iv, 469; see, however, M. Mate, 'The Rise and Fall of Markets in Southern England', *Canadian Journal of History* 31 (1996), 59–86.

[6] See, in general, D. Farmer, 'Marketing the Produce of the Countryside, 1200–1500', *AHEW* iii, 324–430.

[7] C. Dyer, 'The Hidden Trade of the Middle Ages: Evidence from the West Midlands of England', *Journal of Historical Geography* 18 (1992), 141–57.

sellers by making transactions easier and safer.[8] They were equally attractive to their founders and owners, who derived income from stallage (the rent of stalls), from tolls on goods sold, and from fair and market courts.

By the thirteenth century, for reasons that are not fully clear, it was established that the right to hold a market and fair was a franchise (jurisdictional privilege), and in many cases required royal warrant.[9] Grants of markets and fairs were enrolled in great number on the royal charter, patent, and close rolls, and these are a chief source for calculating the number of markets in existence. A market or fair could also be held in various circumstances by 'prescriptive' right without requiring a royal grant. Many but by no means all of these prescriptive markets were investigated and recorded in the various *Quo Warranto* inquiries into royal rights of the late thirteenth and early fourteenth centuries. Thereafter the crown's control over markets and fairs seems to have been exercised fitfully and erratically: escheators, for example, were supposed to inquire into the existence of unlicensed markets, but there is little evidence that they in fact did so.[10] Consequently a number of markets are mentioned only in a variety of miscellaneous sources, such as private accounts and, of course, IPMs; and there are great difficulties in establishing truly comprehensive lists of fairs and markets. The fullest existing list is the *Gazetteer* maintained by the Centre for Metropolitan History, based largely on the chancery enrolments, but also drawing on a variety of other evidence.

The changing numbers of fairs and, more especially, markets have been used by historians to approach two different but related problems.[11] First, the extent of economic expansion and subsequent contraction in the period 1200 to 1500; second, the nature and extent of commercialization in the medieval economy. Evidence from IPMs has something to contribute to both debates. First, though, we must ask what detailed study of markets and fairs can tell us about the value and reliability of the inquisitions themselves.

The IPMs: Evidence for the Existence and Operation of Fairs and Markets

Those who are thoroughly sceptical of IPM extents will be surprised by the frequency with which their details regarding markets and fairs are corroborated by other sources. This is particularly true regarding the dates on which markets and fairs were held. Time and again an IPM's statements confirm the evidence of the establishing charters (which are surely unlikely to have been produced at the

[8] For a detailed discussion, see M. Kowaleski, *Local Markets and Regional Trade in Medieval Exeter* (Cambridge, 1995), ch. 5

[9] J. Masschaele, 'Market Rights in Thirteenth-Century England', *EHR* cvii (1992), 78–89 (79–80).

[10] *SR* I, 241 ('capitula escaetrie'). For one example, see E 153/1214.

[11] For a summary of recent research see J. Davis, *Medieval Market Morality: Law, Life and Ethics in the English Marketplace 1200–1500* (Cambridge, 2012), 9–19.

inquisitions). Examples include the fair on the Decollation of John the Baptist at Latton, Essex; the Tuesday market, and fair on SS Peter and Paul, at Great Limber; the Thursday market and All Saints fair at West Rasen (both Lincs.); and many others.[12] Such correspondences establish a certain degree of confidence in the IPMs' reliability.

The IPMs also, however, record a significant number of markets and, especially, fairs that (for reasons explained above) do not appear in the *Gazetteer*. These include the Wednesday market at Chelsworth, Suffolk, recorded in 1438; the Michaelmas fair at Minehead, recorded in 1428 and 1435; the Whitsun fair at Dunster, Somerset, recorded in 1428; the Martinmas fair at Shaftesbury; and so on. Some items are described a little misleadingly in the IPMs: the fairs at Nymet Tracy, Devon, recorded in 1434, which initially appear to be unrecorded elsewhere, are clearly to be identified with the fairs at Bow, in Nymet Tracy parish, which are well documented.[13] Nevertheless the IPMs are a significant source of new information; and, as is the case at Dunster, this information can often be verified in other sources.[14] The Lincolnshire IPM of Thomas Lord Roos taken in 1430 recorded the existence at Wragby of a weekly market on Wednesdays and an annual fair on the feast of the Ascension; both had also been recorded in an inquisition of 1421.[15] The Wednesday market is known from other sources and is listed in the *Gazetteer*. The fair does not appear there, but its existence is confirmed by an account of 1423–24, when the tolls were leased to John Hancok, forester.[16]

It should in fact be noted that not all the references to fairs in the IPMs can be counted with full confidence. Since *nundinae*, one of the usual terms for a fair, was a plural form, it is often impossible to be certain whether it has a single or plural reference on any given occasion. For example, the toll of *fori et nundinarum* recorded at Kendal in 1445 could refer to a market and fair, or market and fairs.[17] (Two fairs were chartered there.) At Rhaedr in 1425 an IPM likewise records

12 *CIPM* xix.120; xxii.180, 312, 737.

13 *CIPM* xxiii.52, 108, 555; xxiv.240, 470; xxv.107. The fair at Bramber on the feast of Mary Magdalen mentioned in a 1433 IPM (*CIPM* xxiv.117) seems in fact to be the fair at Bidlington in Bramber, and the Tuesday market at Grishaugh in Wymondham (*CIPM* xxiv.122) to be that listed in the *Gazetteer* under Wymondham.

14 For the fair at Dunster see *VCH* draft text (http://www.victoriacountyhistory.ac.uk/sites/default/files/work-in-progress/dunster_economic_history_1st_draft_edited.pdf, accessed June 2015); the 1428 IPM apparently supplies the first evidence of its date on Whitsun Monday, confirmed by Leland in the 1530s (*Itinerary*, I, 166). For other evidence of the Martinmas fair at Shaftesbury, see C.H. Mayo, *The Municipal Records of the Borough of Shaftesbury* (Sherborne, 1889), 17, 19 (but also 23–4 for the Midsummer fair, not mentioned in the IPMs)

15 *CIPM* xxi.845; xxiii.548. The *Gazetteer* records a late thirteenth-century fair on the feast of the Assumption.

16 SC 6/1121/16 m. 17.

17 CIPM xxvi.195, calendared by the present writer with insufficient attention to this ambiguity.

the 'farm of toll of *a fair or fairs* and market (*firma tolnet. mercati et nund.*)'; a contemporary account records two fairs, on the feast of St Clement and the gules of August.[18] (The *Gazetteer* records a single fair occurring on an unknown feast.)

In many cases the IPMs also provide new information even when the existence of a market or fair is recorded elsewhere. IPMs may provide additional information on the days when markets occurred: Friday as the market day at Wakefield (Yorks.); Thursday at Weobley (Heref.); and so on. At Chatham in Kent, where only a single fair of unknown date is recorded in the *Gazetteer*, an IPM of 1424 records fairs on the feasts of St Bartholomew (24 August) and the Nativity of the Virgin (8 September).[19] The IPMs may also provide information about changes of market and fair days, since in a number of cases the details provided in inquisitions conflict with the provisions in the original grants. The market at Penrith (Cumb.), for example, which was chartered for Wednesdays, is recorded in 1440 as taking place on Tuesdays; the market at Great Oakley (Essex), chartered for Thursday, is recorded in 1438 as occurring on Monday; the Appleby (Lincs.) market, originally on Wednesday, is recorded in 1427 on Thursday; the market at Wantage, held on a Monday in the thirteenth century, had moved to Saturday by 1349; and so on.[20] This information is more difficult to corroborate; however, a proof of age taken in 1370 also recorded a Tuesday market at Penrith, suggesting that the market day had indeed changed.[21]

Finally, and perhaps most significantly, the IPMs provide evidence of the continued operation and existence of markets and fairs. This evidence cannot be accepted completely at face value, because of the possibility (in some cases, indeed, virtual certainty) that extents were duplicated from earlier documents, rather than being compiled on the basis of current information. Thus the 1446 extent of Newcastle Emlyn borough, mentioning two fairs whose profits, together with those of the local court, came to £1, was almost certainly copied from an earlier extent of 1429.[22] Accounts of 1421–26 do record both fairs, but the IPM duplication casts some doubt on their continued existence in 1446, even if it might appear unlikely that an escheator would offer to account for income that no longer existed.[23] A similar difficulty arises at Great Bardfield (Essex), where IPMs of 1425 and 1432 both seem to have derived ultimately from an earlier extent of 1398.[24]

18 *CIPM* xxii.510 (C 139/19/32 m. 32); SC 6/1209/17 m. 1d.

19 *CIPM* xxii.311; xxiv.262, 475; xxv.69.

20 C 135/95/7 m. 4; *CIPM* xxi.625, 633; xxii.795; xxiii.576; xxv.104, 517.

21 *CIPM* xiii.66. It is most unlikely that the IPM information derived from the earlier proof.

22 For other apparent examples see *CIPM* xxiii.560, xxiv.84 (Halstead, Essex); xxii.180, 737 (Latton, Essex).

23 SC 6/1166/11–13. Earlier accounts refer only to the Martinmas fair: SC 6/1166/1–3, 5, 7–10.

24 C 136/105/34 m. 39; *CIPM* xxii.499, xxiv.78; C 139/19/32 m. 15, C 139/59/39 m. 22). The 1432 extent includes a scribal error: the extents of 1398 and 1425 apparently refer to farm of lands, fair(s) and market(s) (*firma terr', nundin', et for'*); in the 1432 extent this was miscopied as farm of three fairs and a market (*firma trium nundinarum et for'*).

The possibility that information has been copied from an earlier IPM or from some other document must always be borne in mind. How frequently this happened is unclear, not least because we do not know how many IPMs have been lost. Nevertheless there are a number of instances where details of markets and fairs do not appear to be derived from earlier extents, as for example at Wragby in 1430, Castle Acre in 1440, Kersey in 1425, or Chelsworth in 1438.[25] These markets and many others were presumably still functioning, even if many (as we shall see below) had low valuations and may have been in decline. In many cases IPMs appear to provide the only evidence for the continuing operation of markets, and they provide an important source for tracing the survival of trading institutions in the fifteenth century.

Evidence for the Disappearance of Fair and Markets

The IPMs may also provide evidence for the failure and disappearance of markets, although this too can be difficult to interpret. In particular, the failure of an IPM to mention a fair or market does not provide clear evidence of its disappearance, since comparison with other sources (including other IPMs) indicates that the recording of markets and fairs in the inquisitions is erratic and inconsistent. For example:

(i) An IPM of 1433 records a market at Bungay, Suffolk, together with fairs at the feasts of the Invention and Exaltation of the Cross; an inquisition of 1425 had mentioned only the market. The fairs apparently existed since at least 1307. Similarly the Thursday market at Castle Acre (Norf.), which had been chartered in 1391, was recorded in an IPM of 1440 but not an assignment of dower of 1426.[26] A market and fair were recorded at Wellow (Notts.) in 1438 but had not been mentioned in extents of 1347 or 1427. Both had been chartered in 1268 and were recorded in 1330.[27]

(ii) A market and fair at Somerton (Som.), which had been chartered in 1255, were mentioned in 1411 but not in 1428. Other sources indicate that they operated in the late fifteenth century.[28] Similarly a fair at Ayot St Lawrence (Herts.) was recorded in an IPM of 1375 but not in 1421; it was still being held in 1470–71.[29]

(iii) Two extents of quarter shares of Standlake (Oxon.), taken in 1423 and 1425, make no mention of a market, but a market was certainly operative on a different share of the manor in the fourteenth and fifteenth

25 *CIPM* xxii.504; xxiii.548; xxv.107, 376.

26 *CIPM* xxiv.115, xxii.441; *CIPM* xxii.533 (this does however mention fairs), xxv.376.

27 *CIPM* ix.47; xxii.780 (extent of one third of the manor); xxv.46.

28 *CIPM* xix.865; xxiii.281; *VCH Somerset* iii (1974), 142.

29 *CIPM* xiv.191, xxi.499; BL Harley Roll A. 15.

centuries, and it is likely that all four portions shared the rights and profits of a market.[30]

(iv) The market at Warwick, worth around £5 in the late fourteenth and earlier fifteenth centuries, is not mentioned in extents of 1401 or 1439, yet in both inquisitions the market at Brailes (Warw.) is recorded.[31]

(v) An extent of two-thirds of the manor of Warminster (Wilts.), taken in 1433, makes no mention of the market, even though tolls were worth between £8 and £10 in the 1440s and 1450s.[32]

(vi) Extents of two-thirds of the manor and castle of Arundel (Suss.) in 1421 and 1435 made no mention of a fair court or tolls valued at £5 and over £3, respectively, in about 1400 and of continuing importance in the fifteenth century.[33]

The explanations for these and other omissions and inconsistencies are not always clear. In some cases the profits from markets and fairs may have been included under the broad heading of 'profits of court' (which, in themselves, were somewhat erratically recorded in the IPMs); or they may be included among assize rents or rents and farms.[34] (Both practices are also found occasionally in estate records.)[35] Where the extents concern manors that had been partitioned, or from which dower had been assigned, it is possible that the profits of fairs and markets were not divided evenly (although that does seem to have been the usual practice).[36] In general, however, the most plausible explanation is simply that the existence of markets and fairs was recorded inconsistently according to the quality of the information available to the escheator and/or jurors, and their concern for comprehensiveness and accuracy. It is relevant that neither markets nor fairs commonly feature in the 'model' extents found in formularies; they may not, therefore, have been a feature that escheators consistently recorded or enquired about.[37]

30 *CIPM* xxii.339, 451; *VCH Oxon.* xiii (1996), 191–2.

31 *CIPM* xviii.509, xxv.283 (both based on extents of 1369, cf. E 149/29/9 mm.3, 7); *VCH: Warw.* viii (1969), 480–1.

32 *CIPM* xxiv.50; *VCH Wilts.* viii (1965), 115.

33 *CIPM* xxi.817, xxiv.377; *Two Estate Surveys of the Fitzalan earls of Arundel*, ed. M. Clough, Sussex Record Society 67 (1969) 115; *VCH Sussex* v/1 (1997), 62.

34 cf. *CIPM* xix.1037, Newmarket market valued with court profits (although this might refer to the market court); xxvi.303 (fairs and three-weekly court at Newcastle Emlyn valued together); xvi.677 (court, market and fair at Hunmanby of no value).

35 Withernsea (Yorks.): SC 6/1083/11 (1422–3) refers to profits from two fairs; SC 6/1083/10 m. 2 (1422) refers only to 'diverse rents and farms'; SC 6/1084/1 (1422–3) presumably includes the fairs among 'other minute farms'. An undated fifteenth-century extent of Castle Acre (Norf.) includes £7 11*s* 0*d* 'pleas and profits of court with profits of fair(s)', SC 11/33; an account of 1423–4 for Hackford (Norf.) includes 'issues of market' as part of the £20 farm of the manor (SC 6/1121/16 m. 2).

36 E.g. *CIPM* xix.497, 667; xx.627, 631–2; xxii.523, 705, 706; xxiii.556.

37 See, for example, *Walter of Henley and Other Treatises on Estate Management and Accounting*, ed. D. Oschinksy (Oxford, 1971), 67–72 and 312–13; *Legal and Manorial Formularies: Edited from Originals at the British Museum and the Public Record Office* (Oxford, 1933), xvii–xviii,

For these reasons the failure of a market or fair to appear in an IPM does not necessarily indicate that it had ceased to function, and conclusions from such absences should be drawn only with caution. Even when an IPM mentions one market or fair but not a second or third, we cannot assume that the latter were not in existence: a 1426 extent of Castle Acre refers to a fair but not the Thursday market (chartered in 1391); an extent of 1440 refers to both fair and market.[38]

Nevertheless, again, scepticism must not be taken too far, and the testimony of IPMs must not be dismissed completely. On some occasions the absence of a particular fair or market may indeed be significant. In the thirteenth century the Bardolfs received grants of a Monday market and of fairs on the Exaltation and Invention of the Cross at their manor of Wormegay in Norfolk. An IPM of 1427 mentioned only the fair on the Invention, 12*d* yearly; accounts from the following years stated that a fair had also taken place on the Exaltation, but had made no profit; the market was not mentioned.[39] Similarly Chesterfield (Derb.) had charters for Tuesday and Saturday markets and fairs on the feasts of the Exaltation and Palm Sunday. Only the Saturday market and the Exaltation fair are recorded in an IPM of 1442, and it may well be that the other market and fair had lapsed by this date, since they do not appear in an account of 1474.[40] So too at Withernsea (Yorks.) an IPM of 1438 mentioned only fairs at the Assumption and Nativity of the Virgin, and not the weekly market which had been chartered in 1338 and 1343; an account of 1423 likewise mentions only the fairs, perhaps implying that the market had lapsed.[41] (In all these instances, however, it must be borne in mind that private accounts themselves do not always record markets and fairs with full precision.[42])

The Value of Fairs and Markets

On very rare occasions the IPMs do provide explicit evidence of a market's decline. In 1444 the Wednesday market at Ashill in Somerset was said to be worth nothing 'because not used for many years'. Fairs at Lady Day and Simon and Jude, in contrast, were still worth 2*s* a year. Likewise in 1382 the market at Hanworth (Norf.)

25–9; E 163/24/34. Fairs and markets do, however, figure in the more detailed version of the treatise *Extenta manerii*, see *SR* I, 242–3; *Fleta*, ed. H.G. Richardson and G.O. Sayles, 3 vols (Selden Soc. 72, 89, 99), I, 239–40.

38 *CIPM* xxii.533; xxv.376.

39 SC 6/1307/7 (1428–29). In 1528–29 a fair or fairs (*nund'*) were apparently still in operation, but were not valued separately: SC 12/13/7.

40 *CIPM* xxvi.63; J.M. Bestall, *Early and Medieval Chesterfield*, History of Chesterfield, I (Chesterfield, 1974), 90. C 1/9/332 (1432x43) refers to a single fair (unfortunately the date is lost) and a Saturday market; accounts of the Eyre family, 1472–91, also refer to a fair or fairs at Chesterfield. The date is not given, but the sequence of payments suggests that the Exaltation fair is referred to (Oxford, Bodleian Library, MSS.D.D. Weld C.19/4/2–4).

41 SC 6/1083/11.

42 Cf. Kowaleski, *Local Markets*, 356.

had been 'worth nothing because discontinued for many years'.[43] The association of a nil value with an inactive market raises the question of whether the values ascribed to markets and fairs in the IPMs can be used more broadly as an index of their success or decline. To approach this question we must first consider in more detail the nature and reliability of the valuations in the IPMs.

It should probably be assumed that the values of markets and fairs given in the IPMs are intended either as averages or as maxima.[44] They are thus approximations, since profits from a market or fair could vary considerably from year to year; consequently many are given in round figures, such as £1 or 10*s*, that might otherwise excite suspicion. Because annual profits could vary so much, it is not straightforward to compare the IPM valuations with extant accounts, which often do not survive in lengthy series. Even from such comparisons as can be made, it is difficult to generalize about accuracy and reliability. Nevertheless in several cases the IPM figures are confirmed by contemporary or near contemporary accounts. This seems particularly to be the case when a market or fair was farmed to the local community for a fixed sum, especially when such arrangements were of long standing. Thus the farm of £6 paid (according to an IPM of 1425) by the burgesses for the market at Clare is confirmed by accounts of 1428–29 and earlier, as is the fee farm of £10 similarly paid by the burgesses of Sudbury.[45] The Courtenay share of Crolditch fair in Exeter, worth 10*s* in IPMs of 1420, 1422, and 1441, had the same value in an account of 1422.[46]

The IPMs can also be reliable, it seems, where income was more variable. The figure of £8 given for a share of market and fair profits at Newmarket, Suffolk in an IPM of 1412 fits reasonably well with the evidence of accounts from 1401–2 and 1428–40.[47] More typically, however, the IPMs tend to undervalue, often by significant factors of 50% or more: as at Swaffham, Norfolk, where an IPM of 1437 gives profits of 20*s*, and accounts for 1434–36 average well over £2 12*s*;[48] and as, apparently at, Cottingham, Yorkshire, where an IPM of 1424 records 4*s* 10*d*, and accounts of 1420–21 about 9*s*;[49] or at Thirsk, where an IPM of 1407 recorded market and fair profits of £6 13*s* 4*d*, which had come to over £10 in an account of 1398–99.[50]

43 *CIPM* xxvi.218; xv.609.

44 *CIPM* xxi.827: incomes 'variable but no more than 40*s*', 'variable but no more than 13*s* 4*d*'.

45 *CIPM* xxii.504; SC 6/1113/3 m. 1; cf. G.A. Thornton, *A History of Clare* (Cambridge, 1928), 40–2; G.A. Holmes, *The Estates of the Higher Nobility in Fourteenth-Century England* (Cambridge, 1957), 157.

46 *CIPM* xxi.350, 941; xxv.507; SC 6/1118/6 m. 1.

47 *CIPM* xix.1037 (valued together with other courts); P. May, *Newmarket: Medieval and Tudor* (privately published, 1982), 25, 27–9; P. May, 'Newmarket 500 Years Ago', *PSIA* 33 (1973–6), 253–74, at 263, 268; P. May, *Court Rolls of Newmarket in Suffolk 1408–10* (Newmarket, 1973), 37–8 (and *passim* for profits of the fair and market courts).

48 *CIPM* xxiv.536; SC 6/944/12–14.

49 *CIPM* xxii.332; *VCH Yorks. East Riding* iv.73.

50 *CIPM* xix.315; SC 6/1087/14. However, the IPM extent of Thirsk is ambiguously worded and the value given may relate, more accurately, to a two-thirds share of the manor.

Table 7.1 Relationship between the recorded value of markets (1399–1447) and their survival in the early modern period

IPM value	2*s* or less	3*s* to 13*s* 4*d*	£1	>£1 to £10
No. of markets recorded	13	21	12	17
No. of markets surviving	2 (15%)	18 (86%)	9 (75%)	15 (88%)

In other instances the IPMs are inexact and somewhat misleading. The market and fair at Knighton were valued in a 1425 IPM at £40 (together with mill, demesne lands, and ferry (*passagium*)), those at Rhaedr at £16. A contemporary account shows that the toll of market and fair(s) at Knighton (together with the ferry) were in fact at farm for £20, although it was noted that £40 had been paid the preceding year (the account does not refer explicitly to the farm of demesne lands, so they may well be included here, as the IPM implies). The same account records that a farm of £16 was indeed paid at Rhaedr, but included not only the Thursday market and two fairs, but also the watermill, demesne lands, and meadows.[51]

Such comparisons suggest that the degree, if any, of undervaluation varied significantly from one inquisition to another and that IPMs may occasionally (as Knighton) be over-generous in their estimates. This makes it somewhat problematic to use the IPMs even in calculating the relative values of different markets. Again, though, it would be premature to leap to the overly pessimistic conclusion that the values recorded in IPMs are completely unreliable. Kersey (Suff.), where the market was at farm for £5 in 1385 but worth only £1 in 1425 and 1432, suggests that IPM data may provide some information about the pace and extent of market decline in the post-Black Death period.[52] More broadly, there is an apparent correlation between a market's fifteenth-century value, as recorded in the IPMs, and its apparent chances of survival into the sixteenth century, as illustrated in Table 7.1.[53] (Similar results emerge from combined valuations for fairs and markets, where again an income of 2*s* or less was a likely sign of future failure.)

The surviving markets valued at less than two shillings were Penrith and Hitchin.[54] It might seem unlikely that a thriving market centre such as Hitchin would be of no value, as the 1434 IPM recorded; but the statement seems to have been technically accurate, since an account of 1426–28 shows that the toll was at

51 *CIPM* xxii.510; SC 6/1209/17 (3 Jan. to 29 Sept. 1425), mm. 1d, 2.

52 *CIPM* xvi.314; xxii.510; xxiv.81. SC 6/1001/3 (1398 99) confirms that market toll and pleas were at farm for roughly £5, although there were significant additional profits from rent of stalls.

53 Survival rates based on the lists in *AHEW* iv.468–75; for problems with this source, see below, pp. 113–14.

54 *CIPM* xxiv.251; xxv.517.

farm for £4 13*s* 4*d* yearly, but that the sum had been granted to the bailiff as his fee.[55] Similar circumstances may explain why the market at Penrith was recorded as worthless in 1440.

Fairs and Markets in Proofs of Age

Fairs and markets also feature occasionally in proofs of age. These references demand separate treatment because the documents pose particular problems of interpretation. Proofs of age were part of the administrative process by which heirs who had been in the crown's wardship claimed livery of their estates. They recorded the testimony of twelve jurors who claimed to recall the place and date of the heir's birth and who supported their testimony by referring to contemporaneous events, such as strong winds or football matches. The reliability of these testimonies is often suspect because a number of proofs were copied or adapted from early documents, and other testimonies appear to have been conventional. While this does not necessarily mean that they had no basis in reality, the burden of proof currently appears to lie with those who would argue for the veracity of the testimonies, at least by the fifteenth century.[56]

There are a number of occasions when the testimony regarding markets and fairs contained in the proofs is corroborated by other sources. One proof, for example, referred to the Saturday market at Blandford Forum in 1389; another mentioned the fair at 'Aldburgh' in Holderness on the feast of St Bartholomew, 1377; yet another described the Midsummer fair at South Petherton (Som.) in 1380.[57] Equally, however, on a number of occasions the evidence conflicts, especially in the case of fairs. Thus one proof refers to a fair at Beaminster (Dors.) on 22 June, when other evidence points to 8 September (the Nativity of the Virgin) as the correct date; another describes a fair at Fakenham (Norf.) on 14 November, when other evidence points to fairs there at Whitsun and August.[58] It is sometimes possible that the proofs accurately record a changed feast day. What seems more likely, though, is that jurors treated the date of a fair or market with considerable freedom, because their testimonies had to be tied to heir's actual date of birth. It was no use recalling an event that had occurred several months previously.

The proofs do not, then, provide good evidence for the dates on which fairs or markets were held. They may nevertheless indicate that those events were in continuing operation at the time of the events recalled by jurors, and even at the time of the proofs themselves, since it seems unlikely that a discontinued fair or market

55 BL Egerton Roll 8363; by the 1450s the toll was worth 40*s* yearly (BL Egerton Rolls 8364–5).

56 Holford, 'Testimony', 635–54; see also chapters 9–11.

57 *CIPM* xvii.1320; xviii.858; xix.997.

58 *CIPM* xix.102, 783.

would be recalled. Memories of fairs and markets are not especially common and tend to be associated with places where such institutions are otherwise recorded. This suggests that complete fabrication of such memories, as opposed to manipulation of dates, was unusual.

The possibility of complete fabrication cannot be ruled out, however, which creates a difficulty when a proof is the only apparent source. Examples include the proof taken in 1382 which recorded a 'small fair' at Leckhamstead (Berks.) on the feast of St Valentine, to whom the church was dedicated; or the proof taken in 1444 which described a fair at Little Maldon (Essex) on the feast of St Giles.[59] Giles was the patron of Maldon hospital, which may lend credence to the latter proof; conversely the dedication at Leckhampstead seems to have been to St James, which perhaps casts doubt on the former. The date of the fair had to correspond with the heir's date of birth, and evidently it was felt that the dedication of the local church had to correspond with the feast day on which the fair was held. Nevertheless the possibility that a 'small fair' was held at Leckhampstead (perhaps the feast of St James) remains.

A close study of fairs and markets in IPMs thus has a good deal to tell us about the nature of the documents themselves and their reliability. It is clear that both markets and fairs are recorded incompletely, and that IPM evidence cannot be used negatively (that is, the absence of a market from an IPM does not necessarily indicate its actual disappearance or decline, although it may do so in some circumstances). Where markets and fairs are recorded, though, the IPM evidence is often of high quality, corroborating and sometimes correcting information available from other sources. Even the testimony in proofs of age is often reliable. A note of caution must be sounded regarding the copying of information from one IPM to another, however, and it is also clear that the valuations in IPMs are often underestimates, sometimes by significant factors.

The extent to which accuracy and reliability varied at different times, or between different escheators, is difficult to discern from a relatively small body of evidence. Nevertheless there are interesting patterns in the data that suggest avenues for future research. First, many more markets and fairs are referred to in the IPMs from 1420 onwards. This reflects the fact that manorial extents are much more common in this period, for reasons explored elsewhere.[60] However, the *proportion* of manorial extents referring to markets and fairs is significantly greater in the period 1399–1419. This raises the interesting possibility that although extents were not frequently compiled in this period, a more careful job was done when they were prepared. In contrast, when extents became more commonplace after c.1420 less care may have been taken over their accuracy.

There are also interesting variations between the number of markets and fairs

[59] *CIPM* xv.658; xxvi.156.

[60] Holford, 'Valuations and Extents', 130–2.

recorded in different counties, in proportion to the number of surviving IPM extents. Some of these variations, of course, reflect the distribution of markets and fairs themselves. It is not surprising that IPMs from Norfolk, a county richly endowed with commercial institutions, mention markets and fairs relatively frequently. It is perhaps more surprising that, for example, IPMs from Hampshire and Wiltshire contain relatively few references, or that those from Herefordshire contain a relatively large number. The reasons for these variations require more research, but are likely to reflect both administrative and economic differences. It seems likely, for example, that markets and fairs loom relatively large in the Herefordshire evidence because the county included several lordships in the adjoining Welsh March, whose markets, reflecting patterns of settlement and lordship, tended to be valuable.[61]

Clearly, therefore, the evidence of IPMs and related documents can be problematic and is not always easy to use; but at the same time, they contain much information that is not available elsewhere. What, in sum, can IPMs contribute to our understanding of markets and fairs in medieval England?

First, they can refine our understanding of market networks at a regional and local level. In Norfolk the IPMs add two markets and six fairs to existing lists.[62] These are usually relatively small contributions to the county picture: in Suffolk, for example, the IPMs add only a single location to the total of over a hundred markets and/or fairs, although only a proportion of the latter will have remained active in the fifteenth century. Nevertheless, such additions can add important details to our picture of local trading networks. The same is true of the additional information found in IPMs relating to the dates of markets. Kersey (Suff.), for example, was chartered for a Monday market in 1252; by the fourteenth century IPM evidence suggests that the market day had changed to a Friday. Presumably this reflected competition from the market at nearby Toppesfield (now Toppesfield Hall in Hadleigh), which had also been chartered for a Monday market in 1252.[63] Similarly IPM information on the dates of fairs can refine our picture of their seasonality, and also of the relationship between fair dates and the dedications of local churches.[64]

It must be emphasized that in these local and regional studies IPMs must be used in conjunction with other sources. Since they usually record only the foundations of tenants-in-chief, and even those somewhat erratically, the IPMs give a very patchy picture of fairs and markets both at a regional and at a national

[61] Campbell & Bartley, *Atlas*, 272–3, 290, 301–2.

[62] Norfolk: markets: Babingley; Burnham Thorpe; fairs: Aldborough (apparently); Hingham (2); Watton (3); Castle Acre. Suffolk: markets: Chelsworth. For the fair at Hingham cf. D. Dymond, *The Norfolk Landscape* (1985), 165.

[63] Cf. comments on Kersey in R.M. Smith, 'A Periodic Market and its Impact on a Manorial Community: Botesdale, Suffolk, and the Manor of Redgrave, 1280–1300', in *Medieval Society and the Manor Court*, ed. Z. Razi and R. Smith (Oxford, 1996), 460–1; M. Bailey, *Medieval Suffolk: An Economic and Social History 1200–1500* (Woodbridge, 2007), 120.

[64] Cf. Farmer, 'Marketing the Produce', 339–40.

level. For example, the IPMs from 1399 to 1447 do not record a single market in Cambridgeshire. Several successful markets in that county (e.g. Balsham or Cambridge) were in the hands of ecclesiastics, so do not feature in the IPMs. There were a number of lay foundations in the county, but many (as at Abington Pigotts or Cottenham) seem to have failed to establish themselves or (like perhaps Bassingbourn or Fowlmere) were early failures.[65] Others (as at Barham, Barrington, Brinkley, or Foxton) simply failed to occur in the IPMs because the manors were not extended, or the tenants did not hold in chief.

Considered in its own light the IPM evidence suggests not so much conclusions, as avenues for future exploration relating to the nature of markets in the fifteenth century and their survival into the sixteenth. The IPMs provide a snapshot, even if it is a partial and incomplete one, of the markets founded and maintained by lay landlords. Between 1399 and 1447 almost 75% of these were relatively minor affairs, worth £1 or less (see Table 7.1). That was something of a decline from the first half of the fourteenth century, when under half of the markets recorded in IPMs were worth less than £1.[66] Evidently, and unsurprisingly, the general profitability of markets had declined in an age of contracting population and declining trade. What is perhaps more striking, however, is that so many markets had never been very profitable. Perhaps, as Richard Britnell has suggested, many were originally intended to serve only a restricted area.[67] They were able to play such a function even in a period of economic contraction and many survived into the sixteenth century. We saw above that markets with an estimated annual IPM value of less than 2*s* were highly unlikely to survive into the early modern period. Perhaps more surprisingly, the majority of markets valued at 3*s* or more in IPMs did survive, and the chances of survival did not increase significantly among the groups of markets valued at £1 or greater. Evidently some low-valued markets were in decline, and that decline in some cases proved terminal. But it is also likely that a large number of low-valued markets operated consistently within a limited radius and maintained an existence as institutions of purely local significance. The 'frenzy' of market foundation between about 1250 and 1330, when many local markets emerged, may have been more rational than is sometimes supposed.[68]

It is in any case not easy to assess the survival of medieval markets into the sixteenth century and later. The standard lists of early modern markets were compiled by Alan Everitt in 1967, with some additions in 1978, for the fourth

65 However for shops at (apparently) Bassingbourn in 1438, see *CIPM* xxv.301.

66 Campbell & Bartley, *Atlas*, 301.

67 R. Britnell, 'Urban Demand in the English Economy, 1300–1600', in *Trade, Urban Hinterlands, and Market Integration c.1300–1600*, ed. J.A. Galloway (Centre for Metropolitan History Working Papers Series, no. 3; Institute of Historical Research, 2000), 11. The contrary argument – that the majority of markets were intended to cater for more than local demand – is made by J. Masschaele, *Peasants, Merchants, and Markets: Inland Trade in Medieval England, 1150–1350* (Basingstoke, 1997).

68 Masschaele, *Peasants*, 231.

volume of the *Agrarian History of England and Wales*, and are routinely cited in studies of the decline or survival of medieval markets.[69] Everitt admitted that his lists might be modified by future 'local research', however, and it is clear that a number of such modifications are necessary, at least for the sixteenth century. For example, the market at Hunmanby (Yorks.) was described as 'decayed' in 1382, and was not mentioned in an extent of 1442, but was nevertheless still extant in 1539–40.[70] The nearby market at Filey also survived in 1539–40; neither was listed by Everitt. In Cambridgeshire, the only county where Everitt's list can be checked against a full modern *VCH*, medieval markets are thought to have survived into the sixteenth century at Balsham, Brinkley, Foxton, Gamlingay, Orwell, Sutton, and Swavesey,[71] adding seven further markets to the eight listed by Everitt. (The *VCH* also suggests that Masschaele's arguments concerning failed markets in Cambridgeshire require some revision.)[72] Kowaleski's list for Devon may add nine markets to the 45 listed by Everitt.[73] Similarly the markets in Table 7.1 above valued at £1 or less, which are thought to have failed, include a number which may well have continued into the sixteenth century.[74]

Until our knowledge of sixteenth-century markets is fuller, historians should be cautious in comparing marketing systems c.1300 and c.1600 and in attempting to explain the apparent contrast between abundance, on the one hand, and scarcity, on the other. The IPMs, with their notices of hitherto unrecorded markets and their evidence for the continued functioning of many others, invite fuller study of what exactly changed in the key period between about 1348 and 1500, perhaps suggesting that many marketing systems may have remained localized well into the sixteenth century. For all their difficulties, they can make an important contribution to our understanding of late medieval and early modern marketing.

[69] Britnell, 'Urban Demand', 11–12.

[70] *CIPM* xv.579; xxv.591; *VCH Yorks. East Riding*, ii.240; and cf. *CIPM* xxv.591 for mention of shops.

[71] The Tuesday market at Swavesey was granted by Henry VII in 1505, an earlier Tuesday market possibly having lapsed.

[72] Masschaele, *Peasants*, 184–8 and map on 185.

[73] Kowaleski's criteria for surviving markets was inclusion in Everitt's lists, but she included a market at Sheepwash not listed by Everitt, and also eight markets active in the fifteenth century which may have survived into the sixteenth (pp. 356, 360–7)

[74] For example Brailes (Warw.), see *Ministers Accounts of the Warwickshire Estates of the Duke of Clarence 1479–80*, ed. R.H. Hilton, Dugdale Soc. 21 (1952), 75; DL 29/643/10434; SC 6/HENVIII/3704); Long Stratton (Norf.) and Garboldisham (Norf.). F. Blomefield, *Essay Towards a Topographical History of Norfolk*, 11 vols (1805–10), i.263, v.188 implies that the market at Long Stratton survived until the early sixteenth century.

8

The Structure of the Milling Industry, 1427–37

Matthew Tompkins

In 2006 Bruce Campbell and Ken Bartley brought out *England on the Eve of the Black Death: an Atlas of Lay Lordship, Land and Wealth, 1300–49*. This magnificently detailed analysis of the rural economy in the first half of the fourteenth century used data from the manorial extents contained in IPMs to produce distribution maps and statistics of land use and land values, agriculture, estate and social structure, and other aspects of rural society. It is sometimes said that a similarly detailed analysis cannot be produced for subsequent periods of the late Middle Ages because from the middle of the fourteenth century onwards the extents contained in IPMs become ever less detailed. This is partly true – the later IPMs do indeed lack some of the detailed lists of manorial assets which are numerous before c.1350, primarily those of crops and livestock.[1] But nevertheless they often do provide aggregate data for these assets (for example, the total areas of arable, pasture, meadow and woodland within a manor and their values per acre, or the respective total rents received from its free and customary tenants), and some use can be made of these. In some other categories they provide data nearly as full as those to be found in the pre-1350 IPMs. This paper tests the possibilities through a case study of one type of manorial asset: mills.

Mills are dealt with in Chapter 16 of the *Atlas*. Its 20 pages contain 24 distribution maps and eight graphs analysing the numbers and types of mills and their geographic distributions and values, broken down by power source, function, physical condition and other factors. There is not space here to attempt to duplicate every analysis featured in the *Atlas*, but its major aspects will be covered.

The *Atlas* deals with mills only in the half century before 1350. Two monographs on the milling industry have also been published which cover the later Middle Ages after 1350. Richard Holt's *The Mills of Medieval England* covered the entire period from Domesday Book to c.1500, while John Langdon's *Mills in the Medieval Economy* focused on the two and a half centuries after 1300. Both were based principally on data from manorial accounts and court rolls, however,

[1] After the middle of the fourteenth century IPMs 'became increasingly sporadic in recording manorial assets' (J.R. Langdon, *Mills in the Medieval Economy: England 1300–1540* (Oxford, 2004), 21), and 'far fewer of them include detailed extents, so that by the final quarter of the fourteenth century they are of greatly diminished use as a source of land-use information' (Campbell, *ESA*, 37).

and made little use of IPMs, save that Langdon used data from the IPMs of Edward II's reign to reveal the numbers, types, distribution and values of mills in 1302–27.[2] The great majority of the published *CIPMs* have not abstracted the manorial extents and a substantial research effort was required for Langdon to extract the data from the original inquisitions for that single reign. To have done the same right up to the early sixteenth century would have been impossible. It may also have been thought that the quality of data offered by the later IPMs would not be good enough to justify the effort. Both studies are detailed and comprehensive, so to some extent this paper's IPM-derived data will only be confirmatory of their findings, but it will nevertheless sometimes be able to complement them and to fill gaps in the picture provided by the manorial records.

The problem of the accessibility of the data in the IPMs remains, of course. Only the *CIPMs* for 1399–1447 have abstracted the contents of the extents. For other periods it is still necessary to go to the original manuscript IPMs. Until recently even the data in the 1399–1447 extents has had to be extracted from those nine print calendars manually, volume by volume, via their indexes. Fortunately these nine volumes are now becoming available online through the Mapping the Medieval Countryside website, in an enhanced digital format which will make it relatively quick and simple to extract all references to a topic from all the volumes electronically.

When this paper was written the online calendars were still in preparation. The calendars which were then most nearly ready were volumes 23 and 24, covering 1427–37, so this paper is based on them alone. All references in them to mills were extracted into a database, which has formed the basis of the following analysis.[3] A single decade is rather a short period to investigate change over time (except by comparison back to the 1300–49 data in the *Atlas*), but it will at least reveal regional variation. The years 1427–37 are fortuitously a useful decade to work on. The later fourteenth and fifteenth centuries were a period of depression in the milling industry, which reached its nadir in the 1440s, so this will give us a snapshot of the industry at almost its lowest ebb (Figure 8.1).[4]

The reliability of the IPM extent data, criticised by Kosminsky and others, has been re-established by more recent work by Campbell, Langdon, Dyer, Holford and others,[5] but certain deficiencies of the IPMs from all periods as a source

[2] R. Holt, *The Mills of Medieval England* (Oxford, 1988); Langdon, *Mills*, Maps 1.1, 1.2 and 6.1.

[3] www.inquisitionspostmortem.ac.uk; the extraction was effected by Matthew Holford, without whose computing expertise this paper would not have been possible.

[4] Holt, *Mills*, 159; Langdon, *Mills*, 26–32. Fig. 8.1 is based on the graph at p. 28.

[5] E.A. Kosminsky, *Studies in the Agrarian History of England in the Thirteenth Century* (Oxford, 1956), 63; B.M.S. Campbell, J.A. Galloway and M. Murphy, 'Rural Land-use in the Metropolitan Hinterland, 1270–1339: the Evidence of Inquisitiones Post Mortem', *AgHR* xl (1992), 3–6; J. Ambler and J. Langdon, 'Lordship and Peasant Consumerism in the Milling Industry of Early Fourteenth-Century England', *Past and Present* 145 (1994), 3–46; C. Dyer, 'The Value of Fifteenth-Century Inquisitions Post Mortem for Economic and Social History',

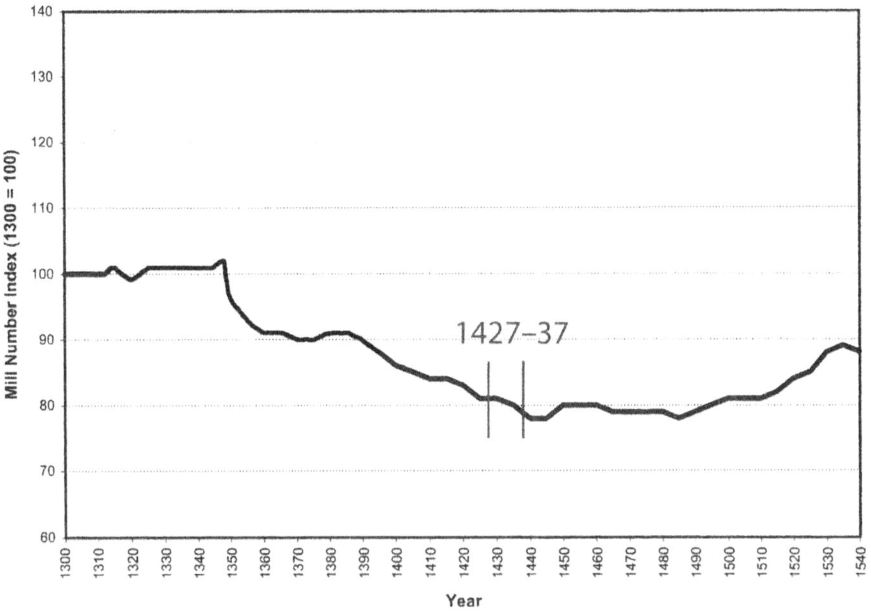

Figure 8.1 Movement of total mill numbers, 1300–1540.

for economic data, especially regarding mills, must be recognised. IPMs record only certain categories of mills, almost exclusively rural mills – very few urban mills are recorded – and principally demesne mills (in this period nearly always leased out, not kept in hand). Tenant-owned mills are seldom recorded, which is unfortunate, as the independent sector was expanding in the fifteenth century. Nor do the IPMs record *all* rural demesne mills. Ecclesiastical estates are not covered (unlike Holt's and Langdon's data from manorial records), and by and large neither are estates of mesne tenants, so gentry lords are under-represented.

It must also be noted that references to mills in the later IPMs are generally somewhat terse, sometimes no more than a statement that there is a mill and its annual value (e.g. 'Great Barton, the mills, annual value 100*s*').[6] For a very few not even a valuation is given. However, a small amount of other details are frequently added. The type of power source is often stated (i.e. whether a watermill or a windmill, or very occasionally a horse-mill and, just once in all nine fifteenth-century volumes, a sea mill).[7]

The *purpose* for which the mill is used is also sometimes stated, though not as often as the power source. Usually it is either a grain mill or a fulling mill (used to full cloth, that is, to beat it in order to shrink the weave and felt the fibres

in *IPM Companion*, 97–115; M.L. Holford, '"Notoriously Unreliable": The Valuations and Extents', in *idem*, 117–444.

6 *CIPM* xxiv.26.

7 At Wrabness, on the Stour estuary in Essex in 1419 (*CIPM* xxi.115).

together). The type of grain is specified only very occasionally (just once in 1427–37: Penshurst in Kent had one mill for wheat and another for malt). Industrial mills other than fulling mills are also mentioned only very rarely (again, just one in our decade: a tanning mill in Cornwall).[8]

Information about the physical infrastructure of the mill and its surroundings is seldom given, except for the statement that it is a water or windmill, or a grain or fulling mill. Occasionally the mill-pond is mentioned, but usually when it has value as a fishery.[9] The seigniorial rights which gave value to the mills, such as millsuit or preferential multure rates, are also seldom mentioned (no doubt partly because by the fifteenth century many manors were no longer enforcing millsuit).[10] *CIPMs* xxiii and xxiv contain just four references to millsuit and none to multure rates.[11]

Bearing these limitations in mind, what can the two volumes tell us about the milling industry in the period 1427–1437?

Mill Numbers and Distribution

Mills were recorded in only 15% of the IPMs in these two volumes (in 203 IPMs out of 1,370): a considerable reduction from 1300–49, when mills were 'recorded by at least half and sometimes well over three-quarters of all IPMs'.[12] It is unlikely that this is due to failure of the fifteenth-century escheators to record mills. It is known that the absolute numbers of mills fell severely during the century after 1350. Mark Bailey found that more than half the manorial mills in Suffolk disappeared in the century or so after 1350. Langdon's national data does not show a decline of quite this severity – he found a fall of one fifth, perhaps one quarter at the most – though it does suggest that East Anglia was one of the regions which suffered most severely.[13]

In all, 464 mills were recorded in 1427–37, located in 327 manors. John Langdon found more than three times as many mills in the 1307–27 IPMs, from almost four times as many manors (1,592 mills in just over 1,200 manors). The difference no doubt reflects the fact that his data came from two decades, not one, as well as the known fall-off in mill numbers during the intervening century.

8 *CIPM* xxiv.549 (Penshurst); *CIPM* xxiii.247 (Tregony, Corn.).

9 For example, Lilford in Northamptonshire, where in 1434 the mill and the fishery in the mill pond were together valued at 6*s* 8*d* (*CIPM* xxiv.252).

10 M.W. Bailey, *The Decline of Serfdom in Late Medieval England* (Woodbridge, 2014), 56, 278–81; Langdon, *Mills*, 286; Holt, *Mills*, 166–7.

11 *CIPM* xxiv.37 (Mosterton, Dors.); xxiii.89 (East Tanfield, Yorks.), xxiii.427 (Nacton, Suff.) ; xxiii.697 (Seaton Delaval, Northum.).

12 Campbell & Bartley, *Atlas*, 280, Graph 16.1(c). The 1327–37 calculation excludes proofs of age but includes all other types of *IPM*, whether or not they record landholdings.

13 M.W. Bailey, *Medieval Suffolk* (Woodbridge, 2007), 233; Langdon, *Mills*, 6, 26–32; and see also Holt, *Mills*, 159–70.

Quite a few manors contained more than one mill (usually two, but sometimes three or more), and these were not just the territorially large manors in the north or west. More than one mill was also common in southern and eastern manors. For example, in Upper Clatford, Hampshire, in 1435 there were 'a watermill, worth 26*s* 8*d* and a fulling mill, worth 13*s* 4*d*', and Penshurst, Kent, in 1436 had 'a house with 3 watermills attached, one for wheat, one for malt, and one for fulling cloth'.[14]

Map 8.1 shows the 327 manors where the mills were found. It should be noted that there are none at all in the palatine counties of Lancashire, Cheshire and Durham, because their IPMs were produced and retained by their palatine administrations and are not included in the published national calendars.[15] There were also no mills from Cambridgeshire, Middlesex and Rutland and just one in Huntingdonshire, while in several counties the coverage is confined to just one part of the county. Some of these gaps in the coverage reflect areas where ecclesiastical landownership predominated – the Cambridgeshire and Lincolnshire Fenland, for example – but others are probably consequences of the data deriving from just one decade of IPMs, and the inclusion of more calendars might have produced denser and more even coverage. Only a few regions in Wales are covered, however, principally Monmouthshire and Gower, and there can be no doubt that here the IPM data can make no claim to be representative of the principality as a whole (which is equally badly covered by the pre-1350 IPMs – *cf.* map 3.6 in the *Atlas*). Subject to these caveats, however, the coverage shown in Map 8.1 is satisfyingly extensive and, if it might be unwise to draw conclusions from it as to conditions in individual counties, it can surely sustain analysis at national and regional levels.

Power Sources: Water and Windmills

The 464 recorded mills can be broken down by power type as follows:

watermills	308
windmills	40
horse-mills	5
tidal mills	0
unspecified	111

The large number of mills of unspecified type is disappointing, as in 1300–49 the power source was specified in 95% of IPMs. The two periods can be compared in Figure 8.2.

It can be seen that the proportions of watermills and horse-mills were much the same in both, but those of windmills and 'unspecified' were very different. It is tempting to suppose that it is simply a case of most windmills having gone

14 *CIPM* xxiv.340 (Upper Clatford); 549 (Penshurst).

15 Mills in Hart and Hartlepool in county Durham do appear in one Northumberland *IPM* (xxiv.693), no doubt due to their location in the wapentake of Sedberge, which was not within the palatinate jurisdiction; *VCH Durham* iii. 191–4.

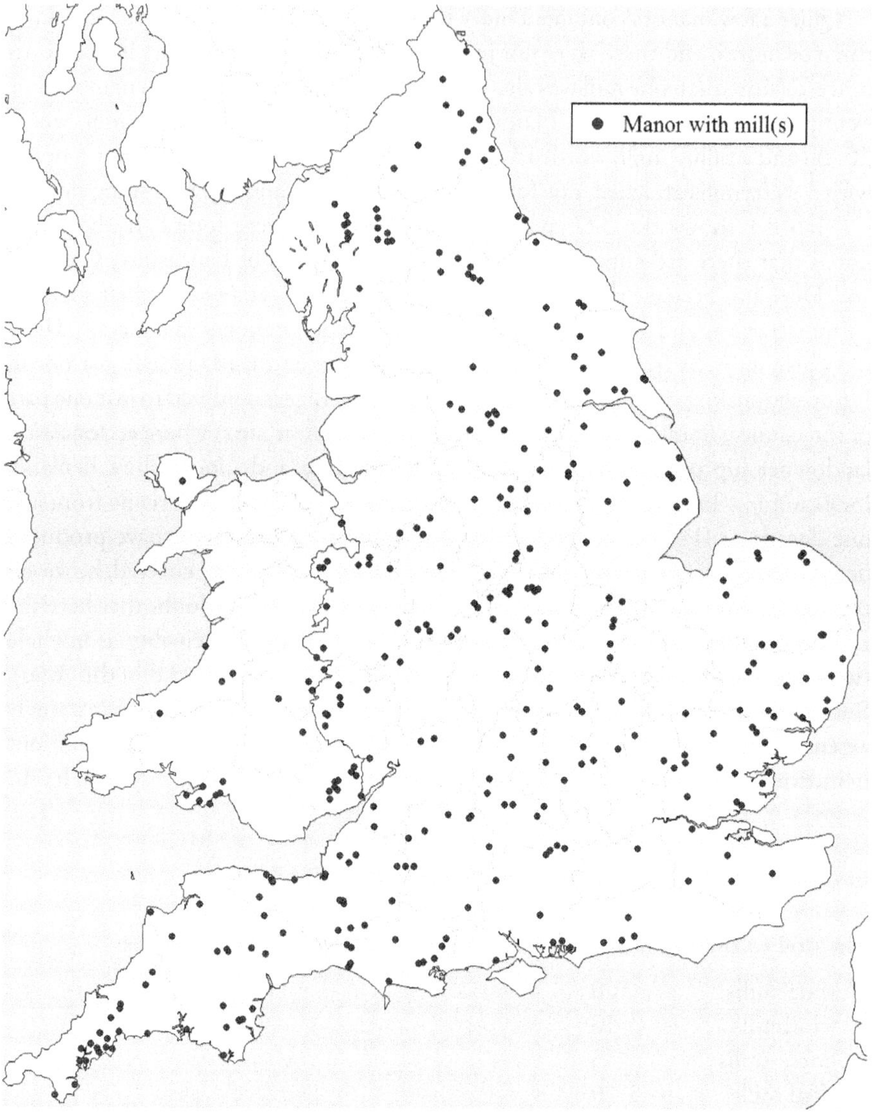

Map 8.1 Distribution of manors with mills recorded in IPMs, 1427–37.

unrecorded as such, and so appearing in the 'unspecified' category, but this is unlikely as it is known that windmill numbers declined between these two periods to a much greater extent than did watermills.[16] It seems likely that, if the power sources of the 111 unspecified mills were known, the number of watermills would increase considerably, making the two pie-charts look rather more dissimilar.

The small number of horse-mills in the IPMs does not reflect their actual

[16] Langdon, *Mills*, 35–7; 'the number of windmills in 1540 was only about 45 per cent of that in 1300', p. 35.

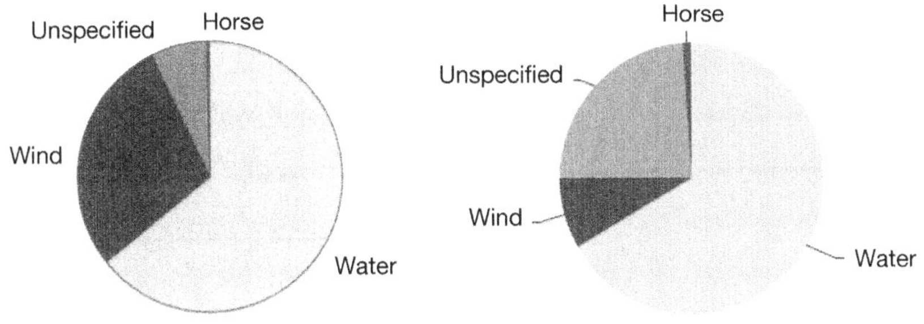

(a) Water, wind, unspecified and horse mills as percentages of total number, 1300–49

(b) The same, 1427–37

Figure 8.2 Power sources: water, wind, horse and unspecified mills as percentages of total number.

Source: Campbell and Bartley, *Atlas*, 297.

numbers, but rather the fact that they were usually owned by independent tenant millers, not by manorial lords.[17] The number of tidal mills in medieval England has been the subject of debate,[18] but it seems certain that they also were more numerous than is suggested by the 1427–37 IPMs, which record none at all (only one is recorded in any IPM between 1399 and 1447).[19] The reason for their absence from the IPMs may be, as Langdon has suggested, that 'their often quite ferocious costs' of construction and maintenance limited them to wealthy institutions, which generally do not feature in IPMs, and that some mills described simply as 'watermills' may in fact have been tide-mills.[20]

Many manors had more than one watermill, though only one had more than one windmill (Longbenton in Northumberland – and one of them was ruinous).[21] In the first half of the fourteenth century manors with both a watermill and a windmill were relatively numerous, especially in the East Midlands and East Anglia – no doubt so that wind power could supplement water power when seasonal streams ran weakly[22] – but in 1327–37 only six of the 40 recorded windmills were co-located with a watermill.[23] It seems that a windmill which was

[17] Holt, *Mills*, 166–7; Langdon, *Mills*, 78–9; *idem*, 'Watermills and Windmills in the West Midlands, 1086–1500', *EcHR* xliv (1991), 434.

[18] W.E. Minchinton, 'Tidemills of England and Wales', *Transactions of the Fourth Symposium of the International Molinological Society* (London, 1978), 339–53, and *idem*, 'Early Tide Mills: Some Problems', *Technology and Culture* 20 (1979), 777–86; Holt, *Mills*, 133–7.

[19] The single occurrence of a sea mill was at Wrabness, near the Stour estuary in Essex, in 1419 (*CIPM* xxi.115).

[20] Langdon, *Mills*, 78–9.

[21] *CIPM* xxiii.378.

[22] Campbell & Bartley, *Atlas*, 281.

[23] Branston, Lincolnshire, both ruinous (*CIPM* xxiv.46); Cottingham, Yorkshire (*CIPM* xxiv.262); Great Bardfield, Essex (*CIPM* xxiv.78); Little Walsingham, Norfolk, 1 ruinous windmill and 2 'mills' worth nothing (*CIPM* xxiv.80); Low Ham, Somerset (*CIPM* xxiii.107); Watford, Northamptonshire (*CIPM* xxiii.213).

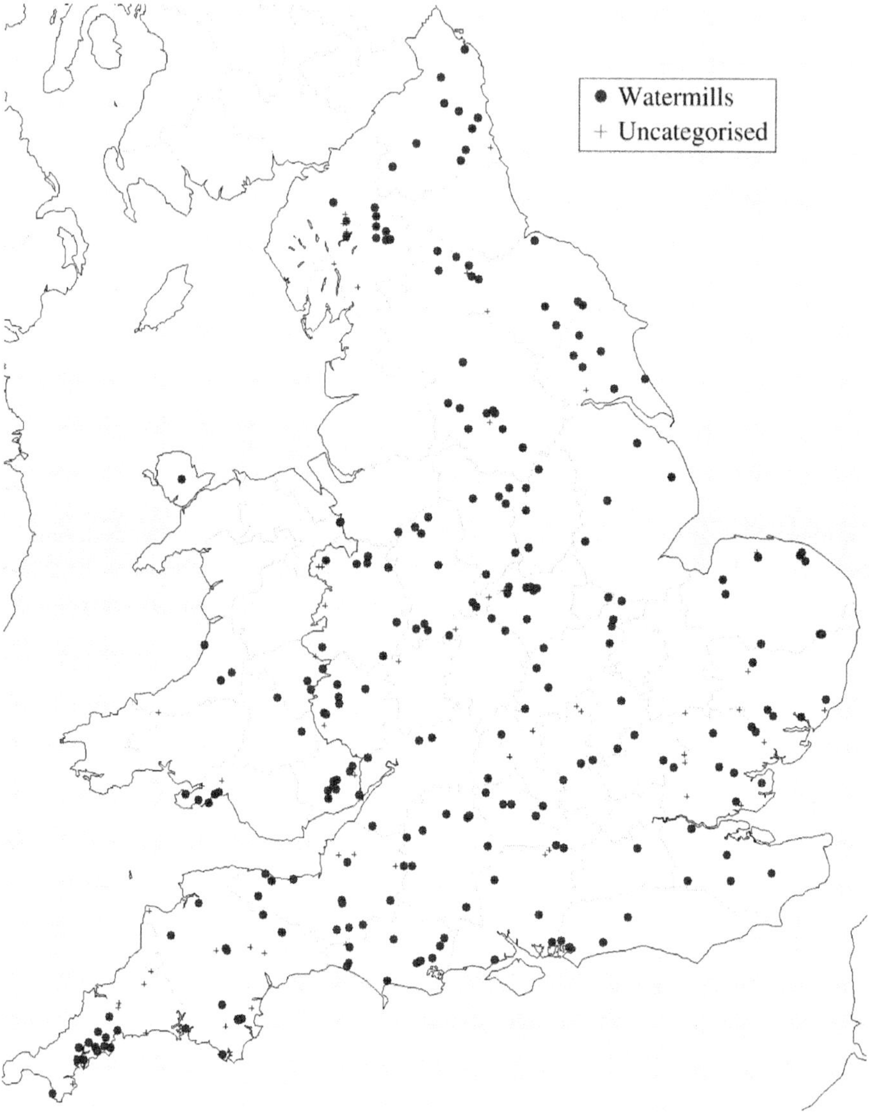

Map 8.2 Distribution of watermills, 1427–37.

supernumerary to a watermill was more likely to close down than was any that was the sole mill in the manor.[24]

Maps 8.2 and 8.3 show the respective distributions of the water and windmills in 1427–37. As might be expected, the watermills are found in all parts of the country, though far from evenly spread across it. Some of the blank spaces are to be expected – the three palatinate counties, and perhaps the Fenland, where

[24] Holt, *Mills*, 34–5, 164; Langdon, *Mills*, 35–6.

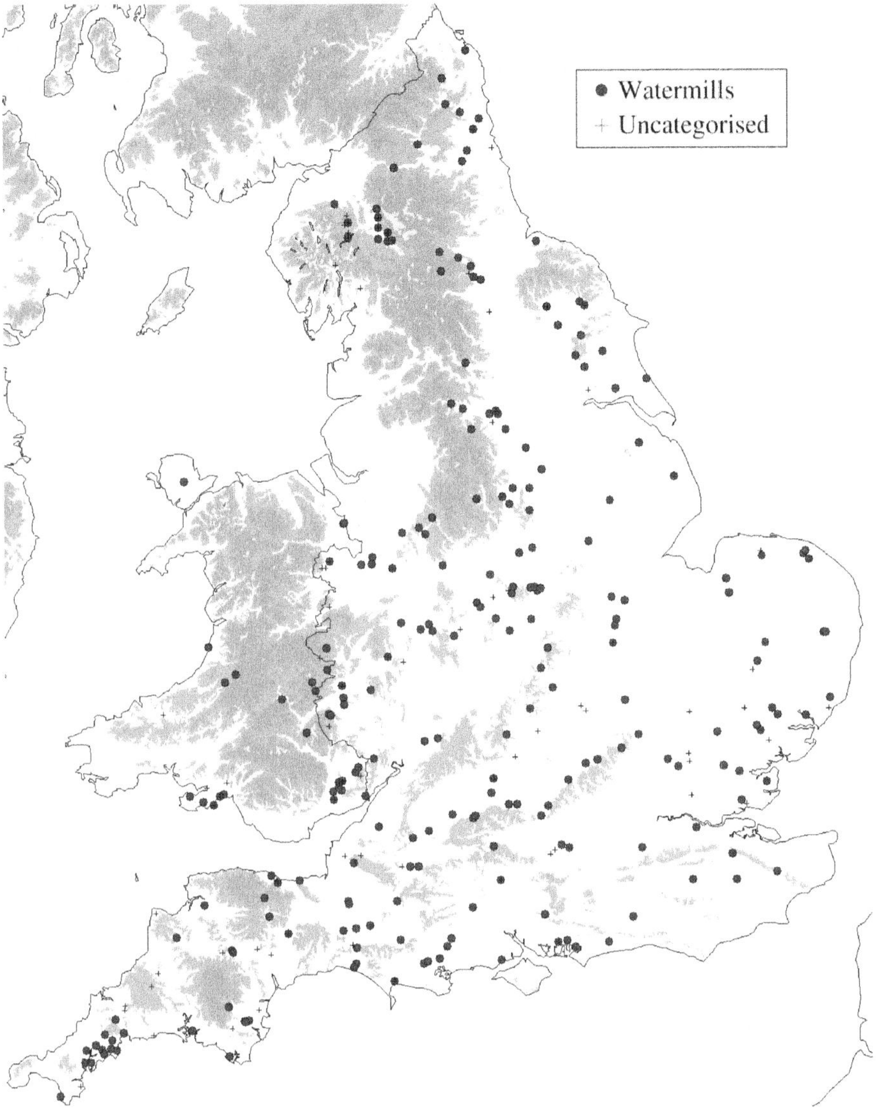

Map 8.3 Distribution of watermills in relation to relief map.

water flows were presumably too sluggish (and where ecclesiastical landlords predominated), but many of the others would no doubt be filled if the data came from more than one decade. In the *Atlas* a fairly clear bias towards 'those parts of the north and west best endowed with sites suitable for the generation of water-power, i.e. fast-flowing streams with a reliable supply of water' is evident[25] – this can also be seen in Map 8.3.

[25] Campbell & Bartley, *Atlas*, 280–2.

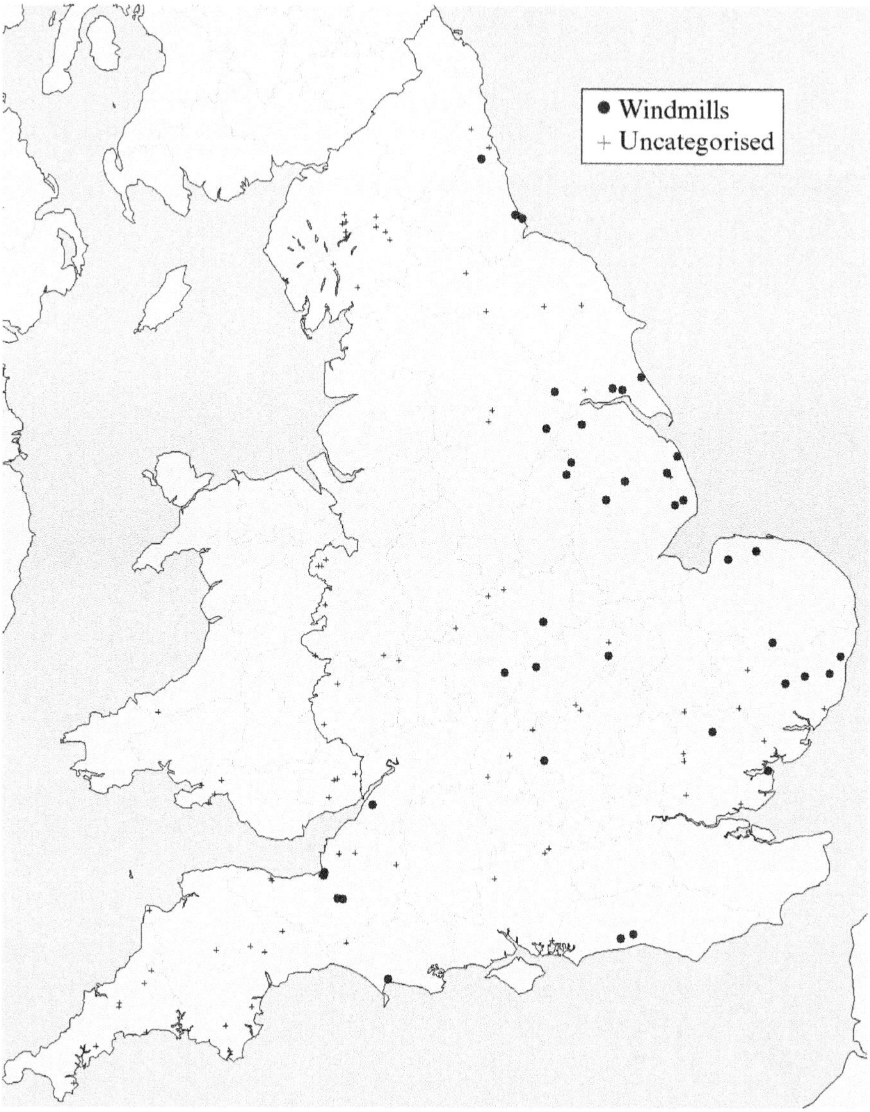

Map 8.4 Distribution of windmills, 1427–37.

Map 8.4 shows a clear bias to the eastern half of the country, with a complete absence from the south-west beyond Somerset, and from the north-west. Although it is based on only a small sample of only 40 mills, data from more than a single decade would probably show a similar distribution, as the eastern bias of windmills was a long-standing phenomenon: this is where streams are more likely to be seasonal and sluggish. Maps 8.5 and 8.6 show similar distributions for windmills in the twelfth century (from all sources), and the first half of the fourteenth century (from IPMs only).

Map 8.5 Distribution of windmills, 1185–1200.
Source: Holt, *Mills*, 172.

It is interesting that the 1300–49 distribution, though heavily biased to the east, also shows a sprinkling of windmills across much of western England – a westward extension largely absent from the 1427–37 map. The fifteenth-century IPMs thus appear to provide evidence not only of the known diminution in windmill *numbers* in the late fourteenth century but also of a *geographical* contraction. This retreat eastwards has not previously been reported, though Langdon has hinted at it in a comment that 'the decline in windmills was especially precipitate in those regions, such as the West Midlands, where they competed with water power for custom', and a suggestion that windmill numbers held up better in 'areas such as the East Midlands and Holderness, ... where

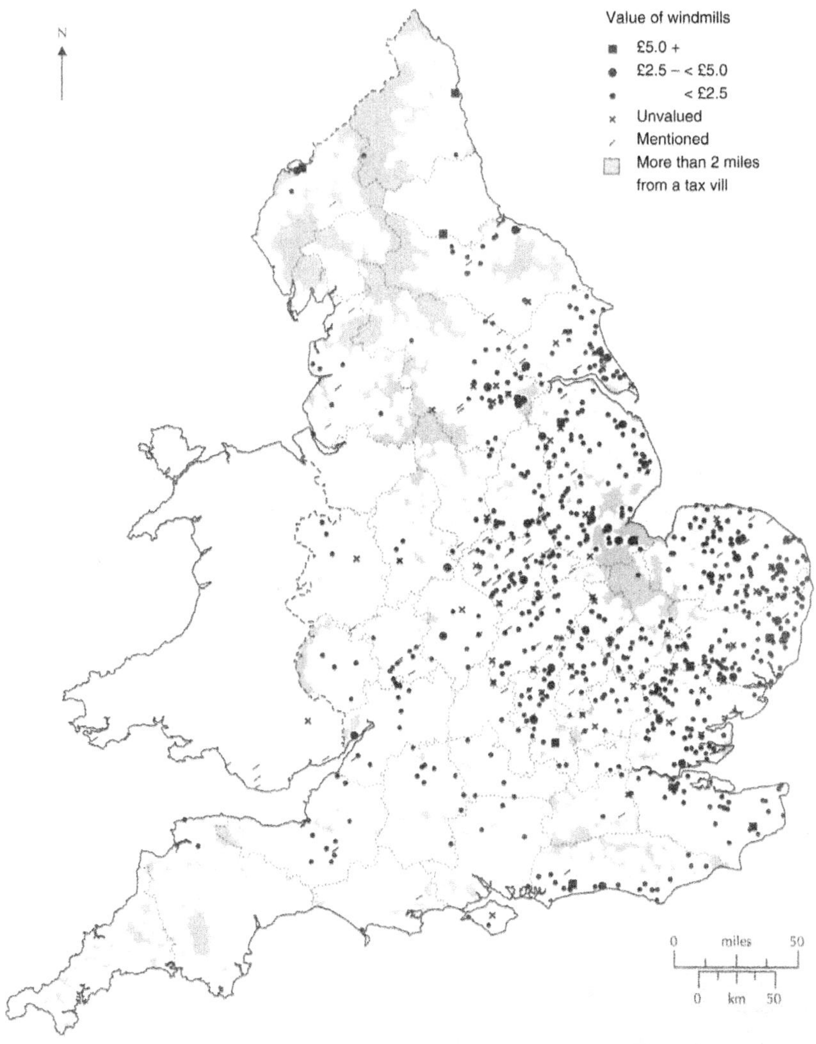

Map 8.6 Distribution of windmills, 1300–49.
Source: Campbell and Bartley, *Atlas*, 294.

there was little in the way of competition from water power'. The 1427–37 IPM data seems to evidence a retreat from nearly the entire western part of the country, however (though it may be premature to assert this on the strength of data from just a single decade).

Types of Mills by Function: Grain Mills, Fulling Mills and other Industrial Mills

If we wish to break the mills down, not by power source, but by type of work done, then the IPMs are not quite as informative as they were for power sources:

grain mills	60
fulling mills	45
tanning mills	1
blowing mills	0
unspecified	358

Slightly more grain mills are recorded than fulling ones, but the absolute numbers are small and the function of three-quarters of the mills is not stated. The same problem arises with the 1300–49 IPMs. Langdon's manorial data, which is much better at recording function, suggests that about 88% of the mills would have been used for grinding grain. Certainly all of the 39 *wind*mills whose function was unspecified would have been grain mills, as windmills were never used for any industrial purpose.[26]

The samples from which the data are derived are small, but nevertheless the geographical distributions of grain mills and fulling mills, in Maps 8.7 and 8.8 respectively, are interesting.

The grain mill map, Map 8.7, shows a distribution largely confined to the far north and south-west (a similar pattern is disclosed by the 1300–49 IPMs), but this clearly cannot have been the case. Grain mills were, of course, ubiquitous, and it must be certain that most of the uncategorised mills were for grinding grain. The explanation for the failure to identify the function of most of the grain mills is suggested by a comparison with the fulling mill distribution in Map 8.8; the areas where grain mills were identified are also the regions where fulling mills occurred. Evidently grain mills required to be identified only in those areas where industrial mills were numerous – elsewhere it could be assumed that a mill was a grain mill. The one region where a cluster of fulling mills is not matched by one of grain mills is East Anglia – but Map 8.4 does show several windmills here, and by definition these were grain mills.

This seems to suggest that the distribution pattern of fulling mills in Map 8.8 (which is again similar to the 1300–49 distribution in the *Atlas*) can be accepted at face value, as showing those regions where they really were numerous. Fulling mills are known to have been in this period particularly a feature of the south-west and north-west, and to a lesser extent East Anglia.[27]

26 Campbell & Bartley, *Atlas*, 282; Langdon, *Mills*, 40, Table 2.3.

27 R.A. Pelham, *Fulling Mills: a Study in the Application of Water Power to the Woollen Industry* (London, 1958), pl. iv; Holt, *Mills*, 153–8; Langdon, *Mills*, 41–6; Campbell & Bartley, *Atlas*, 282–7; L.R. Poos, *A Rural Society after the Black Death: Essex 1350–1525* (Cambridge, 1991), 60–1.

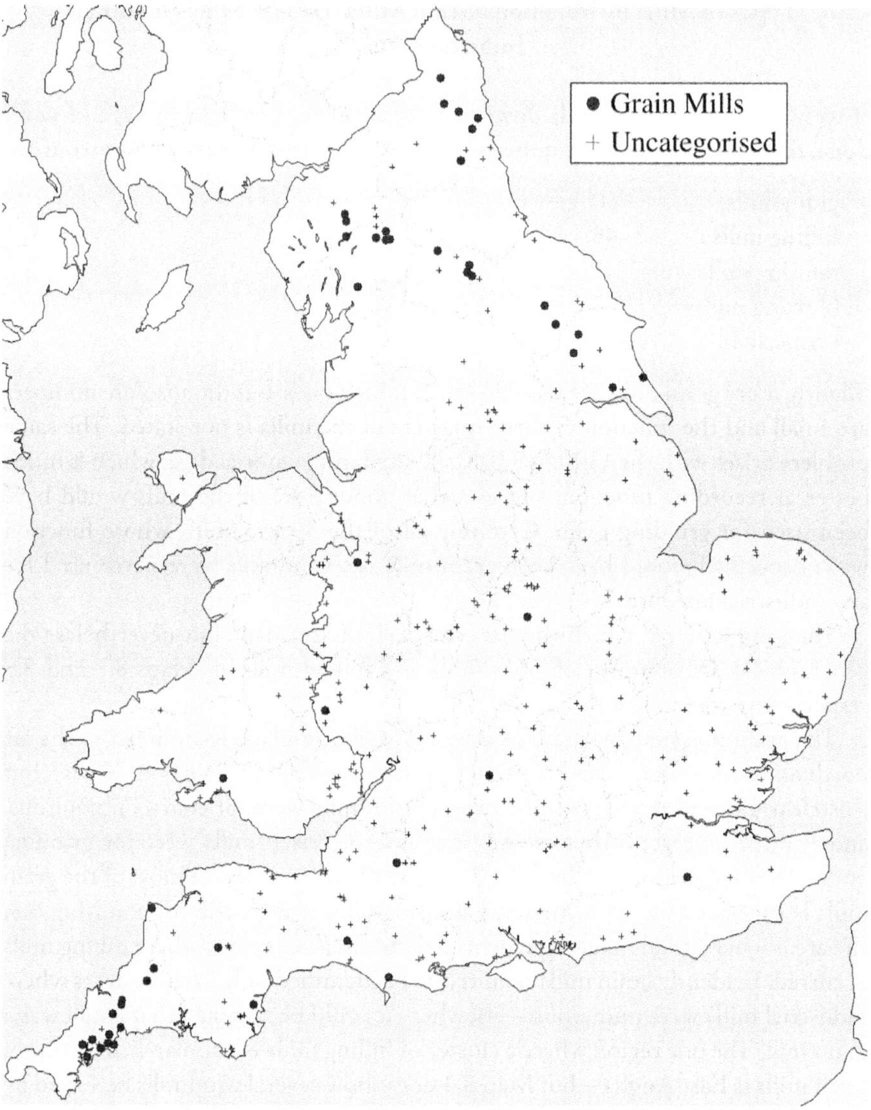

Map 8.7 Distribution of grain mills, 1427–37.

Fulling mills are relatively well recorded compared to other types of industrial mills, which are barely mentioned at all (though this is also a problem in the pre-1350 IPMs, and in fact in all the sources, including manorial records). Only one reference to a non-fulling industrial mill occurs in the 1427–37 IPMs: a mill in Tregony in Cornwall which was 'called Tanmylle' in 1428. Only two more were recorded in the entire half century between 1399 and 1447: a tanning mill in South Tawton in Devon, in 1439, and four blowing-mills, powering bellows for

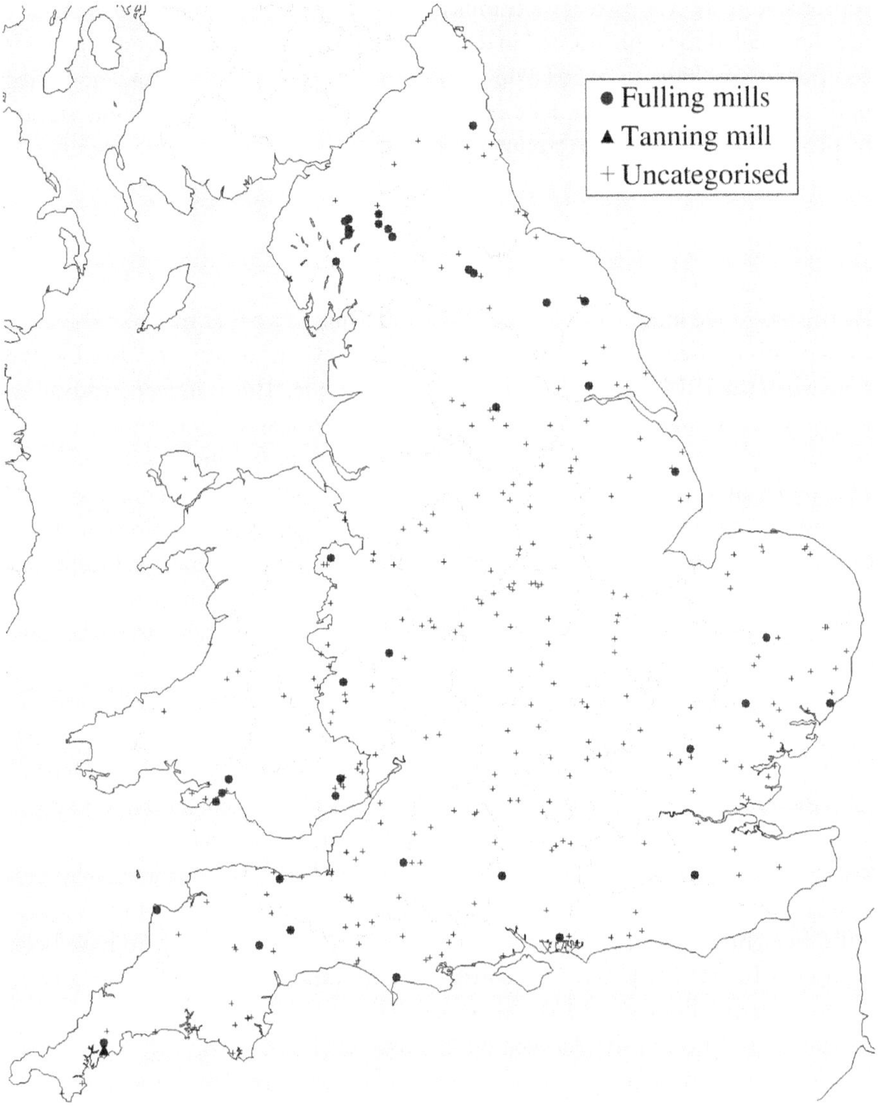

Map 8.8 Distribution of fulling mills, 1427–37.

smelting tin, which occur together on a manor near Bodmin in Cornwall in 1439.[28] Nevertheless other non-fulling industrial mills must have existed. Occasional references to them pop up in other sources,[29] and it has been suggested that they

[28] CIPM xxiii.247; xxv.273, xxv.255 (manor of Newland).

[29] For example, the 1346 court rolls of the manor of Romsley (Worcs.), on the edge of what would later become the Black Country, record a grant to Hugh the Cutler of 'a plot of land with a watercourse to make a building for milling knives, axes and other things pertaining to

comprised up to 1% of recorded mills. John Langdon has suggested that they may have failed to be mentioned in documents because they were usually just one component in a larger industrial unit, for example a forge, unlike grain and fulling mills, which had an independent existence and earned a separate income stream by providing their service to paying customers.[30]

Decayed Mills

At this point we must consider the slightly alarming fact that many of the mills we have been discussing did not in fact exist, or rather, no longer existed at the time when the IPMs which recorded them were made. This is in fact an advantageous defect. It was suggested above that data from just a single decade cannot reveal change over time, but in fact some degree of temporal analysis is made possible by frequent references to mills which had ceased to be operational or even to exist. It is particularly useful because, as already discussed, the preceding half century had seen a considerable decline in the number of operational mills and this defect provides some opportunity to investigate that development.

Of the 464 mills recorded in the 1427–37 IPMs, 60 were stated to be ruinous, waste or dilapidated, or merely the site of a former windmill, and a further 12, though not explicitly described as decayed, were given a nil value, presumably meaning that they had ceased to be operational. Together these comprised 15% of all recorded mills. Most of the 60 decayed mills were expressly stated to be of nil value, and a few were simply left unvalued, though some, curiously, were given a value, ranging from 2*d* to 15*s*. This may sometimes have been the value of the fishery in the mill-pond, or perhaps of the mill building without its machinery, or was perhaps its previous value when it had been operative. Ten of these waste mills, in eight manors in Wales and Northumberland, were stated to have been destroyed by Welsh rebels or Scottish raiders (and some others had greatly lowered yearly values, due to Welsh attacks).

The distribution of the decayed mills can be seen in Map 8.9. Ignoring those damaged by enemy action, there was a particular concentration in the north-east Midlands, and a distinct absence from the south-west and north-west of England and the rest of the Midlands. The sample is fairly small, and it is difficult to be sure whether this is evidence for regional variation in the rate of closure of mills, or just due to differing regional habits of recording, or not recording, decayed assets. Certainly Langdon found that the East Midlands saw the *lowest* fall in

the art of a smith': Birmingham City Archives, 346314. This independent mill was unlikely to appear in an IPM.

30 A.R. Lucas, 'Industrial Milling in the Ancient and Medieval Worlds: a Survey of the Evidence for an Industrial Revolution in Medieval Europe', *Technology and Culture* 46:1 (2005), 1–30, at 25; Langdon, 'Watermills and Windmills in the West Midlands', 436; *idem*, *Mills*, 4–5, 15–26, 35.

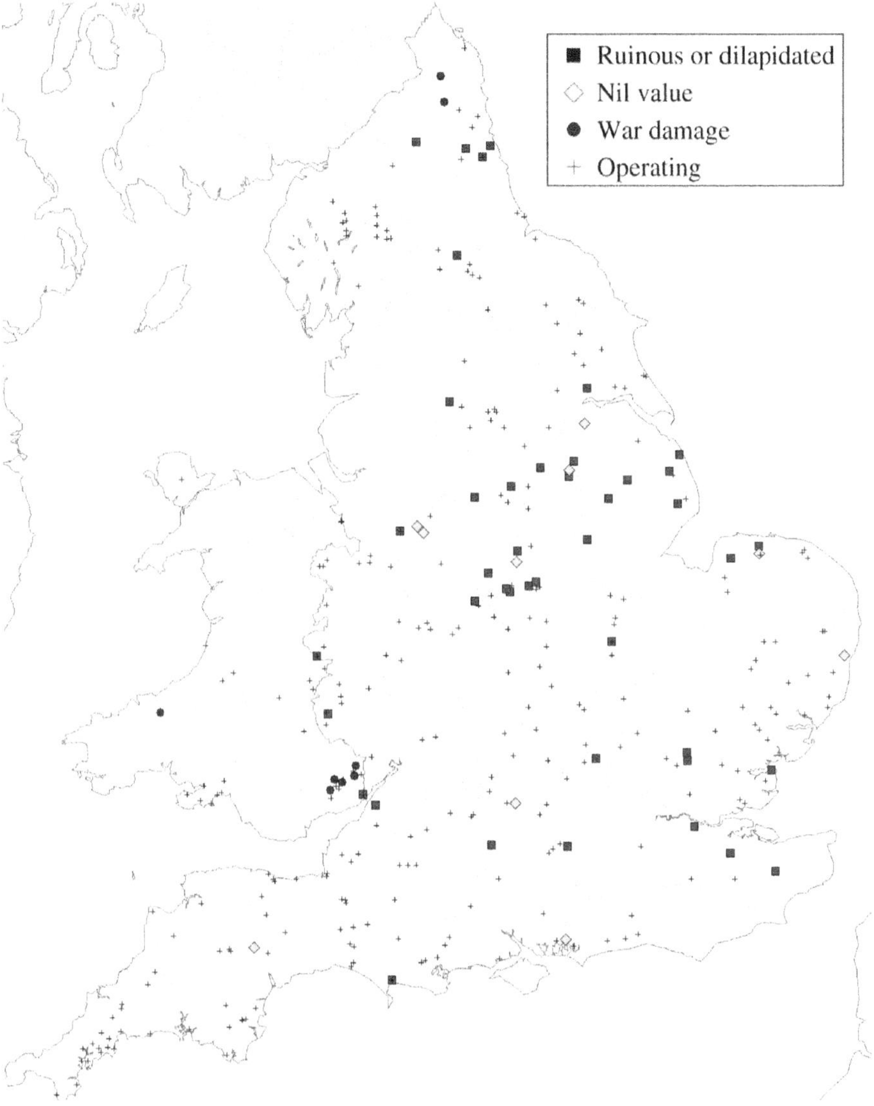

Map 8.9 Distribution of decayed mills, 1427–37.

mill numbers of any region – the opposite of what we see here – but he admitted that this was on the strength of a very small sample of manors and thought that it needed further research. Here perhaps the fifteenth-century IPMs can correct deficiencies in other sources.

In Map 8.10, where the decayed mills are broken down by power source, it can be seen that there is a noticeable geographic bias in the type of decayed mill: in the east they are almost entirely windmills, and everywhere else watermills. This does not give support to the retreat of windmills from the western half of

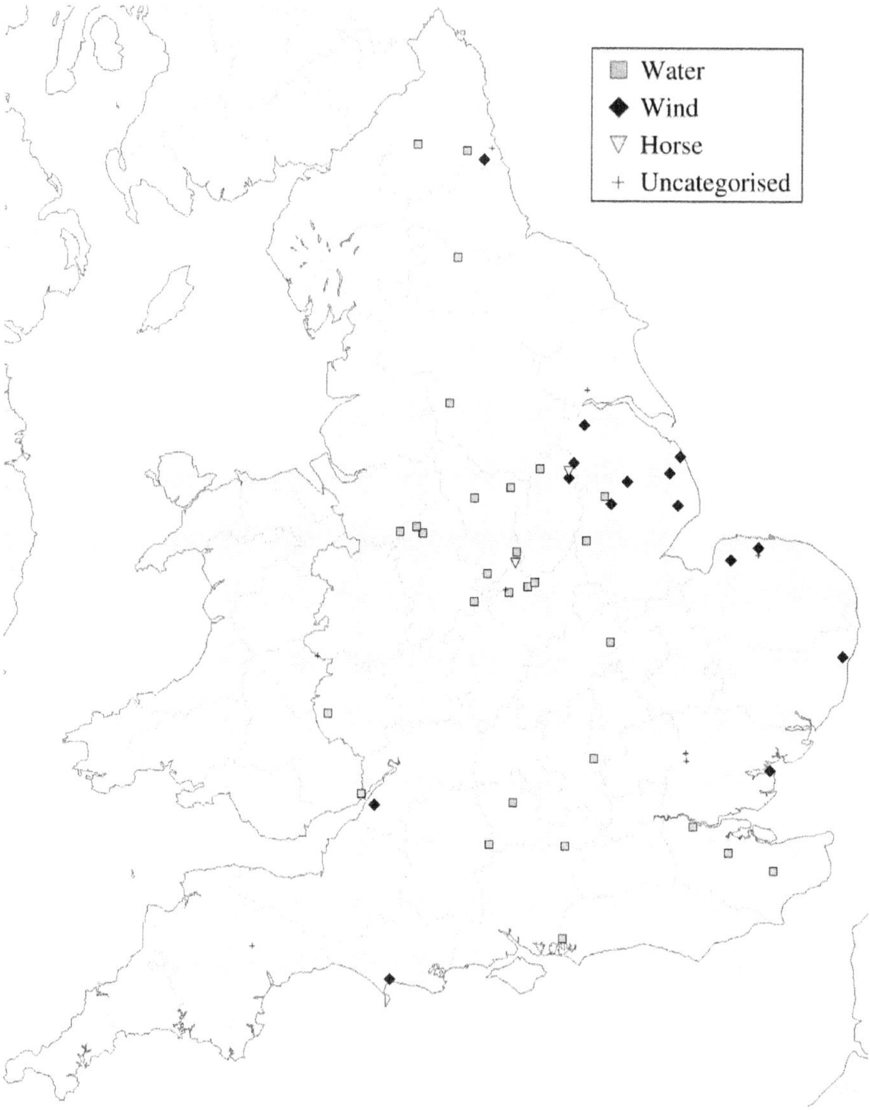

Map 8.10 Distribution of decayed mills, by power source.

the country, which was suggested above – unless the disappearance of windmills from western England had occurred in too distant a period before 1427–37 for the closed-down mills to be remembered and recorded in extents.

The numbers of decayed mills in each category are:

watermills	36
windmills	15
horse-mills	2
unspecified	10

Windmills formed a disproportionately high proportion of the decayed mills. They made up only 7% of all mills (25 out of 392 operating mills), but 24% of decayed mills (15 out of 63). This is unsurprising, in view of Langdon's finding, mentioned above, that windmill numbers fell at a greater rate than watermills during the century after 1350.

Sometimes the rough date at which a mill went out of operation can be discerned from the IPMs. Even within the single decade covered by the present database, manors sometimes appear in two successive IPMs, occasionally even in three, and sometimes a mill is recorded as operational in the first IPM and then as decayed in the next. For example:

- Sandling, Kent: watermill valued at 40*s* in 1429, fallen down and worth nil in 1436
- Blythburgh, Suffolk: windmill valued at 4*s* in 1427 and nil in 1429
- Wallbury, Essex: two fulling mills dilapidated in 1428 but worth 20*s*, in 1436 'greatly run-down' and worth nil.[31]

Of course the earlier extents may not be entirely trustworthy – they can sometimes be shown to have been copied from previous extents with no updating[32] – but the subsequent one at least provides a date by which a mill was definitely no longer operational.

Unit Values

Fully half of the *Atlas* chapter on mills analyses the unit values of mills in a number of ways, to cast light on varied aspects of the milling industry in the early fourteenth century. Most of these analyses could be reproduced using the 1427–37 data (though those which consider change over time would be more interesting if data from more than a single decade could be used). However, we do not have space here to do more than touch on the subject superficially, by considering the ranges of unit values, broken down by power source and by work type.

The IPMs state an annual value for 83% of the operational mills recorded between 1427 and 1437 (i.e., ignoring decayed mills and those valued as 'nil'). In some cases two or three mills in the same manor were lumped together in a single valuation. In the discussion which follows, these joint valuations have been divided equally between the mills to which they relate (but eight mills in eight manors, all in the same county, which were valued jointly have been ignored).

As Table 8.1 shows, the unit values of individual mills varied greatly, from 12*d* (a fulling mill at Newbiggin in Westmorland and another of unspecified purpose at Diptford in Devon) to £12 (a watermill called 'Swanbournemull' at Arundel in

31 *CIPM* xxiii.235, xxiv.628 (Sandling); xxiii.120, xxiii.405 (Blythburgh); xxiii.240, xxiv.629 (Wallbury).

32 Holford, '"Notoriously Unreliable"'.

Table 8.1 Unit values of operating mills: by power source

Values	Highest	Lowest	Median	Mean
All mills (318 no.)[1]	£12	12*d*	16*s*	22*s*
Watermills (236 no.)	£12	20*d*	20*s*	25*s* 4*d*
Windmills (24 no.)	£2	24*d*	10*s*	14*s*
Horse-mills (3 no.)	£1	13*s*	20*s*	17*s* 8*d*

[1] Includes 55 mills for which the power source is not stated, and excludes 60 decayed or nil value mills.

Sussex).[33] Welsh lordship mills close to the English border tended to be particularly valuable: one at Usk had been worth £26 13*s* 4*d* before Glendower's revolt, though in 1432 its value was only £6 13*s* 4*d*.[34] However, most lords derived much more modest incomes from their mills; the mean value was just 22*s* p.a., and the median a mere 16*s* p.a.

Watermills were generally almost twice as valuable as windmills (mean yearly value 25*s* 4*d* against 14*s* for windmills), though they included some of the least valuable mills as well as the most valuable. However, in Figure 8.3, where the 1427–37 mean values are superimposed on the pre-1350 values from the *Atlas*, it can be seen that although the average windmill value in 1427–37 was not greatly lower than that of a century previously, the average watermill value had fallen considerably in the same period. It appears that it was the least valuable, marginal windmills that had gone to the wall in the late fourteenth century.

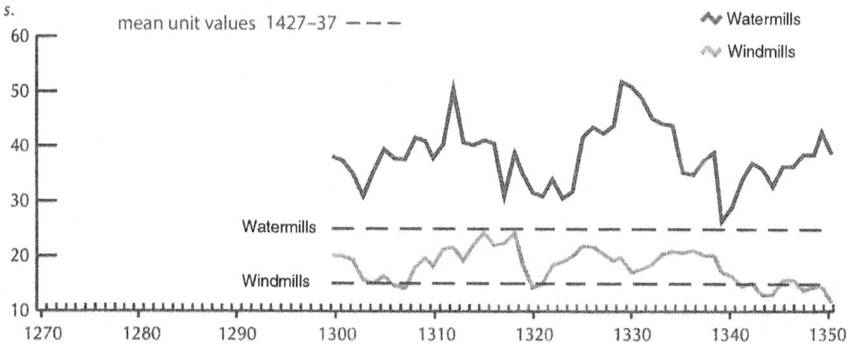

Figure 8.3 Unit values of water and windmills, 1300–49 and 1427–37. Source: Campbell and Bartley, *Atlas*, 297.

[33] *CIPM* xxiv.468 (Newbiggin); xxiii.260 (Diptford); xxiv.377 (Arundel).

[34] *CIPM* xxiv.77.

Table 8.2 Unit values of operating mills: grain versus fulling mills

Values	Highest	Lowest	Median	Mean
All mills (318 no.)	£12	12*d*	16*s*	22*s*
Grain mills (49 no.)	£3	3*s* 4*d*	13*s* 4*d*	26*s* 6*d*
Fulling mills (38 no.)	£1 15*s*	12*d*	6*s* 8*d*	10*s* 7*d*

As Table 8.2 shows, fulling mills were typically less valuable than grain mills, their median value being half that of the median grain mill, and their average value less than half. It should be remembered, however, that for 220 of the valued mills no function was stated, and these included all the higher-valued mills. It is likely that the great majority of them were grain mills, and that if their function were known the difference between the mean and median values of the two types of mills would be greater still.

Conclusion

Although the fifteenth-century extents are in some respects not as detailed as those in the pre-1350 IPMs, this paper has shown that it is nevertheless possible to extract useful data from them and to reconstruct many aspects of the institutional and economic geography of the fifteenth-century countryside as thoroughly and informatively as has been done in the *Atlas*. To some extent the results, as was commented of the *Atlas* itself,[35] are more confirmatory than revelatory, but that is useful, too, and some new insights have been uncovered. The data have sometimes suffered from small sample sizes, but this is in large part due to their derivation from just two volumes of calendars covering only a single decade. The use of data from lengthier periods would ameliorate this problem, and the digitisation of all nine of the 1399–1447 volumes by the Mapping the Medieval Countryside project will greatly facilitate this. When the project's goal of one day making available online the full contents of all the manorial extents in all the medieval IPMs, from 1256 to 1508, is realised, the creation of some very long time series will be possible.

[35] P. Coss, review in *EcHR* lx, 4 (2007), 827–8.

9

Proofs of Age 1246 to 1430: Their Nature, Veracity and Use as Sources

William S. Deller

Records of proof-of-age hearings exist from the second half of the thirteenth until the mid-sixteenth century.[1] The hearings were an addition to existing inquisition *post mortem* arrangements for tenants-in-chief of the crown, the purpose of the procedure being for the tenant-in-chief to 'prove' by means of the sworn testimony of a local jury that he or she[2] was of age and so could enter their inheritance. A key and unique feature of a proof was the requirement for each juror to give a brief account of how he knew the heir's age. In doing so, jurors linked the heir's birth with details of their own personal lives, such as a birth, death or marriage in their family, their presence at the baptism or a reference to some dated document. Historians have long recognised their potential value, containing as they do personal details of the experiences of comparatively humble men whose lives are barely recorded elsewhere. They began to be calendared along with inquisitions post mortem at the end of the nineteenth century.

It is easy to see why historians recognised the usefulness of the calendared proofs, but a problem about using them was identified almost as soon as the first volumes of the *Calendar* were published. As early as 1907, for example, R.C. Fowler pointed out similarities in the sworn statements of witnesses in three proofs from the 1420s.[3] In the same year M.T. Martin pushed back the period when such practice could be detected to 1328.[4] A string of subsequent reviews drew attention to innumerable 'correspondences' within and between proofs as they appeared in the published volumes.[5] By implication it was assumed that

[1] Records of proof hearings (1245–1509) are to be found in bundles in rough chronological order in the following TNA files: C132–42 (one file per monarch, Henry III–Henry VII), E149 (covering Henry III–Richard III), and E150 (Henry VII).

[2] Eighteen per cent of hearings between 1270 and 1430 concerned female heirs.

[3] He said 'they presented features which forbid our receiving them as literal statements of fact. There was an element of 'common form' which 'leads us to infer that the particulars sworn to were fictitious'. R.C. Fowler, 'Legal Proofs of Age', *EHR* xxii (1907), 101–3.

[4] M.T. Martin, 'Legal Proofs of Age', *EHR* xxii (1907), 526–7.

[5] A.E. Stamp, 'Legal Proofs of Age', *EHR* xxix (1914), 323–4; J.H. Round, '[Short Notice] *CIPM* ix', *EHR* xxxii (1917), 453–4; T.A.M. Bishop, '[Review] *CIPM* xi', *EHR* lii (1937),

such plagiarism would, if detected widely, undermine the usefulness of proofs as sources. Continuing hesitancy over their veracity seems to have been a factor in most subsequent discussions.[6]

I

The development of modern electronic databases has made possible the systematic analysis of a whole body of texts over a long period of time, rather than confining comment to ad hoc remarks on single volumes. In this case such a database enabled the wording of all 10,036 jurors' proof testimonies from 1246 to 1430 to be compared, patterns of 'correspondence' between testimonies to be analysed and changes in vocabulary and syntax to be examined.[7] Original proofs for the thirteenth century have been used. For the fourteenth and fifteenth centuries the printed calendar versions have been consulted, randomly supplemented by reference to originals to check translations. All the translations here follow the printed versions.

Before turning to such analysis, however, it is important at the outset to stress that the aim of the record was the production of a valid legal document to trigger the release of land, not to set down accurate eyewitness experiences. In common with most civil and common law actions, by the end of the thirteenth century proof hearings were formal, even formulaic, procedures totally dependent on the writ that initiated them.[8] Record keeping was similarly stereotyped in form and wording: thus we find that the opening juror's testimony, which typically detailed the place and date of the heir's baptism was not, as might appear, the spontaneous utterance of an individual juror but the repetition, habitually word for word, of the text of the *de etate probanda* writ which the heir's family had raised to initiate

437–440; T.A.M. Bishop, '[Short Notice] *CIPM* xii', *EHR* lv (1940), 329; C. Ross, '[Short Notice] *CIPM* xiii and xiv', *EHR* lxxii (1957), 109–11.

[6] The most important of these are: R.F. Hunnisett, 'The Reliability of Inquisitions as Historical Evidence', *The Study of Medieval Records: Essays in Honour of Kathleen Major*, ed. D.A. Bullough and R.L. Storey (Oxford, 1971); S.S. Walker, 'The Feudal Family and the Common Law Courts: the Pleas Protecting Rights of Wardship and Marriage, c.1225–1475', *Journal of Medieval History* 14 (1988); J. Bedell, 'Memory and Proof of Age in England, 1272–1327', *Past and Present* 162 (1999); J.T. Rosenthal, *Telling Tales: Sources and Narration in Late Medieval England* (University Park, PA, 2003), chapter 1 on proofs of age; C. Carpenter, 'Introduction', in *CIPM* xxii (Woodbridge, 2003).

[7] The first recorded proof of age was that for Roger Bertram, which was undated but referred to an alleged majority on 4 December 1245. C132/47/27 (*CIPM* ii.848). The end of the reign of Henry V in 1422 is a convenient end point for this study, though for statistical purposes the sequence has been continued to the end of the decade (1430), since most of the data is presented in ten-year aggregations.

[8] For an account of the proof's early development see W.S. Deller, 'Thirteenth-century Proofs of Age: the Development of a Hybrid Legal Form', *Journal of Legal History* 31 (2010), 245–72.

Table 9.1 Testimony types

Motif/Type	Number of Mentions	% of All Testimonies
Eyewitness to baptism	1,517	15.1%
Reference to writing	1,441	14.4%
Death	1,096	10.9%
Birth	1,073	10.7%
Reference to legal matter	910	9.1%
Transfer of land	838	8.3%
Marriage	818	8.2%
Accident	740	7.1%
Employment or office	697	6.9%
Church reference	633	6.3%
Travel or journey	550	5.5%
Crime or violence	416	4.1%
Leisure activity	417	4.1%
Life stage (other than above)	334	3.3%
Gift	301	3%

the proceedings.[9] Because both jurors and recorders were united in the overriding aim of producing an effective legal document which would facilitate an heir's gaining their inheritance, the range of recollections recorded for each juror was also quickly limited by convention to a 'safe' and fairly narrow set of about fifteen common types, which were repeated in various forms throughout the life of the records (Table 9.1).

Indeed, over the whole corpus of 10,036 separate testimonies recorded between 1270 and 1430, only about 947 or 9% of the whole were what might be described as uniquely personal in the sense that the content or wording does not appear elsewhere in the record. This should not surprise us, given that the whole purpose of the action was not to register personal or even truthful memories but to trigger successfully the heir's legal majority. We are dealing, in short, with a typically conventional legal record where the personal element from the juror was corralled into a set of characteristic motifs which were of proven judicial utility.

Analysis further reveals the incidence of more or less obvious plagiarism permeating the already conventional texts. This involved the repeated use of phrases, sentences and whole testimonies and can be divided into two broad categories. The first comprises the re-use of material from the testimony of other jurors *within the same hearing*. As far as the jury was concerned, the processes behind such repetition can be readily imagined. For jurors,[10] a proof-of-age hearing would probably

[9] The '*de etate probanda*' writ emerged from about 1251. An example for that date appears in *A Formula Book of English Historical Documents*, ed. H. Hall (Cambridge, 1908–1909), part ii, 73–4.

[10] In the fourteenth century fewer than 2% were described as knights. Where the occupation of a juror is stated or implied the most common designation is that of 'servant'.

be a unique occasion in their experience.[11] In its demand that each individual juror should explain how he knew the heir was of age, the procedure was unusual and peculiar to proofs of age,[12] and even at the busiest centres[13] proof hearings were comparatively rare events. It is likely, therefore, that in these circumstances the procedure would have been gone through beforehand and that suitable answers to the crucial question 'how do you know' were discussed, if not rehearsed.[14]

In many early hearings jurors simply referred in their reason for remembrance to the *fama patrie*, or 'report of the county', which neatly transformed the demand for an individual memory into a generalised assurance of what everybody knew. Jurors and recorders also seem to have sought safety in adapted or disguised corporate testimony whereby groups of jurors, or even the entire jury, plausibly swore to their attendance at some common event or occasion – eyres, previous inquisitions, baptismal and purification ceremonies were all popular motifs. Many of these testimonies amounted to a rewording of the *fama patrie* formula: perhaps under pressure from the escheator and his staff, or even the families themselves, the traditional basis for a jury oath was adapted into attendance at a gathering 'when news came' of the birth.[15]

Most common was the record of one juror simply concurring with a previous individual or group: he was recorded as simply agreeing – *concordat* – or saying the same – *idem dicit*. In many cases, though, either juror or recorder felt that more than bald agreement was necessary and the juror was therefore attributed a similar testimony to a previous one. This often resulted in a string of allegedly remembered births, deaths, marriages or other motifs.[16] Sometimes later

[11] The most common exception to this was when two hearings were held very close to one another, especially when the heirs were from the same family, mostly sisters. Examples are the proofs of Elizabeth Stabolgi and her sister Philippa, heard in Lincoln in May 1376 and in April the following year, respectively. Six of the jurors were used on both occasions. *CIPM* xiv.317, 346.

[12] In both criminal and civil cases jurors were typically asked to give corporate testimony or verdict, not individual witness.

[13] The six counties with most hearings between 1270 and 1430 were, in order of frequency, York (81), Essex (58), Lincoln (45), Gloucester (39), Somerset (37) and Northumberland (35). Even the York average was therefore well under a hearing every two years. In the peak years of the 1360s there were never more than 18 proof hearings a year across the whole country. Hearings could never become routine even for the 'professionals' involved, let alone for village jurors.

[14] The note attached to the proof of Laurence de Paveli, the firstborn of twins, is a rare example of such rehearsal being openly articulated; the brothers, it states, 'are twin sons born on the same day but Laurence being the firstborn is his next heir, all of which the said Philip [the other twin] in the presence of his mother and the jurors and also on Thursday the morrow in the presence of the escheator acknowledged to be true'. *CIPM* ii.686.

[15] A typical example, from many, is the testimony of Robert Bosevyle in 1297, who said he was at a feast 'where immediately after the birth of the said Thomas, news thereof came and the guests rejoiced greatly thereat'. *CIPM* iii.437.

[16] To take some early examples: half the jurors for Alice heir of Hugh de Winsor in 1298 mentioned a death as their reason (*CIPM* iii.484), while half the jurors at John Cordboef's

Table 9.2 Percentage of testimonies influenced by others in the same hearing

Year	Influenced Testimonies	Year	Influenced Testimonies
1270–79	38.9%	1350–59	43.0%
1280–89	24.2%	1360–69	50.4%
1290–99	32.7%	1370–79	53.4%
1300–09	42.4%	1380–89	68.6%
1310–19	30.9%	1390–99	52.6%
1320–29	28.6%	1400–09	41.9%
1330–39	36.6%	1410–19	43.3%
1340–49	42.3%	1420–30	11.8%

testimonies were weaker versions of previous ones. Sometimes they were elaborations on what had gone before, but, whatever the process, jurors throughout the life of the proof-hearing procedure continued to utter or be ascribed testimonies that were heavily influenced by those of their fellows. The results of counting such 'influenced' testimonies for each decade are shown in Table 9.2.[17]

The overall rate – about 40% – varied both over time and by location. The highest national rates occurred in the last forty years of the fourteenth century, but throughout the period from 1270 to 1430 well over a third, and in some decades as many as a half, of all recorded testimonies were to some extent 'influenced' by others in the same hearing.[18]

The level of agreeing, 'saying the same' or repeating motifs may be seen as indicative of anxiety within the system, on the part both of jurors and their recorders. They were concerned to establish an acceptable testimony, and uneasiness seemed to be greatest, judging by the degree to which jurors relied on one another, where proof hearings in the county were comparatively infrequent and, so, worryingly unfamiliar. Busy counties like York or Essex had 'recycling' rates within the same hearing of 30% and 35% respectively, as compared with those at less-used counties like Worcester, Devon and Warwick, where rates were as high as 58%, 41% and 43%, respectively.

Lest we dismiss the veracity of the records too readily, however, where a testimony makes reference to a 'checkable' event such as a battle, treaty or royal

proof in 1297 favoured a birth (*CIPM* iii.487), as did six of Richard de Dummer's in 1317 (*CIPM* iii.484).

[17] There is obviously a degree of subjectivity in ascribing a testimony as 'influenced' by another, unless it is a straight copy, and even then the correspondence may be coincidental. In practice, copied testimony is usually quite easy to spot. Only the most straightforward examples are included .

[18] Of course, to be influenced in the choice of a remembrance motif by one that a juror had just heard, or even discussed before the hearing, does not make that testimony false: the original memory may have simply served as a trigger for another genuine remembrance. On the other hand, it may have led to the manufacture of testimony that jurors had seen was acceptable.

occurrence,[19] the overwhelming impression is of an honest recall of clearly remembered episodes with personal as well as 'national' significance.[20] It could be argued that jurors who referred to datable events were untypical by that very choice: such public references would not be chosen by someone who was intending to deceive. Nevertheless, the obvious conclusion from these texts is that jurors were typically anxious to offer an appropriate testimony in an unfamiliar situation. Many tended to copy or adapt the recollections of their colleagues, but most seem to have taken their oath reasonably seriously and offered a testimony that was at the very least plausible.[21] Some made a definite effort to be accurate, while others went along with what their colleagues were saying or had prepared beforehand.

In comparison with the jurors, the escheators[22] and their deputies, the sub-escheators, who often conducted the hearings, tended to be substantial landowners in the county. They were professional administrators[23] of similar social backgrounds to sheriffs[24] and often moved through various posts in the legal and administrative system,[25] most of which required detailed legal knowledge, if not legal training.[26] They commanded a considerable staff[27] and their offices were subject to a constant stream of writs and royal instruction; twice a year

[19] There is reference to events that are datable in 148 testimonies – about 1.4 % of the whole. Of these, only 6% appear to be misdated and in only a handful of cases was there any likelihood of deliberate deceit.

[20] Even mistakes seem t be the result of honest muddle rather than deceit, as in the testimony of Geoffrey de Bronnesle in 1328. The first juror stated the heir's birth as 7 November (the feast of St Leonard) 1307, making him just 21. This was Geoffrey's memory. He 'knows it because, on Sunday next after the Purification, 1 Edward II, before the said feast of St Leonard, the said king married Isabella, queen of England, at Westminster; and he (Geoffrey?) passed the night before the celebration of the said nuptials at the Tower of London'. The Sunday after Purification in 1307–8 fell on 5 February 1308, but if he meant the one before the actual birth that would bring it to the previous year – 35 Edward I (or 1307). In any case Edward married Isabella not in Westminster but in Boulogne on 25 January 1308. Geoffrey may have confused this with Edward's coronation, which took place on 25 February 1308. It is possible that Geoffrey meant to deceive, but much more likely that he mixed up the two royal events. *CIPM* vii.172.

[21] Rosenthal, *Tales*, xvi.

[22] From 1340 they were appointed by the chancellor, treasurer, chief baron of the exchequer and justices. Statutes of 1331, 1368 and 1472 required that they be men of property appointed for one year. H.M. Jewell, 'Local Administration and Administrators in Yorkshire 1258–1348', *Northern History* xvi (1980), 15–40.

[23] M.J. Bennett, 'Provincial Gentlefolk and Legal Education in the Reign of Edward II', *BIHR* lvii (1984), 223; H.M. Jewell, 'Local Administration', 7.

[24] W.A. Morris, 'The Sheriff', *The English Government at Work*, ii. *Fiscal Administration*, ed. W.A. Morris and J.R. Strayer (Cambridge, MA, 1947), 100.

[25] R.F. Hunnisett, *Medieval Coroner* (Cambridge, 1961),116.

[26] A. Musson and W. Ormrod, *The Evolution of English Justice: Law, Politics and Society in the Fourteenth Century* (Basingstoke, 1999), 55.

[27] As well as a sub-escheator, staff would have included bailiffs, stewards, clerks and various petty agents: Morris, 'The Sheriff', 100; Jewell, 'Local Administration', 102–40.

Table 9.3 Percentage of 'borrowed' testimonies

Year	Corresponding proofs	Year	Corresponding proofs
Pre-1300	—	1360–69	68.9%
1300–09	—	1370–79	57.8%
1310–19	13.3%	1380–89	48.0%
1320–29	32.4%	1390–99	40.7%
1330–39	42.1%	1400–09	35.5%
1340–49	46.9%	1410–19	23.8%
1350–59	56.7%	1420–30	49.5%

their accounts were examined at Westminster.[28] As well as ensuring that records remained within the accepted legal conventions, their actions probably account for the second broad type of recycling whereby testimonies *echo those found in other proof hearings*, ranging from the re-use of similar phrasing to the wholesale copying of virtually complete texts.[29] For rates of such 'correspondence' see Table 9.3.

Rates of 'correspondence' seem to be related closely to the total number of proofs recorded at the time. Copying peaked in the 1350s, 1360s and 1370s, when recorded testimonies for each decade were running in excess of 1,000. They reached similar proportions only at the end of the period, in the1420s, when the number of recorded testimonies again topped 1,000. The more hearings there were in the system, the higher the proportion of such 'borrowing' seemed to be.[30]

A possible explanation is that, in common with all medieval bureaucracy, a problem for the system's operators was not so much the production of records as their retention and retrieval. No doubt copies were kept by local escheators, but, since there was a high turnover of personnel – in theory the escheator changed annually – and they were under constant pressure of business, it does not appear that the system retained knowledge of its textual product beyond a year or two at most – certainly up to the1350s.[31] Even at chancery, proofs were retained in

[28] E.R. Stevenson, 'The Escheator', *English Government at Work*, ii, 140–5.

[29] A recycled element is more likely to be connected with escheators if it exists in two or more proofs taken at separate times. This is because a juror's influence was typically likely to be confined to a single hearing. It becomes progressively more likely if one instance of possible copying is found alongside a group of similar examples. Caution has been used in ascribing 'correspondence' and only instances where wording is almost identical or clusters of motifs are repeated together have been included in Table 9.3.

[30] It seems that escheators or their clerks tended to 'borrow' whenever the system was at its busiest – that is, when it was under most pressure to produce a suitable record and when the availability of previous proofs, either in the heads of participants or in written form, was likely to be the greatest.

[31] This impression is strengthened when the rates in particular counties are considered. The five busiest counties had the following scribal 'borrowing' rates: York 50.6%, Essex 56.9%, Lincoln 60.0%, Gloucester 53.9% and Somerset 54.1%. By contrast, the proportions in counties where proofs were heard less frequently were as follows: Cornwall 11.1%, Leicester 22.2%,

bundles in rough chronological order and could be retrieved only with expert and inside knowledge.[32]

Another key factor in plagiarism rates was rapid change within the system. In November 1323, for example, the two large escheatries north and south of the Trent were reorganised into eight regional escheatries. The effect on text production was immediate: in the five years before the reorganisation the average number of proof hearings that took place each year was five; in the five subsequent years the average was two. Similarly, the proportion of proofs with material 'borrowed' from other proofs rose from 26% in the previous five years to 46% in the next five. Thus the system produced fewer hearings and more of them were copied.[33]

If we consider the type of material that tended to be recycled most frequently, it is certainly true, as historians have suggested,[34] that 'correspondences' appear most commonly between more vivid and unusual motifs, but this may simply be due to the fact that violent events or vivid accidents are simply more unusual and so more noticeable.[35] For example, of the total number of references to births by jurors (11% of all testimonies), 29% occur in proofs where some or all the testimonies bear a marked similarity to testimonies in one or more other proofs. But, while references to accidents comprise only 7% of all testimonies, a much greater proportion – over half (55%) – occur in proofs with 'borrowed' material.

When the opportunity arose, some escheators had little compunction in recycling wholesale any testimony material that had worked in the past. One blatant example (from many) are two proofs which took place in 1350, one in March of that year in Essex for the majority of John de Burgher,[36] the other in May in Kent for Nicholas de Huntyngton.[37] The first jurors in each case had as their reason 'his name is entered in the missal of the said church on the feast of St Gregory 2

Middlesex 22.2% and Rutland 33.3%. Moreover, within busy counties, the peak years of the 1350s, 1360s and 1370s saw 'recycled' testimonies in York running at between 70% and 100% of the whole; in Essex comparable rates were between 66% and 100%.

32 'Whatever the ingenuity of the medieval mind, it was unable to develop a workable and widely accepted method for finding documents once they had been stored.' M. Richardson, *The Medieval Chancery under Henry V* (List and Index Society, special series 30, 1999), 23. No indexing or even alphabetical ordering existed throughout the period.

33 This may well have been due to a diminution of political consent under the Despenser regime, rather than the change of system per se. Certainly when the young King Edward III bowed to pressure and reverted to the old system in February 1327, the average number of hearings per annum during the five years that the system lasted before further change rose to six and the 'borrowing' proportion dropped to around its old rate at 29%. But when, between July 1332 and December 1335, escheatries were again recast into eight regional groupings, the annual rate of hearings remained steady at six, as did the 'borrowing' rate at 29%.

34 See notes 5 and 6; and S.S. Walker, 'Proof of Age of Feudal Heirs in Medieval England', *Medieval Studies* 35 (1973), 310.

35 Carpenter, 'Introduction', 35.

36 *CIPM* ix.591.

37 *CIPM* ix.590.

Edward III' in exactly the same form of words. It was the same with the following jurors, whose testimony was a near-verbatim copy of each other's, with only the names and ages changed. What the maker of these records probably did was to put into the mouths of jurors the exact testimonies which had already been recorded and which he probably had to hand, with only the substitution of new and plausible local references. Perhaps the second hearing never took place but the escheator knew the names of those who had been summoned and so could insert existing testimonies, or the meeting did take place, but it either was not recorded or a substitute record was thought preferable. Examples of directly copied proofs like these, unquestioned by the system, are scattered throughout the record.[38]

These examples are at the extreme end of plagiarism. More common was the reworking of testimony as a sort of template into which plausible local detail could be inserted. A testimony that referred to a death which was recorded in a church missal first appeared in Dorset in 1304 and was most probably based on a not uncommon practice at the time.[39] One further instance appeared in Essex in 1311,[40] before a burst of six between 1332 and 1336, three of them in Essex, followed by examples from Bedford, Stafford and Cumberland. It disappeared in the 1340s, then re-emerged in Surrey in 1351 and was repeated 24 times over the next 20 years. From the 1330s, the pattern of the motif remained constant: the person whose death was cited was referred to by name and usually by their relationship with the juror; and the church where the missal was located was also named. Often the form of words was identical from example to example, or with only minor variations.[41] The advantage of such a form was that it allowed the local detail – the dead person, the church – to be fitted into a ready-made testimony, known to be acceptable.[42]

Networks of professional influence or exchange may have lain behind such rapid – and temporary – dissemination. If such repetitions had been the result of chancery activity, it is less likely that motifs would have arisen and disappeared in such various ways and with such regional flavour. They may reflect informal

[38] Seldom with quite the assiduity of the Kent and Essex examples, but examples of similar plagiarism can be detected in the following: *CIPM* vii.630 and 631 from Essex; *CIPM* vii.61 and 76 from Cumberland; *CIPM* xi.545 and 553 from Suffolk; *CIPM* xi.548 and 549 from Sussex; *CIPM* xii.268 and 269 from Somerset; *CIPM* xii.378 and 384 from Hereford; *CIPM* xiv.168, 299 and 302 from York.

[39] *CIPM* iv.238.

[40] *CIPM* v.286.

[41] An example was Alan de Arkelby, who 'knows it because, on the day on which the said John was born there died one John, father of the said Alan, whose death was entered in the missal of Brigham'. *CIPM* viii.76.

[42] Other instances were a robbery motif, featuring the place of the robbery, which most examples were careful to mention, and the proving of a will coincidental with the heir's birth. The temporal pattern of both was the same as the death-plus-missal testimony, with an early isolated example, followed by more extensive repetition, starting in the 1330s. However, the regional patterns were different in each case.

and quite short-lived contacts which were facilitated by the nature of the escheators' work. At Easter and Michaelmas, each escheator visited Westminster to account for his financial stewardship that year. The process took several weeks and counties were seen in order, allowing plenty of time for contact between local escheators and with chancery and exchequer staff. It is likely, too, that there was direct contact between neighbouring pairs of counties, which could also have fed into the process.

The degree to which the process was underpinned by written exchange in the form of past or model proofs, or formularies, or other guidance, is unknown, but it is certainly true that from the mid-fourteenth century the tendency grew to repeat the exact or very similar wording of a motif. A single example will illustrate the point. References to football flourished briefly between 1420 and 1425; there were eight examples, all from Lincoln southwards. The first – from Lincoln – simply mentioned that the juror was playing the game when he heard of the birth. All the subsequent examples, however, were local variations (from Essex, Oxford and Sussex) on the same template and each included the breaking of a left leg.[43]

Given the systemic nature of textual repetition within and between hearings what use can historians make of the material? Two broad approaches suggest themselves. The first centres on the examination of comparative frequencies in the production of different types of remembrance motif. Thus, if we find (and we do) that jurors or recorders chose at particular times in the fourteenth century to record more mentions of death than at other times, or to recall crimes and violence more, we can begin to draw tentative conclusions about what was on their minds at the time and, even, what might have been happening in society at large.[44]

Even where statistically significant variations in mentions are not apparent, a second approach, that of close examination of differences in the vocabulary and style of testimony expression, can yield positive insights. For example, subtle variations over time in the way a familiar motif was expressed – how a wife was referred to in a marriage reference, what detail was thought relevant in a crime recollection – can tell us much about the mentality of participants, irrespective of whether they were individually aware of it or not.[45] Both methods take account

[43] The later wording was 'John Grenewey, 46 years and more, was playing football (*ad pilam pedalem*) at Little Laver with his fellows immediately after Thomas's baptism and broke his left shin (*tibia*)'. *CIPM* xxii.360. All subsequent examples use the same wording, except for the carefully allowed-for local detail. *CIPM* xxii.361, 364, 528, 531, 665.

[44] An example of this is the fourteenth-century expansion of references to writing, discussed in W.S. Deller, 'The Texture of Literacy in the Memories of Late Medieval Proof-of-age Jurors', *Journal of Medieval History* 38.2 (2012), 1–18.

[45] For examples of this approach see B.R. Lee, 'A Company of Women and Men: Men's Recollection of Childbirth in Medieval England', *Journal of Family History* 27.2 (2002); B. Gregory Bailey et al., 'Coming of Age and the Family in Medieval England', *Journal of Family History* 33.1 (2008); W.S. Deller, 'The First Rite of Passage: Baptism in Medieval Memory', *Journal of Family History* 36.1 (2011).

of the conventional and repetitious nature of the texts, to a degree bypassing the notion of intentionality: for the purposes of the historian it does not matter that a juror repeated a fellow's testimony or that a recorder borrowed material from another record. Provided that the repertoire of choice remained sufficiently wide, what was chosen for borrowing is as potentially revealing as an individually original (or even truthful) testimony. Given a large-enough database, particular distortions are subsumed into wider statistical or semantic trends and, since jurors referred to a comparatively wide range of life experiences, useful insights can be gained into the experience of men whose lives are otherwise unknown and into their lives and culture.

II

To illustrate the fruits of such an approach, the rest of this chapter will examine what jurors had to say about their employment and their experiences of buying and selling. From what may seem a narrow focus, valuable insights will be gained into the development of that 'marketing and commercial mentality',[46] that social and economic ambition, that individualistic approach to life, traditionally said to be a mark of early modern capitalism but now seen as having much earlier roots in the medieval period.

Of the 719 testimonies that mention a juror's occupation, about a third describe the juror as a 'servant' or 'in service'. Many others imply that status without stating it directly. Within the group there is a clear bias towards top-end jobs:78 bailiffs, 46 clerks, 28 stewards, 15 butlers and 13 esquires, but only three carpenters, two carters and one thresher. (Jurors were selected for their knowledge of the heir, so, naturally, many tended to be recruited from the higher-status servants and dependants of the heir's family.)

In many remembrance records, to be employed was to gain a named position, an 'office' (*officium*), the obtaining of which was often marked with ceremony and paperwork. Henry de Neuland, was in his forties when he attained the post of steward to John le Chaumberleyn, 'and made oath to him to hold his courts there, and well and faithfully to serve them'.[47] Stephen Paule gained 'the office of bailiff of the honour of Peverell, by the demise of Richard Martel', at the younger age of 22 and he remembered the occasion 'by the date of his commission'.[48] Jurors often stressed the length of time they had spent in service.[49]

46 C . Dyer, *An Age of Transition? Economy and Society in England in the Later Middle Ages* (Oxford, 2005), 244.

47 *CIPM* viii.67.

48 *CIPM* vii.172.

49 Nicholas de Burton was typical in the gratuitous detail he added to his eyewitness testimony. 'The deponent himself was present at the baptism. He has been in the said parson's service for 22 years, and the said heir was born in the second year of such service'. *CIPM* xiii.319.

Such men clearly gained status from their association with important families. Robert del Grene typically stressed his indispensable role in the heir's family. 'He was of the counsel of John's father and was present in the castle at the time of the birth, so that he remembers by the death of the father.'[50] Many others emphasised that they were members of the retinue of a person of consequence. John de Thrillewall, for example, seemed to claim a vicarious prestige from the deference in which his master was held. 'He was at Penrith in the retinue of Sir Gilbert de Welton, then bishop of Carlisle, when John de Eglesfeld came to the bishop and humbly asked him to confirm his daughter, which was done in sight of the deponent.'[51] Prestige was not the only reward on offer. Roger de Waltham obviously made quite a bit of money from his attachment to a bishop. 'He was at that time esquire to a certain bishop called "Seint Nicholas bisschop" and was rewarded with divers gifts to the value of 40*d* out of reverence for the said bishop as he served his office bearing a staff in the bishop's presence.'[52]

Jurors eagerly grasped status by association. Richard de Rugge, for example, recalled getting in first with important news. 'He was in the service of John de Eyton the father, and first announced to him the news of the said Thomas's birth.'[53] Similarly, Stephen de Dalham was keen to emphasise the extent of his responsibilities. 'He was servant of Thomas de Lovetot, the father, and had the administration of all the goods of his manor.'[54] John Lygearde neatly combined his intimacy with the heiress's father and his own sensitive discretion. 'He was in the service of the said Thomas Hildeyerd, and was sitting before him to render his account, and hearing a report of the said Elizabeth's birth he immediately retired from the said account.'[55]

The form of the record stresses the closeness of the dependant to the superior: the most common form of words to express membership of a household was *familiaris in domo* and the verbal form for entering the service of a lord was *stetit cum* – literally 'he stayed' or 'stood with'. The vocabulary of position holding leaked down into comparatively lowly roles. Roger Edmund, for instance, recalled 'that in the week after the Sunday Katherine was born he was made apprentice to the office (*ad officium*) of baker'.[56] In addition to the usual service specialists like bailiffs or stewards, all sorts of tradesmen like carpenters, bakers, cooks, gardeners, carters, threshers, cobblers, falconers, cow keepers and brewers, as well as professionals like auditors and attorneys, find a place in the testimony. Each craft or expertise (*artificiolum*) conferred a certain, if sometimes limited, status on its possessor: the texts placed a value on naming it in the record.[57] Thus Robert and

[50] *CIPM* xiv.162.
[51] *CIPM* xiii.66.
[52] *CIPM* xv.159.
[53] *CIPM* v.541.
[54] *CIPM* vi.196.
[55] *CIPM* vii.544.
[56] *CIPM* x.395.
[57] Even a humble baker, the appropriately named John Baker, was typical in foregrounding his own position before describing what he actually did – and then in selecting a moment

John Blod described themselves, or were described, as *coopertores* (roofers), a fact not altogether relevant to their testimony,[58] while John Dawe served the family 'in the office of cow keeper' (*officio custodis vaccarum*).[59]

So attached were some jurors to the family they served that they were passed from member to member as need arose. Luke Bodin's progress was typical. 'At the time the said Geoffrey was born and before, he was bailiff of Geoffrey de Lucy his father, and keeper of his manors and remained with him for 14 years and afterwards with Ellen de Lucy, grandmother of the present Geoffrey, for seven-and-a-half years.'[60] More menial servants were expected to rally round in emergencies, even to the point of doing unfamiliar jobs for friends of their masters, though always with a keen sense of their position in the hierarchy:

> William Barker and William Weston were in the church on the day of the churching of the mother of John Conquest, and afterwards at the feast with Henry Conquest the father. Willam Barker was staying (*stetit cum*) with William, rector of Marston Moretaine, who was godfather. William Weston was with the rector as bailiff and rode to the feast. There William Barker was a servant in the kitchen and served William Weston in the hall.[61]

Apart from all these workers who were no doubt kept fully occupied, much service, particularly higher-status service, seemed to have consisted, in some part at least, of hanging around waiting to be useful. Members of the retinue (*comitiva*) appeared to be frequently on hand to accompany women on journeys or to take messages. Other servants made much of their publicly noticeable, if not exactly onerous, role. Thomas Sharp, for example, 'held the stirrup of Thomas of Woodstock, earl [*sic*] of Gloucester, godfather, when he descended from his palfrey at the church door and held the palfrey whilst the duke was in the church'.[62] When they did have some responsibility, they made the most of it. John Asshebrok, one feels, enjoyed recalling the (to him) importance of his role, though in essence his job was delivering letters. 'He was at the time in the service of the heir's father and was charged with (*super*) divers letters into the counties of Wiltshire, Stafford, Northampton and Leicester to divers of the father's friends (*complicibus et amiciis*) for joy (*pro leticia*) of the birth of the said heir.'[63]

It would be wrong to give the impression that the testimonies depict an uncomplicated world of contented long-term dependency. For while many jurors recalled the completion of their service with the death of their master – such as

when he was centre stage. 'At the time of her birth he was servant and baker to Richard her father and he carried three hot loaves to the church for eating at the time of her baptism'. *CIPM* xxii.367.

58 *CIPM* x.537.

59 *CIPM* x.537.

60 *CIPM* v.227.

61 *CIPM* xviii.665.

62 *CIPM* xix.655.

63 *CIPM* xii.87.

Roger de Hegham, who stated 'he was with John de Orlaweston and took his robes all his life'[64] – others remembered shorter periods of service. John de Grofham, for example, said 'that he was in the service of William de Moyne, knight, and in five years received from him five gowns, and for two years following he was with the rector of the church of Sawtry'.[65] Jurors frequently depicted service as a career which offered advancement, Richard Menell typically remembering a birth because of his own promotion. 'He was then a clerk in the house of the said John and Elizabeth, and received an esquire's robe at Christmas following.'[66]

Some combined periods of service with looking after their own property. Geoffrey de Stanfordham, for instance, remembered 'because for a long time previously he had been in the service of the prior of Eynsham and at Christmas day before the said Margery's birth when he had received his robe from the said prior, with his permission he went to his own house at Stanfordham'.[67] For others it was a phase in their lives. Roger de Eynton's experience was common: 'He was with the said John de Northwode, at the time of the birth of the said Robert, and two years afterwards Robert, his own father, died, and he withdrew because he was his father's heir, and he has cultivated his land now for twenty years since his father's death.'[68] Some positions of service ended with marriage. John de Burton, for example,

> left the school of Nottingham by the advice of Thomas de Stapelford, rector of the church of Trowell and became clerk with the said Thomas from the aforesaid day to the same day seven years after, on which day he married Joan, daughter of Nicholas de Sandiacre, with whom he has lived now for fourteen years.[69]

Testimonies were careful in their expression of the termination of service – few seemed willing to go on record as getting the sack. Most jurors simply 'left', or 'withdrew' – most often at Michaelmas when contracts came to an end. Occasionally a juror stated baldly that he had been 'removed' from office,[70] but it was rare for any further detail to be given. An exception was in the case of William Herre, who hinted at family tension when it seemed a young child was taken into wardship against the wishes of his mother. What part William played in it we do not know:[71]

> Hugh, son of William de Braytoft, was taken into the wardship of the lord of Willoughby by reason of his minority and he, the said William Herre, at the same time was servant of Maud, late the wife of the said William de Braytoft, and was

64 *CIPM* v.153.
65 *CIPM* xi.550.
66 *CIPM* xiii.292.
67 *CIPM* iv.58.
68 *CIPM* vii.696.
69 *CIPM* vii.172.
70 E.g. *CIPM* iv.49; viii.399.
71 Though the fact that he was giving evidence for a Willoughby heir might be a clue as to where his sympathies lay.

> removed from office by reason of the taking of the said heir and twenty-one years and more have elapsed since then.[72]

Most common is evidence of a hard-headed and business-like relationship between master and servant. For many jurors a key point in their recollection of service was the rendering of their annual account – over thirty make this the central point of their testimony.[73] That they were right to be anxious is revealed in the fate of William le Smyth, who remembered that 'he was bailiff of Warin the father of his manor of Braybrooke and made account and upon that account was £20 in arrears, for which he was arrested by his body and sent to Northampton gaol until he should pay the aforesaid money in full'.[74]

Some jurors mentioned the wages they received for their service, most commonly the robe or gown they were given as part of their annual stipend, often at Christmas. John de Bassinburn, for example, 'was esquire to the boy's father, entered his service in the same year and received robes from him'.[75] Even within this conventional testimony, there is a keen sense of demarcation. Superior servants were quick to mention their more generous entitlement. Griffin Kylbrest 'was retained by John Skydemore, knight', as 'keeper of Kentchurchpark for four years', for which he received 'two gowns as livery' each year.[76] While earlier examples foregrounded length of service, and were mostly silent on the actual value of the wage, by 1329 Ralph le Brewere was recollecting 'a robe in two parts with four ornaments (*garneamentis*)',[77] and by 1400 it had become common to mention cash wages. William Hovell, for example, testified in 1427 that 'he had a red gown, price 26*s* 8*d*, for his labour'.[78] Indeed, the typical fifteenth-century testimony mentioned first the money received, before the traditional robe or gown – John Cukhook, a butler, recalled 'five marks years yearly and two gowns as livery'.[79]

There is no doubt that many jurors' memories dwelt on the possibility of unusual reward associated with an important birth. Over three hundred testimonies mentioned a gift or reward connected with an heir's birth and baptism, many of them made to dependants of the family. What stuck in many jurors' memories was the unusual generosity of such rewards. William de Brumptone remembered that he 'announced to Sir Robert de Schelt that the lady had borne a child, who

72 *CIPM* ix.451.

73 Of course the occasion provided a usefully dated document.

74 *CIPM* xi.378. Indeed, many masters had an even more direct approach to staff discipline: William Taillour, a comparatively high-ranking chamberlain, 'was not present in the chamber on the arrival of Sir Ralph from the chase', so 'Sir Ralph struck him on the neck and felled him to the ground'. *CIPM* xvii.430.

75 *CIPM* v.68.

76 *CIPM* xxiii.596.

77 *CIPM* vii.249.

78 *CIPM* xxii.825.

79 *CIPM* xxiii.596.

gave 2*s* and a gold ring'.[80] Robert Scot got ten times as much when 'immediately after the said John's birth he hastened to the earl of Lancaster, deceased, and brought him the news of the said John's birth, for which the said earl gave him 20*s*'.[81] Such largesse was obviously eagerly sought after and much talked about. Ralph Ardern heard about this example at third hand. 'His father and mother were at the house of Thomas earl of Warwick at Salwarpe and told him of the birth, and that Peter Holt received £10 for taking the news to the earl'.[82] Only the richest households could afford generosity on this scale. More usual was an extra gown for a lucky messenger.[83] Sometimes a messenger's reward might be of practical use to him, like a horse[84] or a pair of shoes;[85] but equally it might be some luxury item.[86] In a few cases the reward was a tenancy on the family's lands.[87]

For some jurors the recollection of such transitory generosity contrasted sadly with more usual circumstances. John Chestervile was one of several jurors who stated his resentment openly. 'William gave him 40*d*, and never before or after that day did he give him a penny.'[88] Many gifts were designed to trigger the memory of the birth in the future and were more in the nature of mementoes than serious rewards. Richard Colvill, for example, testified to a common practice. 'On that day he was charged by the said lady Katharine's steward to bring home 24 bows, which the said steward bought and gave to divers servants.'[89] In another household all the yeomen were given new hose.[90]

Less mentioned than paid service were duties to the community. From 1382 a few jurors recalled holding the office of town constable;[91] and from the 1420s, jurors often mentioned the process of their appointment or dismissal in the position. Richard Hynton, for example, remembered being 'discharged from the office of constable of Leigh by a justice at sessions of the peace held at Gloucester on the day of William's baptism'.[92] Conversely, John Shadde recalled his appointment with considerable pride. 'He was made town constable at the court leet held at Salisbury at the great request of the whole community of the vill of Salisbury

80 *CIPM* v.152.
81 *CIPM* vii.250.
82 *CIPM* xviii.855.
83 Which was what John o the Wolde received when 'he announced it to the child's father'. *CIPM* xii.176.
84 *CIPM* xiv.62.
85 *CIPM* xvii.955.
86 As in the case of John Broun, who received 'jewels to the value of 100s'. *CIPM* v.157.
87 E.g. 'Thomas Ayre, aged 50 years and more, agrees and says that on that day he was at Bothal with Robert Bertram, knight, his grandfather, when the latter received news of the birth of the said heir and gave the messenger a husbandland in Stainton for life'. *CIPM* xiv.62.
88 *CIPM* xx.131.
89 *CIPM* xvii.576.
90 *CIPM* xii.382.
91 The first example is William Addison from York. *CIPM* xv.893.
92 *CIPM* xxi.875.

and, in open court, was sworn to perform this office.'[93] Half the constables from the 1420s specified that they were 'elected' to the post.[94] It seems that some jurors were conscious of the special nature of these community positions. When church wardens remembered giving account of their stewardship, their testimonies adopted a different pattern from the one where servants were reporting to masters. The process does not appear less rigorous – three Gloucester jurors were appointed to audit 'the expenses of the churchwardens (*procuratoribus ecclesie*) in repairing and improving the church';[95] and in Essex the 'convents' between masons repairing the church and the church wardens were carefully recorded in the church psalter.[96] However, what may be hinted at with respect to church wardens and other community posts is the greater personal involvement of the participants and their consciousness of the trust placed in them by the community. Indeed, three Shropshire jurors were unique in testimonies that refer to rendering account by mentioning the attainment of a surplus.[97] John Folebroke was similarly proud when his initiative gained its reward. 'He was churchwarden of that church, then in great need of repair, and for this reason he came to the church that day. He saw the parson baptise Philip. A little afterwards, at his request, Philip father of John father of Philip, offered 100*s* for the repair of the church.'[98]

Seventy-eight jurors testified to buying and 36 to selling a wide range of goods and services.[99] The rate of mention was on an upward trend throughout the period, with a marked growth from the mid-fourteenth century and then another burst at the beginning of the fifteenth. One of the most memorable deals was the buying and selling of horses: 25 jurors remembered such a transaction, 19 of them being in the early years of the fifteenth century. Thirteen jurors recollected the price paid: the cheapest horse cost 20*s* shillings,[100] the most expensive £10. Jurors typically recalled something about the particular animal, mostly its colour, but often some more telling detail. William Drwe, for example, remembered being summoned to the church – a frequent location for horse dealing – so that Isabel Roudon could buy his 'palfrey' to ride on a pilgrimage to Bridlington. He remembered fondly that 'the horse was the best and most sure-footed that he had ever ridden'. As such, he drove a hard bargain, charging Isabel 10 marks 6*s*

93 *CIPM* xxii.366.

94 E.g. *CIPM* xxii.419, 423. Regarding another commonly mentioned post, John de Sogedon and Madok le Yong also stated 'they were elected wardens of the guild of St Katharine the Virgin at Hynton by the brethren of the gild'. *CIPM* xv.449.

95 *CIPM* xiii.285.

96 *CIPM* xiv.167.

97 'They rendered their final account as wardens of the goods of the parish church of Pontesbury before the parishioners there and had a surplus of 32*s* 6*d*.. *CIPM* xv.660.

98 *CIPM* xxii.530.

99 The purchase and transfer of land is a larger and separate topic and will be excluded here. It is discussed in W.S. Deller, forthcoming.

100 Not, as it happened, a bargain – it died 'on the same day': *CIPM* xx.267.

8*d* (£7) for it. Marks of attachment, even affection, often accompany memories of the buying or selling of horses. William Monk, for example, remembered the rather elaborate name of the horse he sold for the large sum of £10. It was called '*Skottysh geldyng Swyft for the Nonys*' – and at that price and with that name it had clearly been bred for speed.[101]

If not the animal itself, jurors recalled the thrill of the deal, though Benet Chamberleyn's experience was too good to be typical – he bought a black horse for 10 marks and sold it 'the next day' for 20.[102] There is some evidence of an established dealer network – Isabel had 'often' summoned William Drwe to buy horses. Robert Knyth was described as a horse dealer (*corsour*) and the person he sold a horse to bought it 'for his own use', i.e. not to sell on.[103] John Steyk bought three horses at Fakenham fair, whether for himself or to trade we do not know.[104] Whether buying or selling to neighbours or through dealers, horse trading had the excitement of risk, which made it memorable.

Risk was mitigated by the face-to-face nature of the trade and the support of written contracts of sale, particularly when payment was delayed, as it often must have been, considering the sums involved. John de Backworth was typical in getting a written 'obligation' from the purchaser when he sold a horse for six marks. Richard de Routh 'gave his bond' to pay 'next Easter' when he paid 100*s* for a horse in January.[105] One of the memorable aspects of William Drwe's testimony was that Isabel 'paid there and then' for the palfrey, which was probably unusual. A tone of guarded reciprocity suffused many of these testimonies, only occasionally distinguished by exceptional good or bad luck – the beast sold on for a big profit, or, conversely, its dying almost immediately – or, as in John Russell's experience, recalled in a breathless narrative of exceptional gentlemanly conduct. He described how he

> sold a palfrey that day to John de Courtenay, knight, Philip's father, for £10 legal English money on condition that it proved the best of John's horses. Afterwards that same day, the horses ran about the great close called 'Leypark' near the church, and John de Courtenay's horse suddenly fell and injured itself. Nevertheless John de Courtenay, knight, by his grace gave 40*s* to John Russell by way of compensation for the devaluing of the horse.[106]

Other commodities besides horses were the subject of jurors' recollections of buying and selling. Livestock like pigs, sheep, cows and oxen were all mentioned occasionally, but failed to attract the frequency or excitement of horse dealing. Usually such a trade had to be memorable for something, in addition to the

101 *CIPM* xxi.874.
102 *CIPM* xix.999.
103 *CIPM* xix.782. 'Corsour' was a recorded surname by the beginning of the fifteenth century e.g., *CIPM* xx.129.
104 *CIPM* xix.783.
105 *CIPM* vii.695; xix.781.
106 *CIPM* xxii.530.

simple purchase. William Budd, for example, recalled the purchase of twelve pigs for 33*s*, but the significance for him was, one imagines, in the closing phrase 'and two died immediately'.[107] Similarly, of John Swynton's 12 cows costing 100*s*, which followed William Budd's sheep suspiciously quickly in the same hearing, 'one proved worthless'. More commonly, a sale was remembered for its direct connection with an heir's birth rather than for its own sake. Animals were sold, for example, to be consumed at a mother's purification feast, where often entire cows were needed for the celebration.[108]

For other agricultural trade to be worthy of record, it had to be on quite a large scale. The smallest quantity of grain mentioned was the purchase of two quarters of wheat by William Moumbrey from the heir's father, but here the significance lies in the fact that he saw the infant while doing the deal.[109] More typical were bargains for between 20 and 100 quarters[110] of wheat, oats and pease, but even these are too infrequent for any hint at the size and nature of the trade.[111] Unlike for horses, prices were seldom recorded. Another common type of transaction was the purchase of the tithe in grain or livestock from the local clergy. Sometimes it was the purchase of the winnowed grain taken from storage in or near the rectory. More usually it was bought off the field or stack (*tassum*) in tithe sheaves (*decimas garbas*). The tithe of lambs could also be traded in this way.[112] Sometimes the trading of ecclesiastical surpluses could be on quite a large scale, as when Richard Hayward bought 'a barn full of corn' from 'the bailiff of the prebend of Codworth' in Somerset in 1369.[113]

Buying timber for building was a steadily memorable event: jurors described going to a particular wood and buying either standing trees, or, more usually, already felled logs.[114] Transport of the timber to the place where it was needed was commonly the job of the buyer, unless an owner made it a sign of favour to do so.[115] Oak was the preferred construction material, though ash was also mentioned.[116] In most cases timber was purchased for a specific building project from a nearby wood; there is no evidence for a more widespread trade in timber, though there are a few instances of the large-scale purchase of more easily transportable coppice wood. When a group of four men bought all the underwood cut on a

107 *CIPM* xx.267.
108 E.g. *CIPM* xix.392, 780.
109 *CIPM* xiv.300.
110 A fourth part of a hundredweight, or 28 pounds.
111 E.g. *CIPM* x.530; xiii.60; xiv.300; xviii.664.
112 Thomas Clere paid 5 marks 6*s* 4*d* for the tithe of lambs to the parson of Ashbrittle in Somerset. *CIPM* xx,272. We do not know how many he got for this price.
113 *CIPM* xii.268.
114 E.g., *CIPM* xxiii.140.
115 William Moure received three cartloads of oak wood from the heir's father 'that he might bear witness to and keep in mind his son's age'. *CIPM* xii.268.
116 Where oak and ash were mentioned together in the same testimony the amount of ash compared with oak was a third or half the quantity. *CIPM* x.331; xiii.137.

seven-year cycle from the park of Sir Ralph Basset for £10, the sum paid, indicative of large quantities, makes it likely that the men were trading the wood rather than using it themselves. Similarly, William Stephene's purchase of '400 faggots' from a Middlesex wood may have been aimed at the London firewood market.[117]

Occasionally there are glimpses of dealing in other agricultural commodities. Tanning, for example, was recalled from Southampton to Newcastle: in the former town Valentine Hamond was apprenticed 'to the art of a skinner' (*pelliparii*) while in the latter John Cotam was described as a 'barker' or tanner. A group of testimonies from Somerset and Wiltshire in the 1350s and 1360s referred to giving a deerskin to a favoured retainer straight from the hunt as a reminder of an heir's birth;[118] but the more common dealing was in the commercial sale of hides from domestic animals. John Cooke remembered his mundane journey 'with some cow hides' only because his horse broke a leg.[119] John Pyle was in Wimborne Minster 'to buy undressed hides in the market' when he heard about the birth.[120]

On a much bigger scale was the reference to trade in wool and finished cloth. The wool trade with Flanders was the subject of three Lincolnshire references in the 1350s. Each testimony described 'crossing the sea' with wool for sale, and one mentioned the buyers through whom the sale was made. Each merchant also ordered his affairs before the trip by feoffing his land to trustees.[121] Another juror, this time from York, headed for Calais to make his sale in 1384.[122]

Many jurors stressed the difficulties of trading. For example, William Smyth of Dorset recalled going in 1412 to Blandford Forum market and buying 20 stone of wool for 10 marks; he was stopped by bailiffs, who alleged he was a burgess of Wimborne Minster and should not be trading in Blandford. William must have been ready for such hitches because he was able to show them 'letters patent of the duke of Lancaster' (the lord of Wimborne) and was discharged.[123] If internal bureaucracy was bad, abroad was even worse. Henry Arden was a large-scale merchant with important connections. In 1321 he remembered financing the purchase of cloth for the purification of the mother of John Grey, giving John's servants £6 for the purpose. With the residue from £100 he traded (*mercatizavit*) and went to Flanders, where along with ten others (who collectively lost an alleged £1,000), his goods were confiscated – in retaliation for which 'the king granted them an arrest upon the Flemings'.[124]

If the problems were great, the rewards of the wool trade were equally so. In 1380 three Shropshire jurors recalled paying 100 marks for wool in a single

117 *CIPM* xxii.529.
118 *CIPM* x.450, 645; xi.379.
119 *CIPM* xvii.430.
120 *CIPM* xix.997
121 *CIPM* ix.451, 592; x.194.
122 *CIPM* xix.139.
123 *CIPM* xix.997.
124 *CIPM* vi.336.

deal,[125] and from one estate in 1393 the reeve gave his lord £23 4*s* 4*d* from the sale of wool.[126] The wool trade was recorded across the country as a source of ready money,[127] and sometimes even a substitute for it, alderman Nicholas Whyte of Grantham, for example, finding it more convenient to give his sister and brother-in-law twenty sacks of wool than coin of the realm.[128]

Trade in finished cloth can also be faintly discerned. Several jurors mentioned the work of tailors. In the thirteenth century they seemed to have been quite rare specialists attached to a great household. Sir Emery de Samand, for example, had his own tailor whom he used as a messenger to announce his heir's birth. But from the 1280s the trade began to appear as a common surname for jurors across the country, increasing in frequency from the 1350s onwards.[129] Several jurors recalled apprenticeship in the craft, which seemed to have attracted sub-specialisms from an early date. In 1297 Walter Whyte apprenticed his son *in Draperia Londonis* (which could refer to a drapery shop or quarter), while in the city of York in 1307 a juror's son 'was apprenticed to shear cloth'.[130] Similarly, from 1320 the trade of fuller was mentioned, the name itself becoming a common surname thereafter.[131]

Mention of ready-made clothes was comparatively rare, even well-off heirs' families tending to buy cloth to be made into garments in the home, red being the most commonly mentioned colour.[132] While most everyday clothing was made within the household,[133] the best-quality garments were often made by specialists. In the case of John Parlebyn, for example, who sold 'an ell of light cloth (*una ulna panni levii*) called "Clathe of lake" for a "Crisssom cloth" to be made for John Mitford', the heir's father', the christening garment was probably made by an outsider. This was certainly true of Elizabeth Fienles' purification 'gown and dress', which was made by the local tailor.[134]

It was the luxury trade that jurors tended to recall most, their memories retaining objects of unusual opulence often associated with the baptism ceremony

125 *CIPM* xv.448.
126 *CIPM* xx.131.
127 John Belfeld, from Downham in Lancashire, remarked casually in 1324 that he was at church 'to sell wool and lead'. *CIPM* xxii.365.
128 *CIPM* xxiii.139.
129 Variations of 'Tailor' appear in testimonies at least 60 times. Numbers of mentions peaked in the 1350s (7), 1360s (9) and 1370s (15).
130 *CIPM* vi.191; vii.170. The London drapery trade seems to have become firmly established: in 1404 Richard Elys was placed with a draper there 'to serve faithfully as a live-in apprentice for ten years'. *CIPM* xxii.677. In 1406 a juror's son was apprenticed 'in the drapers' guild for eight years'. *CIPM* xxiii.140.
131 A juror in 1384 'carried a fulled cloth with Stephan the fuller' to the heir's house. *CIPM* xix.350. The surname appeared eight times between 1320 and 1427.
132 E.g., *CIPM* xix.342, 348.
133 Robert le Vyte saw the infant heir when he came to collect 14*s* for 'a cloth of russet' he had sold the family, presumably to make up at home.
134 *CIPM* xix.349.

or the purification celebrations. Thomas Fox, a 'skynner', remembered that he sold to Sir Robert Lisle, the heir's grandfather, 'a fur of pure grey' to wrap the infant, which cost the mind-boggling sum of 100*s*. Lots of jurors remembered the colour and richness of the baby's wrappings, which were often brightly coloured red or gold, in silk or linen.[135]

Contacts in the wine trade were also at a premium before a baptism or churching, and no fewer than 52 jurors from all over the country between 1362 and 1430 mentioned wine in their testimonies.[136] Some, like William Bailiff and William Fenssh, were probably on the wholesale side, one travelling to Gascony for his stock, the other to Bordeaux.[137] Most jurors were involved in a smaller way, particularly on the transportation and consumption side. The preparations surrounding the celebrations were remembered as particularly accident prone by many jurors. One beat his servant for spilling a jar of wine intended for the church; another was a servant himself and broke 'the lights' while carrying wine.[138] These were small-scale incidents compared with what happened to Henry Somer: he was 'driving a cart with a pipe of red wine past the churchyard to the manor and rejoicing and delighting in the birth of Maurice ... in such excitement Henry Somer neglected the cart ... so that the wine was totally lost'.[139] The suspiciously alcoholic factor in all these events was made explicit by four Worcester men, who 'were present at the baptism and drank wine, which was brought to the church, and such was the effect that they could hardly walk out of the church'.[140]

Many jurors tended to dwell on the quantity of the wine available: often large amounts frequently delivered quickly. In 1389, for example, Henry Dunstan rode to the nearest market town – Newcastle – on the day an heiress was born in order to buy three casks (*loginas*) of wine, and he reported no trouble obtaining such an amount.[141] Roger Bailey from Hereford 'sold the father a tun (*dolium*) of red Gascon wine for the churching of Maud, the mother'.[142] He was also clearly able to lay his hands on a large quantity of wine without problem.

From the end of the fourteenth century, jurors began to be more discriminating in their wine memories. In 1399 John atte Priours remembered carrying two gallons of 'sweet wine' from Beverley. Three London jurors made a further

135 Apart from its richness, the christening garment came in a variety of colours and textiles – white, red or gold being the most remembered. Reference to silk came from all parts of the country and seems to be confined to wealthy families; linen was confined to two mentions from a single Essex hearing. *CIPM* xvii.1110.

136 The wine trade is also discussed below, in chapter 12.

137 *CIPM* xi.387; xv.657.

138 *CIPM* xvii.576, 955.

139 *CIPM* xix.343.

140 *CIPM* xx.263.

141 *CIPM* xix.342.

142 *CIPM* xix.780. Although often used as synonym for cask or barrel, the tun from the mid fifteenth century came to be used as a measure of definite capacity, 'usually equivalent to two pipes or four hogsheads containing 252 old wine gallons'. *Oxford English Dictionary Compact Edition*, ii (P–Z), 464.

distinction in 1402: they referred to 'jugs of sweet wine called "bastard" and "Romeney"'.[143] In 1410 a further wine type was mentioned by a Hereford juror – 'a sweet red wine called "Osey"'.[144] Evidence of similar sophistication in the trade was shown by the choice of red or white wine which four Kent jurors remembered in the same year.[145] A decade later the choice at one Norfolk baptism was between 'clarrey' and 'malvesy'.[146] In common with the development of many luxury trades, the accoutrements of consumption also grew more sophisticated: from the second decade of the fifteenth century several jurors recalled the silver vessels in which wine was served after the baptismal service. In this later period the drinking memories also tended to feature the elegance of the occasion rather than the amount of alcohol consumed – one or two silver pots, as opposed to a cask or pipe, and the guests are 'refreshed' as opposed to merely 'drinking'.

As well as celebration, the birth of an heir was often marked by gift giving of various kinds. The rewarding of dependants who brought the good news has already been mentioned, but the heirs themselves were often the recipient of luxury objects, particularly in gold and silver. From 1308 to 1431 nine jurors recalled the heir being given a gold ring, sometimes with a cash gift (ranging from 2*s* to 20*s*) Little was revealed about the origin and trade in such things. The weight of the testimonies was on the rarity and value of the objects. For William Jacob, the ring he gave to the heir was possibly an heirloom. 'He gave a gold ring in which a precious stone was set which he greatly valued.' Robert Hildeyerd was able to distinguish the stone in his ring as a sapphire, but Baldwin de Brugge was more hesitant – he gave 'a gold ring having in it a stone called a "dyamand"'.[147] In addition to rings, gold was given in the form of gold coinage.[148] At York in 1404 such coins were still the object of some wonderment for juror Thomas Frere, who recalled being shown a hoard worth 100*s* given to a servant by the happy father.[149] This was not unusual – as late as 1431 John Welweton of Somerset confessed, when he was given two nobles by the heir's grandmother, that 'such things he had never before had'.[150] From 1404 the custom of giving the infant 'a purse of gold' was remembered, perhaps because of its rarity as well as its monetary value.[151]

Silver was mentioned almost twice as frequently as gold. The objects given – apart from money – were mainly cups or goblets of various sorts. These were more everyday than the gold presents, often being mentioned as part of a more

143 *CIPM* xviii.670.
144 *CIPM* xix.780.
145 *CIPM* xix.784.
146 *CIPM*, xxi.758.
147 *CIPM* vii.245, 544; xiii.293.
148 First minted in England in 1344, the noble being coined from 1351. *A New History of the Royal Mint*, ed. C.E. Challis (Cambridge, 1992), 163–8.
149 *CIPM* xviii.997.
150 *CIPM* xviii.602.
151 *CIPM* xviii.998.

general exchange of tokens which took place after the infant's baptism.[152] Instead of being given by the donor himself, it was sometimes left to servants to make the delivery.[153] The giving of silver seems to have grown in popularity over a comparatively short period – over 65% of examples were from the 1420s and 1430s – and occurred over a wide geographical area. It seems that more people from that time could afford to give silver. Another custom of giving silver was the present to the heir of 'a little silver bell', which, it was often stressed, was given 'immediately' after the baptism, possibly with the intention of distracting the child as well as providing a memorable gift.[154]

Away from luxury goods and trade in agricultural commodities, there occur in the record occasional or even single mentions of what may well have been regular and large-scale trading, but which were too habitual to be particularly worthy of memory. The purchase of food, for example, was seldom commented on outside the special demands of baptismal or purification celebrations. An exception was Roger de Ewelme, who was employed 'for a long time' as purveyor (*creditor et provisor*) in Henley for the heir's family, the Greys of Oxford, which he supplied with 'victuals'.[155] Two jurors mentioned servants of the heir's family, part of whose job was to journey to the local market town for supplies, with an emphasis on more luxury food or drink that could not be produced at home.[156] Regular suppliers, local networks and later payment seem to be characteristic of the trade.[157]

In conclusion, we can see that many of the jurors who mentioned their jobs and their trading were, in their mostly 'middling' status within a deferential society, anxious for a position with a powerful family, or for some similar secure occupation. Those who achieved such a role often took vicarious pride in the status of the family they served and their own importance to it. Social ambition and a keen awareness of relative wealth and status, even, perhaps especially, over such small marks of distinction as the quality of their robe, or the opulence of their reward, lay behind many testimonies. Some jurors recollected the excitement of trading, especially horses; a few still harboured resentments over deals that had gone wrong long ago, and more fondly remembered a quick profit. Credit and written

152 The most frequent motif coupled a silver cup for the heir with a reward of 6*s* 8*d* for the nurse, e.g. *CIPM* xxiii.417, 423, 731.

153 John Pullayn was a link in such a chain of delivery. 'He was deputy to Peter Bukton, knight, then keeper of Knaresborough forest. Peter gave him two deer and a silver goblet to deliver to William Ingilby (the heir) on the day of the baptism'. *CIPM* xxiii.309.

154 The 'silver bell' motif was recorded nine times between 1409 and 1431, mainly from the south of the country but as far north as York and as far west as Somerset.

155 *CIPM* vi.336.

156 Ralph Smyth, for example, 'was at Nottingham to buy wine and other victuals'. *CIPM* xviii.999.

157 At the other end of the social scale, three London testimonies from the 1390s referred to the fast-food business in the city. They recalled that 'on that day Thomas Sprotburgh, cook, was put in the pillory for selling a stinking eel pie and other unwholesome victuals', and a similar punishment followed four years later when Roger Sprayge was caught selling 'stinking rib of beef and other unwholesome victuals'. *CIPM* xvii.957, 958.

contracts were common. Jurors were fascinated by luxury goods and they noted, eagerly, their cost. Several expressed awe at the sight of large sums of coinage. From these testimonies emerges a picture of an individualistic, ambitious, materialistic society, many of whose members were narrowly centred on their own commercial and social advancement.

10

What Went On in the Medieval Parish Church, 1377–1447, with Particular Reference to Churching

Katie Clarke and Michael Hicks

The jurors at proofs of age were never eye-witnesses to the birth itself, for men were barred from the birthing chamber.[1] Midwives and other females at the birth never testified. Instead, several of the proofs detail, as mnemonics (reminders), the journey to tell the father of the birth. John Speman recollected being sent, on 1 August 1385, to London from Datchet, Buckinghamshire to alert John Arundel's father to the birth.[2] Will Dickon, on 17 September 1381, was present when the father was informed.[3] What the jurors recalled was the ceremony of baptism, often witnessed whilst attending mass or some other service. Proofs of age therefore focused not on the birth of the heir, but on the baptism, a formal religious rite that was generally conducted on the same day or the very next day. Medieval babies were baptised at once, so that if they died they were nevertheless eligible for salvation. It was the christening that made them Christian. Proofs of age record only the *live births* of future heirs that *survived*. There are many cases like Hugh Willoughby, baptised at Risley (Derb.) in 1413, who was not the eldest son at birth, but who succeeded to the family inheritance after the deaths of his elder brother and his father.[4] It was permitted for weak children to be christened privately, by lay people, even by midwives, but none is recorded in the proofs, presumably because any heirs so baptised did indeed die. The vast majority of baptisms happened in parish churches, a very few in monasteries or private chapels. Proofs of age give us a snapshot of what was going on in a particular parish church at a particular point in the church calendar.

The baptism service involved both sexes, but it was also differentiated by gender in ways that stressed female inferiority. Only a girl child was exorcised at baptism.[5] The proofs of age are the principal source for churching, the service of purification of the mother following each pregnancy that presumably occurred millions of times in the later Middle Ages, thousands of times in every parish

1 D. Youngs, *The Life Cycle of Western Europe c.1300–c.1500* (Manchester, 2006), 45.
2 *CIPM* xviii.384.
3 *CIPM* xviii.405.
4 *CIPM* xxiv.567.
5 J.D.C. Fisher, *Christian Initiation: Baptism in the Medieval West*, Alcuin Club xlvii, 160–63.

church. Churching was a ceremony that has been rather neglected: it alone placed women at the centre of religious practice.

It is a problem of course that the narratives in the proofs of age are often repetitive, duplicate one another and can hence be factually incorrect, but the stock memories they record had to be credible to contemporaries in order to be accepted and are therefore usefully indicative of the sorts of things that happened on these occasions. Telling use has been made of such stock memories in school exercises by Professor Nicholas Orme, and of real findings in coroners' inquests by Professor Barbara Hanawalt.[6] Not all proofs contain such data, focusing instead on national disasters and personal accidents. Occasionally proofs elaborate illuminatingly on the particular circumstances of a specific baptism in what appear to be a series of eyewitness accounts. Sometimes testimonies recognisably refer to the particular church: St Edmund's College at Salisbury, for instance. It is rare for them to identify architectural features, such as the crypt at St John's Bristol – the now redundant church atop a city gate – as in 1393.[7]

I

The parish church was a public building that was served, for the congregation of a defined area, the parish, by the parish priest, an uncertain complement of other clergy, and the parish clerk. At the high altar in the chancel were celebrated everyday canonical hours – prime, lauds, terce, matins, sext, nones, vespers, compline – and the high mass. These offices required the presence only of the priest himself and of a clerk to say the responses. None of the regular hours is mentioned in any of the proofs, presumably because normally no layman attended. Mass was different. Not infrequently the witnesses to the christening had been in the church to attend mass. Such references are quite common.[8] Calculations of the dates show that laymen might attend mass not solely on Sundays, but throughout the week. Mass began the day for at least some workmen and travellers. Thomas Eyre was in the church of Waddon (Cambs.) on 17 September 1381 to hear mass when he saw Thomas Chalers baptised.[9] There were five witnesses to John Dynelay's baptism at Downham (Lancs.) in 1424, who had actually been attending mass at the same time: afterwards one travelled on to Pontefract (Yorks.), another to Stoneyhurst (Lancs.), and a third went on pilgrimage to Rome. The fourth had travelled to Downham from Grindleton (Yorks.) and the fifth was in the company of Sir Richard Haughton.[10] Far from being commonplace, their

[6] B.A. Hanawalt, *The Ties that Bound* (1986); N. Orme, *English School Exercises 1420–1530* (Turnhout, 2014).
[7] *CIPM* xxi.371.
[8] *CIPM* xv.76; xvii.274.
[9] *CIPM* xviii.1178.
[10] *CIPM* xxii.356.

testimony suggests that a special reason was needed for laymen to attend a weekday mass.

Departure on pilgrimage appears to be such a reason. Sometimes proofs explicitly record prior attendance at mass by pilgrims; in other cases when the pilgrimage served as an aide memoire, the testimony does not actually state that the pilgrim was in church at the right moment, though this perhaps was implicit. Destinations cited were Jerusalem, Rome, Compostella, and the shrine of St William of York. Some visits to the Roman curia may have been on business.[11] Very unusually, one hopes, on 8 September 1362 a priest Sir John Lancy and his woman, Joan Winkman, did penance around the churchyard of Hungry Hattele (Cambs.).[12] In Cardiff another church was re-consecrated after pollution by the spilling of blood.[13] Those who came for business meetings, such as the repayment of debts, sometimes went to mass first before going to work. At least sometimes lovedays were preceded by mass[14] and/or followed by one.[15] Ten middle-aged men dated a christening in 1415 at All Saints Newcastle to the memorable sermon there by Master Robert Harding that they had attended.[16]

It is never recorded whether the mass mentioned was the main parish mass, a chantry mass, or one of the supplementary masses that every priest was required to celebrate every day. The daily liturgy around the high altar took place regardless of any other services that happened in different parts of the church, even at the same time – chantry masses, obits, funerals, baptisms, and marriages. John Long was reading the third morning lesson at Horseheath (Cambs.) on Thursday 8 December 1379 when he heard the baby cry.[17] Then, as now, weddings were surely planned in advance to occur on particular dates. Baptisms and funerals had to be staged at short notice. Proofs of age demonstrate how several services happened at the same time or, alternatively, in sequence, one after another. Most churches had more than one chaplain to handle these simultaneous commitments.

Baptism was a sacrament conducted around the parish font, which was a permanent fitment located at the west end of the church. There was never more than one font. Many of the fonts described in the proofs survive today, as at Boreham in Essex, or were transferred to the new church, as at Charfield in Gloucestershire. On 4 April 1427 at Wellington in Herefordshire the ceremony was enlivened when the cover fell off the font and was damaged: another witness recorded injury to the officiant too, who could not walk home.[18] Presumably the officiant was usually the parson – an ambiguous term that can denote the rector, vicar, or curate – but sometimes particular chaplains or monastic superiors were

11 *CIPM* xviii.1178; xxi.147; xxii.356; xxiv.563; xxv.428; xxiii.309, 422, 691, 722; xxv.128.

12 *CIPM* xvi.341.

13 *CIPM* xx.184.

14 *CIPM* xxii.365.

15 E.g. the famous loveday at St Paul's in 1458.

16 *CIPM* xxiv.456.

17 *CIPM* xviii.673.

18 *CIPM* xxvi.142.

brought in by the baby's family. The mother was almost never present.[19] The infant was carried by a woman (often the midwife) from the place of birth to the church, preceded by bearers with unlit candles. Often the water in the font was warmed. There were three godparents, two of the same gender as the baby, one of whom raised the infant to the font, pronounced its name, and, at least sometimes, chose the name. It was usually the parish clerk who held the book from which the priest read or who jotted the details in the missal, almost invariably now lost. Chrism oil, fire, salt, and the ringing of bells are occasionally mentioned. The standard ritual required a basin and ewer (and presumably towels) for the godparents to wash their hands, two pots of wine or mead for them to drink in the church, and bread or cake to eat.[20] More drink apparently was supplied for other attendants, perhaps outside the church. The basin, ewer, and pots in the proofs were generally of silver, brought from the infant's home. Remember, the baptisms in the proofs related to future heirs, aristocratic children from families who could afford wine and silver vessels on such special occasions. There was plenty of scope for further elaboration and additional ritual. Godparents gave gifts to the child – then, as now, silver goblets were commonplace – and sometimes to the mother. Often the proofs record the appointment of a wet nurse and her reward. Afterwards the congregation processed homewards, preceded by torches, now lit, perhaps for a feast.

Babies, of course, do not come to order. They can be premature or overdue. Regrettably, some were miscarried or stillborn. The precise date for any birth and therefore baptism could be only predicted a day or so in advance and the sex, boy or girl, which determined the gender balance of godparents, not at all. Preparations had to be made very quickly, or at least their finishing touches. Stocks of candles, wine and so forth had to be procured: christenings could be expensive. On the day of the baptism of his son Thomas, Robert Brown postponed payment to two creditors because of the christening, failed to pay a supplier of 3,000 lathe nails, and refused any discount on a horse that had subsequently died.[21] Even the father might be elsewhere and might have to be notified or fetched: Richard Hankford, father of Thomasina Hankford, was hunting.[22] Godparents had to be finalised, notified and fetched. Messengers were despatched to them, to the father, and to absent grandparents, not all of whom managed to attend the baptism. At Risley church (Derb.) in 1413 the font was swathed in red cloth for the baptism of Hugh Willoughby.[23] For the peerage, greater grandeur was sought. In 1406 at Belvoir (Leics.), St Mary's church was decked out with cloths of silk and gold

[19] 'the mother was obviously still in bed', but her testimony might be reported by another, see M. McGlynn, 'Memory, Orality, and Life Records: Proofs of Age in Tudor England', *Sixteenth Century Journal* 40 (2009), 689, 695.

[20] *CIPM* xxi.144.

[21] *CIPM* xxvi.354.

[22] *CIPM* xxiv.720.

[23] *CIPM* xxiv.567.

and the font with cloth of gold and red for the baptism of Thomas, younger son of William Lord Roos. In 1407 at Temple Hurst (Yorks.) the altar was hung with ten cloths of gold and the font with silken hangings for the baptism of John, younger son of John Lord Darcy. Similarly, in 1410 Tattingstone church, Suffolk was hung with ten cloths of gold and the font with ten white silken cloths. In each case the witness was sent to check the arrangements out for the father or grandfather.[24] Baptism was clearly a secular event that needed to be done properly and was expected to convey the wealth and status of these families to much more than a purely local audience.

Proofs of age tell us that the baby inherited when he/she achieved his/her majority: it does not follow that the baby was heir when born. Often he/she was not. At birth John Holland and Hugh Willoughby both had older brothers.[25] Daughters like Christine and Ellen Sumpter were not scheduled to succeed: they became heiresses only when their brother, John Sumpter, predeceased them.[26] One might suppose that younger sons or daughters were greeted with less enthusiasm, less expense or less celebration than their predecessors, but this does not appear to have been the case. The joy of the departing congregation – another stock memory in the proofs of age – applied equally to daughters and sons. Fathers of new-born babies were particularly approachable and conciliatory.[27] They rewarded those bringing them news of the birth and gave money to the church fabric. Edmund Cheyne appears a unique exception: perhaps it was irritation at the birth of a second heiress that caused him to beat John Cutting 'so he despaired of his life' and to break the head of a clumsy servant 'with a stick that he used to have in his hand'.[28]

Many witnesses fixed the date of a birth with reference to other vital events. Often they recorded other births – of their own offspring or others – marriages, betrothals, and occasionally banns (as on Sunday, 25 April 1381 at Welshpool in Powys),[29] and the funerals of parents, children, or wives, and the celebration of first masses.[30] It is not always clear that the other birth resulted in baptism that same day, or indeed that the other religious service that served as a reminder to the jurors even took place in the same church. Just occasionally proofs state explicitly that the baptism or funeral took place in a different church.[31] However, a considerable number of testimonies record such events in the same church on the same day. Particularly common were baptisms of newly born children. This was

24 *CIPM* xxiii.139, 150, 596, 598.
25 *CIPM* xxiv.567, 720.
26 *CIPM* xxii.538. For the context, see *The Armburgh Papers: The Brokholes Inheritance in Warwickshire, Hertfordshire and Essex, c.1417–c.1453*, ed. C. Carpenter (Woodbridge, 1998).
27 See e.g. *CIPM* xxii.530.
28 *CIPM* xxvi.352.
29 *CIPM* xv.659.
30 See M. Hicks, 'Landmarks in Life: Vital Events and Vital Statistics from the Proofs of Age' (2012), www.blog.inquisitionspostmortem.ac.uk.
31 *CIPM* xxi.147.

true at Spotborough (Yorks.) on 15 August 1397 and at Stamford (Lincs.) on 25 March 1397.[32] As many as four baptisms took place at Harewood (Yorks.) on 18 October 1416.[33]

Sometimes the proof states explicitly that this other baby was baptised immediately before the heir in the proof or, more often, immediately after the heir.[34] Many such babies subsequently died in infancy. For every live birth, there should have been a churching 40 days later. In contrast, weddings were surely scheduled in advance, but nevertheless they used the same building in which the canonical hours and baptisms took place, and might coincide in time. Henry Threlkeld's baptism at Threlkeld in Cumberland in 1398 was observed by four men attending a wedding in the same church at the same time.[35] Similarly the marriage of Katherine Spot at Gnosall (Staffs.) in 1394 followed immediately after the baptism of Thomas Chalton.[36]

Christenings and marriages were classless events, in which the humble shared in and benefited from the decorations provided by the rich. Funerals, in contrast, were not classless. The office of the dead, in shorthand *Placebo* and *Dirige*, embraced both the church service and the interment; the requiem mass was on the morrow. Only very occasionally do the proofs refer to the church service (and never to the requiem mass) or to the funeral mass the next day. The proofs habitually record interments. Most such burials were outside, in the churchyard, but some were within the church. There were two burials at Fulbourne (Cambs,) on 12 September 1399: of Richard, brother of a witness, in the churchyard and of Alice, his sister, in the church itself. Alice's interment must at the least have involved the fashioning or opening of a vault and the restoration of the church floor: quite a disruptive process.[37] Similarly one witness's brother, William, was buried in the churchyard at Besford (Worcs.) and his sister Joan in the church.[38] At least some funerals, presumably the simplest, were held on the day of death. Many deaths of those who had long been ill were anticipated and planned for. Obits, most probably one-off anniversary services, are recorded, for example at East Tytherley (Hants.) in 1414.[39] Parents and widowers requested masses for the soul of the departed at Macworth (Derb.) in 1420.[40]

It is often said that churches were public buildings that were used for a variety of purposes. The proofs of age provide confirmatory evidence for this. Leases, deeds, loans, and the repayment of loans are recorded. Those present in Walton church (Lancs.) on Wednesday 7 December 1379 were there to catch up on

32 *CIPM* xxi.147, 216.
33 *CIPM* xxv.131.
34 *CIPM* xxi.672; xxii.673.
35 *CIPM* xi.368.
36 *CIPM* xxi.671.
37 *CIPM* xxi.874.
38 *CIPM* xxvi.335.
39 *CIPM* xxiv.567.
40 *CIPM* xxi.670; xxiii.418.

the news from Ireland, to attend a loveday and a cockfight, to buy corn, and to meet a man from Liverpool; and in three other cases, all in Lancashire, to hear mass before going to Bootle to purchase fish, to buy two oxen at Kirkdale, and to view a wreck and corpse on the beach at Litherland.[41] Contrasting uses indeed. The infants' fathers, such as Sir Philip Courtenay in 1406, John Lely in 1424, and Edmund Cheyne in 1427, were busy men. Lely bought a horse, accepted two homages, and terminated a dispute on the day of his son's christening.[42] Some of these transactions were happening anyway. It was pure chance that the pre-arranged arbitration in the case of Gargrave *vs* Clyve at Bristol coincided with the baptism of John Solers in 1393. Sometimes, however, business drew individuals to the church, to catch a godparent or, more often, a father. William Thornhull tackled Abbot Nicholas of Shrewsbury about business at Moreton Corbet (Salop.) on 8 December 1383 when the abbot baptised Robert Corbet.[43] It was to secure forgiveness for a grievous wrong that Guy Puke tackled Sir Philip Courtenay in 1404. Courtenay was in a good mood at the birth of his son and heir: he also mediated an agreement between William Jow and the other godparent and contributed generously to the church fabric.[44] Mediators persuaded John Lely to end a disagreement with a certain John Sergeant.[45] Could a father refuse such a request on the day of his son's baptism?[46] Edmund Cheyne and Robert Brown show that he could. Lovedays coincided quite often with baptisms. In another instance the baptism preceded a cockfight:[47] could it really have been staged in church? Baptisms, churchings, marriages, and funerals were common occurrences that brought the aristocracy together in congenial mood. They were at least as common as county courts and quarter sessions. Baptisms were opportunities, therefore, to witness one another's deeds, enfeoffments, arbitrations, and so on.

II

Baptisms and churchings give the lie to the general consensus that women were not seen or heard in the medieval church and had no role in religious practice. Admittedly, women were never ordained, but neither were they passive recipients of a religion run by men. Churching and baptism were the two religious services that demanded the participation of female laity. Laywomen managed the birth, they were integral to the baptismal rite, and they were central to the

41 *CIPM* xviii.677.

42 *CIPM* xxv.522.

43 *CIPM* xviii.1148.

44 *CIPM* xxii. 530.

45 *CIPM* xxv.522.

46 Is there a parallel here with modern Sicily? 'by tradition no Sicilian can refuse a request on his daughter's wedding day': M. Puzo, *The Godfather* (New York, 1969), 25.

47 *CIPM* xxii.165.

ritual of churching. Male jurors recorded female participation in both baptisms and churchings. They feature also in other sources, in the *Paston Letters* and at episcopal visitations. The churching ceremony features in breviaries, the principal service book of the medieval church, and in churchwardens' accounts, but the proofs of age are the best and most neglected source.

Women do occur in the proofs. They participated in the baptism service in their roles as godmothers, midwives, wet nurses, and birth companions. More light is cast by the service books. Children could be christened only once, that is, have the baptismal phrase spoken over them, according to ecclesiastical law. It was normally the midwife who carried the child to the church and confirmed the baptismal status of the baby. If the life of the child was in immediate danger during and just after the birth, canon law permitted the midwife to speak the baptismal words over the baby. They might also perform a type of caesarean operation if the mother died before the child was fully delivered in order to christen the baby. The key words could be uttered in Latin or the vernacular – 'I cristene the[e] N, in the name of the fadir and of the sone and of the holy gost. Amen.' While it was anticipated that a man took precedence over a woman at a lay baptism, if a woman was more conversant with the words she was expected to recite them – and men were not usually present in the birthing chamber. In practical terms, a woman always spoke the words in an emergency. It was more important to perform the ritual correctly than to prefer one sex over the other. The water used had to be pure and fresh. Either it was sprinkled over the child or the child was dipped. If dipped, ideally this was done three times, although once could suffice. The priest could complete the ritual in the church but had to ask the midwife, prior to the church baptism, whether the vital phrase had already been spoken.[48] The role of the midwife was therefore pivotal. If the baptism had already taken place, it was the midwife present at the birth who confirmed this and who had most probably uttered the necessary words. Other females were witnesses.

While baptism was a service that included men and women (godparents and supporters), the ritual of churching was specifically a laywomen's rite. It was performed to spiritually cleanse a woman after childbirth. Perhaps originally a recognition of the sinfulness of women, it came to be a celebration of motherhood, enjoyed not just by women but by the whole of society, and was repeated again and again. The length of time between the birth and a woman's re-entry into church life through the churching ritual was determined by custom, canon law, and, probably, the health of the mother. This ritual indicated the month of the birth, and so the age of the heir. It developed to allow the mother to re-enter the church after childbirth and was a service in which many women participated. Although impossible to document (churchings generated no records), there should have been at least one churching per baptism of a live baby. Since actually the ritual should have been repeated for every case of childbirth that the mother

[48] Fisher, *Christian Initiation*,179.

survived, churchings ought to have been celebrated even for the large number of still births and deliveries of infants that did not achieve maturity. Conceivably there were many more churchings than live births and baptisms of live babies. Thousands of mothers should have been purified many times over, year after year. Some women were ineligible: barren and, in theory, unmarried women would not be churched. These were not insignificant in numbers: up to 40% of laywomen, it has been estimated, did not marry.[49] Moreover, the churching ceremony involved women other than the purified mother. All laywomen could participate in churching, even if peripherally, as they supported female relatives and friends, and most are likely to have done so many times.

Some women admittedly evaded the ritual and were prosecuted at archdeacons' courts for non-participation.[50] This evasion may have had a financial reason, since a fee was commonly charged. Giving gifts or money to the parson at the time of churching was not a requirement but an expected custom, despite a decree of 1293 that stated churching should be free.[51] Funding a feast may also have been a deterrent. A few churchwardens' accounts reveal how much churchings cost, and thus how many there were. At Scarborough (Yorks.) in 1435–36 each churching cost between 1½*d* and 3*d*. At Great Yarmouth (Norf.) in 1452–53 takings of £1 14*s* 2½*d* indicate that the churchings totalled between 137 (at 3*d*) and 274 (at 1½*d*) in one year.[52] The £2 14*s* 8*d* received by the wardens of King's Lynn (Norf.) indicate that there were between 221 (at 3*d*) and 442 churchings (at 1½*d*) in 1487–88[53] – more than one churching (and therefore more than one baptism) a day. Churching was an extremely frequent rite of passage: yet another formal mechanism for meeting, celebration, and the transaction of business.

Birth and baptism, the proofs report, were joyful occasions. Churching also was often associated with celebrations. A royal churching was described by the Hungarian Leo of Rozmital.[54] Rozmital was a guest at the celebrations for the churching of Queen Elizabeth, wife of Edward IV. He described a ceremonial procession to the church, the return to an elaborate feast, and gifts distributed to the guests. Similarly William Cely in Calais wrote of a churching to George Cely in London in 1482. William Cely wrote that 'she [his wife] should have raiment [...] against her churching, as she had the other time'.[55] George Cely was expected to provide the finery for the churching feast, again.

For every pregnancy that a woman survived, she was purified. It was an important, if routine, ritual. Descriptions of the churching ritual appear in

49 B.A. Barr, *The Pastoral Care of Women in Late Medieval England* (Woodbridge, 2008), 83.

50 N.J.G. Pounds, *A History of the English Parish: the Culture of Religion from Augustus to Victoria* (Cambridge, 2000), 222–3.

51 Ibid.

52 *Catholic England: Faith, Religion and Observance before the Reformation*, ed. R.N. Swanson, (Manchester, 1993), 150–63.

53 Ibid.

54 *The Travels of Rozmital, 1465–67*, ed. M. Letts, Hakluyt Society 2nd ser. cviii (1957).

55 *The Cely Letters 1472–1488*, ed. A. Hanham, Early English Text Society 273 (1975), 167.

contemporary records and missals. In the Use of Sarum, it was the godmother's responsibility to ensure that the mother was churched.[56] Purification allowed the mother to re-enter the church after the birth of her child; she was forbidden to do so until the ceremony had taken place. The parish chrisom robe, when it had been borrowed, had to be returned, and this was done as part of the churching.[57] Because of the delay between birth and churching, it is probable that there was more than one robe available in a large parish. Churching also marked the time when a married couple could resume sexual relations:[58] an important event for the male jurors, all of whom were probably husbands. Mirk stated: 'For and she [the woman] have been at his [the husband] bed before, she must take her penance and he, both.'[59] Both were seen as equally culpable.

Breviaries record how the mother processed to the church, veiled, and probably accompanied by female relations and friends.[60] The brief ritual began with the priest meeting the woman at the church door, or at a special seat. The woman waited outside the church until the priest spoke the correct form of words. He then sprinkled the mother with holy water and led her by the right hand into the church saying 'Thou shalt purge me, oh lord, with hyssop'.[61] She then moved to the altar and gave a candle to the church. At the subsequent mass, the mother expected to receive the bread before the rest of the congregation.[62] Churching was a rite which linked every mother, from a poor peasant to a queen, and allowed women a central role.

Churchings in the proofs of age are reminders of the baptism by jurors who recall the central presence and purification of a mother in the church. In several of the proofs, the churching of the mother of the juror was witnessed a few weeks after the birth and this ritual was cited. Male witnesses recollected attending church for (or at least during) the actual churching ceremony, often having been present at the baptism, or saw the service happen while they attended mass or happened to be in the church for secular reasons. Isabel, the daughter of William Wight, was born about the time that the mother of John Bocking of Suffolk was purified in 1350. In July 1430, Thomas Boure remembered that the churching of his wife was on the same day as the heir's baptism. William Wreghte of Hartfield was in East Grinstead in Sussex when Thomas Seintcler, the heir, was born on 28 October 1401. He saw the mother churched on 11 November.[63] This was an

56 Fisher, *Christian Initiation*, 178.

57 Ibid. 178.

58 *Mirk's Festial: a Collection of Homilies by Johannes Mirkus (John Mirk)*, ed. T. Erbe, pt 1, Early English Text Society, extra series 96 (1905), 59.

59 Ibid.

60 K.L. French, *The Good Women of the Parish: Gender and Religion after the Black Death* (Philadelphia, 2008), 61.

61 Ibid.,164. Mirk also describes the priest taking the mother by the hand and leading her into the church, Erbe, *Mirk's Festial*, 59.

62 French, *Good Women*, 61–2.

63 *CIPM* xxii.325.

unusually short time between ceremonies – only two weeks. Thomas Hulnewode was in Thorpe-le-Soken (Essex) with Joan, his wife, when Walter Howse was baptised (16 May 1402) and he and his wife were there again for the mother's churching on 24 June, five and half weeks later.[64]

Similarly Robert Aston was in Selmeston in Sussex with his wife, Joan, when William Selwyne was baptised on 24 August 1403. He was present again for the churching of Alice, the mother, on 21 September – a more usual time span of four weeks.[65] Gifts were given to prospective jurors to aid remembrance. John Radeston remembered the gift of three ash trees in the wood of Corston (Wilts.) from John Inge to aid recollection of the baptismal date of John's daughter – 1 October 1355.[66] Five other jurors were each given one arrow after they had breakfasted with John Inge on the day of Margery Inge's churching, so that they would remember that date.[67] It is not clear why this was significant. The proofs reveal that churching also took place throughout the week: John Badcock attended the purification of the mother of Walter Fitzwalter on Tuesday, 20 July 1400.[68]

After the churching ritual came the celebration.[69] The mother had survived childbirth and associated fevers. Survival was worth celebrating. Simon Luscote used as a reminder the churching feast for Pernall, the mother of Alice St Omera, for a baptism on 25 March 1340.[70] Several proofs indicate how fathers prepared for the feast. John Ulshore remembered selling a pipe of red Gascon wine to the father of Robert Constable against the churching of the mother, at a cost of 100*s*. At the proof of age for John Kyriel (born 2 October 1307 at Walmer, Kent) Alexander Oxeneye remembered travelling to Ypres to buy 'whole cloths' to make new robes for Nicholas and Rose, the parents, for Rose's purification.[71] John Urbtiaco used the memory of a hunt in 1345 as a reminder. He and John Moelles took six bucks in Stoke Trister park (Som.) for the feast that followed the churching of John's wife: a further indication of the general celebrations. Will Barker remembered the churching and accompanying feast as the reminder for the birth of John Conquest in 1379.[72] It was not only the parents who prepared for the feast. John Bernard remembered giving John ap Harry, the grandfather of the heir, a pipe of Gascon wine (128 gallons) at the baptism for the churching of

64 *CIPM* xxii.328.

65 *CIPM* xxii.502.

66 *CIPM* xiii.45.

67 CIPM xiii.45. The jurors were William Drury, William Brouk, Robert Bosgrove, John Machon and John Tailour.

68 *CIPM* xxii.119.

69 H. Leyser, *Medieval Women: A Social History of Women in England 450–1500* (London, 1995), 130–31; P.J.P. Goldberg, 'Life and Death: the Ages of Man', in *A Social History of England 1200 – 1500*, ed. R. Horrox and W.M. Ormrod (Cambridge, 2006), 415.

70 *CIPM* x.289.

71 *CIPM* vii.19.

72 *CIPM* xviii.220.

Elizabeth, the mother. The proofs describe the gifts that were given to the mother, further emphasising the importance of the day. The wife of Richard Mansey gave a cock to Margaret Seyntcler at her churching on 11 November 1401.[73]

The mother was at the centre of the celebrations, both religiously and socially. Evidently husbands were expected to hold a feast as part of the celebrations.[74] Since witnesses were often of humbler birth, the churching data – and hence the feasts – apply not just to the elite but those of more modest rank. The rite was so popular that it survived the Reformation. With a small alteration to the words, the Catholic purification became the Protestant thanksgiving. A description of churching by Thomas Delony from c.1598 indicates a happy female gathering:

> Sutton's wife of Salisbury which had lately been delivered of a son, against going to church, prepared great cheer: at what time Simon's wife of Southampton came hither, and so did divers others of the clothiers' wives, only to make merry at the churching feast.[75]

This description shows that women continued to enjoy the female celebration of churching, despite changes in religious practice and belief. They were willing to travel relatively long distances to attend. The service still existed until well into the twentieth century.

Baptism and churching were therefore religious rituals in which women played prominent roles. The midwife was the link between the birthing chamber and the church. She alone could provide the information which dictated the fullness of the church baptismal service. Women participated in and were central to the churching ceremony. It was an important part of a woman's ritual and procreative life. While it can be argued that women were part of the other sacraments, churching was an important female rite. The proofs of age reveal that men, the only jurors, were conscious both of the ritual and of its concomitant feasting. That churching was fixed within a few weeks of the birth made it into a secular legal milestone: an indication of the birth date. Such memories show churching to have been a significant religious and secular occasion that touched every church and was constantly reiterated everywhere.

III

None of these churchings is recorded in other sources. Indeed none of the other services or witnesses in the proofs of age feature elsewhere. Some testimonies are so circumstantial that they read like eye-witness testimony. Proofs were governed

73 *CIPM* xxii.325.

74 French, *Good Women*, 64.

75 'The Pleasant History of Thomas of Reading', *The Works of Thomas Deloney*, ed. F.O. Mann (Oxford, 1912), 260. While the extract was written after the Reformation, the survival of the ritual suggests that women enjoyed participating in churching.

by a great deal of convention, just like the underlying ceremonies, but that really is the value of them today. They recount events that bore the ring of truth for people at the time. Robert Armburgh, for instance, did not try to traverse the proofs of age of the Sumpter girls.[76] They provide vivid insights to the many functions exercised each day by the medieval church. They remind that the parish church was a public building that housed many events, often arranged at short notice and simultaneously, that required frequent attendance by and beyond the parochial community, quite apart from the obligatory Sunday worship. That those involved in one service overlapped with attenders at another is hardly surprising in a small church like that at Little Somborne in Hampshire, consisting only of a nave and chancel. At least the aisleless St John's in Bristol had a crypt. Multiple altars and multiple staff were not luxuries. The proofs of age also remind just how many vital events and vital statistics are lost from late medieval England. Proofs of age are actually the principal evidence for the actual performance of church services and rites of passage, and almost the sole source for the churchings that were a universal feature of everyday medieval life – of every medieval parish church – and a symbol of the prominence of women in medieval religious practice and society. They demonstrate concretely how busy medieval churches were, with planned events (weddings, churchings, and arbitrations), unpredictable rites of passage (baptisms, funerals, requiem masses), month's and year's minds, and chantry masses squeezed in alongside the daily canonical hours. No wonder there was work for several priests (and clerks, choristers, and sextons) in every church.

76 Many other tactics were employed to secure their lands: *Armburgh Papers*, passim.

11

Retainers, Monks and Wine: Three Insights into Everyday Life

MICHAEL HICKS

Witnesses to proofs of age testified unconsciously to their assumptions, habits, and expectations across a whole range of topics. Such data illuminates aspects of everyday life and fills gaps in the formal record. This chapter demonstrates the utility of this material with reference to three contrasting themes: bastard feudalism, monasticism, and the wine trade. It is based on the published calendars xv–xxvi (1377–1447); since, however, proofs of age are a retrospective source that looks back 14, 16, or 21 years from the date of the inquiry, some data stretches even further back in time.

I

Historical knowledge of bastard feudalism, like most fifteenth-century topics, is imperfect. The classic sources popularised by K.B. McFarlane and N.B. Lewis are the indentures of retainer in peace and war sealed to mutual advantage between a lord and a retainer on a specific occasion and creating a contract for life.[1] This is the spirit usually inferred for less formal records, such as baronial letters patent that conferred annuities or appointments, their enrolments, or the mere listing of annuities in ministers' and receivers' accounts. What service the retainers performed is not generally specified in such sources, indentures of war being limited to one campaign. At another extreme of aristocratic entourages there was the household, for which the key functions – cook, butler, the chamber, and stable

[1] K.B. McFarlane, 'Bastard Feudalism', *BIHR* xx (1945), 26–9; N.B. Lewis, 'The Organisation of Indentured Retinues in Fourteenth-Century England', *EHR* xxvii (1945); see also J.M.W. Bean, *From Lord to Patron: Lordship in Late Medieval England* (Manchester, 1989). A complete edition of indentures of retainer hitherto unpublished is in 'Private Indentures for Life Service in Peace and War 1278–1476', ed. M.C.E. Jones and S.K. Walker, *Camden Miscellany* xxxii (1994), 1–190. Several have been discovered since 1994, e.g. A.J. Pollard, 'An Indenture between Richard Neville, Earl of Salisbury, and Sir Edmund Darell of Sessay, North Riding, 1435', *The Fifteenth Century* xiv (2015), 67–75; an indenture of 1474 of Richard Duke of Gloucester retaining Sir John Savile (d. 1482), www.savilehousehold.co.uk/the-saviles/html, accessed 8 December 2015.

– are inferred, for every lord needed to eat, drink, dress, and travel. The personnel are seldom identified.[2] Servants in action do crop up accompanying their lords, delivering messages, fighting, drawing up rentals, and delivering monies, but generally their functions have to be deduced. Similarly the reasons for such retaining tend to be explained in political terms, often correctly, like the 2,000 Stafford knots (badges or armbands) that Humphrey Duke of Buckingham had prepared at parliament time in London in 1454, or the appointment by George Duke of Clarence of Sir Robert Welles 'great captain of Lincolnshire' as steward of his lordship of Calceby (Lincs.) during the Lincolnshire Rebellion in 1470.[3] It is usually mere speculation that the lord wanted his men to riot, to overawe his enemies or determine elections, to make an impressive escort for him at parliament, to serve him at table, or to decorate the household. From 1390, moreover, the statutes of livery limited retaining to members of the household, lawyers, and estate officers, only peers being permitted to retain non-resident gentlemen and higher ranks, and then only for life. Occasional prosecutions for infringements are recorded,[4] but were the recruiting practices of the great really distinct from those of the gentry? The proofs of age can supply data to fill some of these gaps: not merely hard fact, but also insights to the spirit of service.

Inquisitions *post mortem* are excellent sources for the feudal tenures that may or may not have still constituted genuine bonds between lord and tenant. They inform more fully how sub-tenancies were exploited by the crown than what use was made of them by their immediate aristocratic lords. Just occasionally IPMs reveal the names of estate officers and annuitants, too. Proofs of age contain rather more of these kinds of information. It was common for lords and tenants to take the opportunity of the baptism to perform and receive homage and to swear fealty. In 1406, for instance, William Hartford did homage to William Lord Roos for a tenement at Belvoir (Leics.). Hartford had a certificate of homage to prove it. So had Simon Horne of Daventry (Northants.) for the homage that he performed to William Lord Zouche at Haringworth (Northants.). Two tenants did homage at the christening of their lord's son at Herstmonceux (Suss.). Homage was rendered to James Butler, Earl of Ormond for lands at Kivernoll held of the lordship of Kilpeck (Here.) and to Lord Zouche for a tenement at Selby.[5] In 1424 John Lely of Drax (Yorks.) took the homage of William Mascall and John Thomason for land that they had inherited. None of these certificates of homage now survives. Other proofs record how other notable godparents, the abbot of St Albans and bishop of Hereford, also took homages at christenings in 1413.[6]

2 There are a limited number of livery or check rolls, see K.B. McFarlane, *Nobility* (Oxford, 1973), 109–11; see also *The Household Books of John Howard, Duke of Norfolk*, ed. A. Crawford, Richard III and Yorkist History Trust (1992), xxxviii–xliii.

3 *Excerpta Historica*, ed. S. Bentley (London, 1831), 283.

4 G. McKelvie, 'The Legality of Bastard Feudalism: Statutes of Livery, 1390–c.1520', Winchester University, PhD thesis (2012), ch. 3.

5 *CIPM* xxiii.139, 140, 150, 316, 691; xv.160; xvii.430.

6 *CIPM* xxv.522; xxiv.125, 126.

Richard Basy is revealed as steward of courts and John Manby as doorkeeper of Middleham Castle to John Lord Neville in 1382.[7] Proofs also reveal that Ralph Earl of Westmorland, earl of Richmond for life, appointed Edward Skelton as his feodary of Richmond in 1418, that in 1408 Bishop Langley of Durham appointed John Halburn as his bailiff of Allerton, that in 1420 John Holgyls held a court in his capacity as (estates) steward of Sir Richard FitzWalter, in 1372 that 'the lady' of Sir Ralph Cromwell gave livery to John Grayne their gardener at Coningsby; and that in 1416 Edward Burnbury was councillor of Sir John Colshill. Were historians otherwise aware that the substantial gentry had councillors or councils? In 1398 Robert Northwood and Thomas Hurst were servants of the father of the baby John Frogenhale: rather menial service in Hurst's case, judging from his paltry reward of 4*d*.[8] This sort of information is useful, but it does not carry us very far.

The christenings recorded in the proofs brought together the families and connections of the aristocratic babies. There was considerable ritual to the baptismal service that demanded a parade of torches, ewers, basins, pots, towels, and bearers of each. Although each notice was extremely short, the font and often the church were decorated with red cloth, silken cloth, and cloth of gold. It was a display of wealth and splendour, that was clearly designed to impress not just local people – parishioners – but the eminent visitors who came to the sacrament. 'Many magnates' crowded around the font at Tattershall (Lincs.) in 1372.[9] When the earl of Warwick's son Richard was christened at Salwarpe (Worcs.) in 1382 by Henry Wakefield, bishop of Worcester, supported by the abbots of Evesham and Pershore, the prelates brought their own esquires with them.[10] So too did the abbots of Shrewsbury and Haughmond in 1383 for the baptism of Robert Corbet at Moreton Corbet (Salop.).[11] The christenings of Richard son of John Lord Strange of Knockin at the church of St Bartholomew the Less in Smithfield in 1381, of Edmund Holland later earl of Kent at Brockenhurst (Hants.) in 1382, and of John Mowbray the future duke of Norfolk at Calais in 1390 were particularly splendid occasions.[12] Philip Lord Darcy at Temple Hurst (Yorks.), Richard Lord Scope at Bolton (Yorks.), and William Lord Zouche at Harringworth (Northants.) commissioned as expensive displays as possible. Richard II's nephew John, the offspring of the king's half-brother John Holland and Elizabeth of Lancaster, earl and countess of Huntingdon, was born at the earl's palatial Dartington Hall in Devon and baptised in the parish church. Although John was a younger son, the ceremonial was very grand. The abbot of Tavistock and prior of Plympton were godparents, the prominent gentry Sir John Dynham, Sir John

[7] *CIPM* xviii.997.

[8] *CIPM* xvii.181; xxi.307; xxiv.129; xxv.129, 525.

[9] *CIPM* xvii.430.

[10] *CIPM* xviii.855

[11] *CIPM* xviii.1148.

[12] *CIPM* xviii.944, 979; xix.336. Edmund and John were then younger sons.

Pomeray, Peter Edgecombe, and John Hull esquires are recorded as attending, and there were 24 torch bearers amongst whom the earl's household men, John Hukston and Warin Berkeley, survived to testify at the proof of age 21 years later. In 1381 there were six torchbearers at the baptisms both of Alan Buxhull and, at Middleham (Yorks.), of John son of Ralph Lord Nevill.[13] Godparents and other guests brought attendants with them and sometimes their whole households. Henry Scrope was born at Bolton Castle and baptised nearby at St Oswald's chapel. His parents were Richard Lord Scrope of Bolton and Margaret, daughter of Ralph Earl of Westmorland by his first countess. Lord Scrope rode in person to Middleham Castle to secure as godmother Westmorland's second countess Joan Beaufort. His brother-in-law Henry 2nd Earl of Northumberland, husband of the earl's daughter Eleanor, and Sir Ralph Eure were the godfathers. As befitted such high-ranking sponsors of such a high-born baby, the earl and countess each gave him a gold cup as their christening presents and Eure 10 marks in gold. Northumberland was preceded to the chapel and castle by his sword, borne point uppermost by Brian Daywell, and was accompanied amongst others by the 23-year-old Nicholas Baildon on a stock gelding that the earl had given him.[14]

No wonder therefore that the father of the infant, and indeed others, took the opportunity to take homage, to make grants, to seal deeds, and to reconcile disputes.[15] When local notables met together to seal deeds, which has been interpreted as proof of political association or dependence,[16] they may have been convened instead or additionally for christenings of someone's baby, or even weddings or funerals. Even when the baby was a younger brother or sister, there was joy and celebration, and fathers especially seem to have been more approachable and easier to make peace with. The proofs indicate that christenings were often also lovedays.

Only one proof of age mentions the classic indenture of retainer, that of William Ryler of Brightwell by Sir Thomas Sackville at Stonor (Oxon.) in 1393 for life in peace and war for 10 marks a year. 'He knows the date by that of the indenture.'[17] Other formal retainers and annuities, not explicitly by indenture, do occur. Henry Percy, 1st earl of Northumberland, retained John Curson at a christening in 1397 and Gilbert Lord Talbot retained John Doff at Ightfield (Salop.) in 1401: how paid and whether for life was not recorded.[18] Lesser men of course rewarded on a more modest scale. Thomas Carlton clerk was granted a tenement for life for good service to Sir John Loudham. There are quite a lot of such gifts. Some such grants were quite formal: the tenement at Great Tey

[13] *CIPM* xviii.670; xxi.149; xviii.997.

[14] *CIPM* xxv.446; Griffin ap Harry also had his sword carried before him, *CIPM* xxiii.598.

[15] For dispute resolution, see M. Hicks, 'Reconciling Disputes: The Evidence of the Proofs of Age 1360–1447', www.blog.inquisitionspostmortem.

[16] M.C. Carpenter, 'The Duke of Clarence and the Midlands. A Study in the Interplay of Local and National Politics', *Midland History* xi (1986), 23–8.

[17] *CIPM* xx.265.

[18] *CIPM* xx.844; xxi.147.

(Essex) bestowed on Richard Abraham by Sir Walter FitzWalter in 1400 was by letter patent sealed with FitzWalter's armorial seal.[19] Thomas Coggeshall also used his seal of arms to grant a holding at Boreham (Essex) to his serf Henry Netley in 1417.[20] An armorial seal was rather grand for a mere gentleman like Coggeshall and certainly for the villein Netley.

Lords also made formal appointments of their estate officials and household men. In 1408 Sir William Skipwith retained John Trypoke of Harburgh (Lincs.) as his rent collector, an office Trypoke still occupied in 1429. In 1377 Robert Hawley, grandfather of the baby, retained John Rothwell clerk to hold his courts at Riby and elsewhere in Lincolnshire. In 1406 Sir John Skidmore appointed Gilbert Kilbrest as keeper of his park of Kentchurch for a four-year period at a fee of £2 and two gowns of livery each year. William Lord Zouche appointed William, Parker to be his parker of Harringworth Park (Northants.) in 1403. William Sallow was contracted for a year as *donsel* (a gentleman attendant) to the abbot of Abbey Dore in 1415. In 1409 Sir Gilbert Debenham retained John Cukhook for life as his butler at five marks (£3 6*s* 8*d*) a year and two gowns of a valet's livery. William Davy and Thomas Kene remembered the birth of Robert Poynings in 1382 because both had been retained the previous year of counsel with a robe and a pension by written instrument of the baby's father, Richard Lord Poynings.[21] Unexceptional in type, these grants are of interest since they relate to landholders whose status was the lowest rung of the peerage or below. It is also of interest to find reference to formal deeds making unseen appointments about which we normally know nothing.

The proofs also record another aspect of service: default and punishment. Two accountants built up arrears due to their masters. Whereas Sir John Pomeray acquitted his receiver William Rider at the Holland christening, John Weryng's debt was not drawn to his master's attention by his auditors, who committed him instead to Exeter gaol.[22] Presumably he had entered a recognizance on taking up office. Such events remind that good service was required and checked up upon – the lord's resources must not be misappropriated by his officers – and that here were penalties for default; also, in this case, that day-to-day oversight and some quite serious responsibility was delegated by the lord to estate managers.[23] Who was really the lord?

All these arrangements so far comply with the statutes of livery and were therefore legal. One possible exception are grants for terms less than life. The statutes permitted the distribution of a lord's livery to those who were menial servants, estate officers, or learned in the law.[24] Edward Burnbury was of counsel

19 *CIPM* xxi.270; xxii.189.
20 *CIPM* xxiv.128.
21 *CIPM* xviii.316, 990; xxii.526; xxiii.140, 419, 596, 597.
22 *CIPM* xxiv.124; xxi.149.
23 McFarlane, *Nobility*, 51–3.
24 M.A. Hicks, *Bastard Feudalism* (Harlow, 1995), 130.

to Sir John Colshill. Not all these transactions, however, strictly complied with the statutes of livery. Only peers could retain those beyond these categories. Strictly speaking, the knight John Chandos, although lord of Fownhope in Herefordshire, should not have retained the esquire John Russell for life at a fee of 40*s* in 1410, nor should Sir Thomas Rempston have retained John Scarlet for life at a fee of £5 in 1406, nor in 1414 should Sir William Cromwell have retained Richard Northorp of Sausthorp. Was the John Curson who retained William Riselyn for his own life at 20*s* a year in 1413 the same John Curson who was retained by the earl of Northumberland 17 years earlier?[25] None of these offenders was called to account or prosecuted. They do not feature in the livery cases recorded in the court of king's bench. This suggests that the statutes themselves had little impact on actual practices. Livery was still distributed, whatever the law said. It was only when there was trouble that prosecutions ensued.

Of course these are the characteristic bastard feudal transactions – the extraordinary appointments that McFarlane and Lewis illuminated. We know, however, that the feeing of retainers was quite unusual.[26] They were too expensive. The scores of annuities of £20 or more bestowed by John of Gaunt, the richest medieval magnate, were exceptional elsewhere. Even those subsidised by the crown and bestowed by such wardens of the northern marches as the earls of Northumberland and Salisbury were generally more modest in value.[27] Actually the core of every connection was the household: indeed, bastard feudalism is really another name for service. The proofs contain constant references to servants, usually without stating functions. The most common function mentioned in the proofs of age is that of the butler, who had to provide wine for the godparents and others after the baptism, and thus crops up in the proofs of age. Hence we are particularly well informed about butlers. We can identify the butlers of Sir Robert Scales, of two priors of Deerhurst, of Margery Lady Moleyns, Sir Richard Berners, Sir Gilbert Debenham, Gilbert Denys, Henry Heton, John Lilburne, and John Veel.[28] John Druer served William Payn, Richard Parker served Sir Thomas Romsey, John Myste served Walter Romsey, and John Sly died in Sir Thomas Romsey's service.[29] Andrew Lambert was chief butler to John Lord Montagu for the baptism of Thomas Montagu, the future earl of Salisbury, at Shenley (Herts.) in 1388 (a serjeant of the buttery is also mentioned) and William Garvey was chief butler of the earl of Suffolk in 1397. Thomas Sharp held the stirrup of the earl of Warwick and held the earl's palfrey during the service.[30] Robert son of

[25] *CIPM* xxi.844; xxiii.139, 716; xxiv.567, 721.

[26] M.A. Hicks, *Bastard Feudalism* (1995), 29–32.

[27] J.M.W. Bean, *The Estates of the Percy Family 1416–1537* (Oxford, 1958), 85–98; A.J. Pollard, 'The Northern Retainers of Richard Nevill, Earl of Salisbury', *Northern History* xi (1976), 67–8.

[28] *CIPM* xviii.1123; xix.342, 347; xxi.672, 875; xxii.367; xxiii.417, 596, 721; xxiv.132. Berners' baker is also identified, *CIPM* xxii.367.

[29] *CIPM* xix.655; xx.843; xxiv.268.

[30] *CIPM* xix.655.

Robert Thorpe attended the christening at Croft (Yorks.) in 1381 in his capacity as chamberlain of the baby's grandfather John Clervaux.[31] Three chamberlains were present at Thomas Swinford's baptism in 1372: Gilbert de Beseby, chamberlain of Katherine Swinford, mother of the baby; the unnamed chamberlain of John Worksop clerk, Thomas's godfather; and the chamberlain who failed to make the necessary preparations at Tattershall (Linc.) and was struck by his master, Sir Ralph Cromwell.[32] Edmund Pugeon was retained as chamberlain of the abbot of Pershore in 1403.[33] William Cramlington was steward of the household of Sir Thomas Umfraville in 1391 and William Smethcote was steward of the household of Roger Corbet in 1385.[34] In 1391 William atte Hull was employed by Sir William Bonville of Shute explicitly to carry messages for him throughout England, receiving as emoluments a robe and 20*s* a year.[35] In 1408 Robert Winsbury esquire rode with Sir Gilbert Gamage and Nicholas Knyvet rode with Sir John Pauncefoot, both to Rogiet church (Gloucs.); Richard Boteler was butler of Sir William Gamage. In 1409 William Parsons accompanied Abbot Richard of Abbey Dore.[36] Occasionally, however, it is stated explicitly that those checking the church decorations were the father's servants, that the messengers despatched to the priest, father, grandparents, and godparents were the father's servants, at least some of whom were generously rewarded, or that those bearing the torches, silverware, and wine from the baby's home were his servants. At the christening of Joan daughter of John St Aubyn at Combe Raleigh (Devon) in 1410, when William Faringdon and Walter Batston carried the water to fill the font, Gilbert atte Wood, Henry Frank, Walter Tracy, and Thomas atte Tone carried the bread and wine for the godparents after the baptism 'according to custom'. William Flay junior held the candle. John Hylman, John Hendy, and Henry Godford were despatched to fetch the godparents, and John Karswell to fetch the parish chaplain. Hylman, Hendy, and Godford staffed the St Aubyn household. Probably the others too.[37] Indeed most probably all performers of such tasks served the babies' parents. Such miscellaneous duties were the bread-and-butter duties of most of a lord's staff.

It is striking that there is no apparent differentiation between the peerage and the gentry. Great lords might have a buttery department rather than one individual butler, but everybody needed service in this area and all had a butler. There was a distinction in numbers, not in functions: one person in a genteel household equated to a department in an earl's establishment. One area where proofs of age do cast some light is in the estimated age of the jurors at the time of

[31] *CIPM* xviii.953.
[32] *CIPM* xvii.430, 576.
[33] CIPM xxii.674.
[34] *CIPM* xviii.1148; xix.1005.
[35] *CIPM*xx.131.
[36] *CIPM* xxiii.417, 598.
[37] *CIPM* xxii.823.

the proof of age, from which their age at the time of the baptism can be calculated. All the St Aubyn household men were in their twenties at the time. What is not clear is whether, 21 years on, they were still household servants. Alive, yes. Local, yes. Still committed to the family, yes. But still working in the same household? The same doubt applies to estate officers. Nor is it clear whether these servants had married or not. Household lists are static records, snapshots. The proofs do not clarify whether in this period household service was something performed by celibate young men, or a life-long career. Apart from wet nurses, recruited as required, well rewarded, and presumably therefore highly valued, no female servants feature in the proofs, not even the ubiquitous laundress.

All the duties described so far are decidedly civilian. In two cases, however, retainer was for war only. In 1400 Roger Erlich was retained at Wooton with John Croft esquire to serve for one year in the safekeeping of the Scottish marches: which is particularly interesting evidence of subcontracts on the Scottish border.[38] It was for the French war in 1413, however, that John Brugge of Staunton on Wye was retained by John Lord Talbot (the future earl of Shrewsbury) for a year in peace and war.[39] Baptisms are dated by the battle of Shrewsbury in 1403, a well-known event,[40] and by Lollard rebellions, but this is not where the proofs tell us anything new. Proofs in the marches of Wales took place in a land of war, where Prince Henry rode through Little Dewchurch en route from Monmouth to Hereford and where John Andrew, mercer, was robbed of his goods by Welsh rebels at Catsash. Despite such perturbations, the christening at Rogiet nevertheless took place.[41] Otherwise unrecorded conflicts are recorded with the Scots: in 1410 when Richard Bardell's brother was killed, in 1412 when Nicholas Egremont was captured, and when John Lamonby was slain (in 1424?). At Ilfracombe (Devon) in 1421 raiding Bretons nearly captured William Orchard's ship.[42] Such incidents that are scarcely recorded elsewhere are very small additions to the history of the wars in which fifteenth-century England engaged: like the novels of Jane Austen, one would hardly know of the wars from the proofs of age. Wars were fought elsewhere, yet explain plenty of the premature deaths in the inquisitions *post mortem*. War featured most, as one would expect, on the borders and marches, yet these small incidents indicate how it impinged.

II

A second and quite different topic that is illuminated by the proofs of age is the religious orders – monks, canons, nuns, and friars. Most religious lived in

38 *CIPM* xxii.357.
39 *CIPM* xxiv.125.
40 *CIPM* xxii.529: William Elys was wounded in the head and shin.
41 *CIPM* xxiii.140, 417.
42 *CIPM*. xxii.824; xzvi.143, 148, 334, 586.

monasteries, always consisting of churches, residential buildings arranged around cloisters, often substantial agricultural complexes, and the estates that funded them. Title deeds, often registered in cartularies, and ministers' accounts document the estates, obedientary accounts detail the internal economy, bishops' registers and visitation records reveal elections and the quality of management, and other aspects of monastic life emerge from service books, library inventories, tax assessments, and chronicles. In this list of potential sources the inquisitions *post mortem* feature relatively little. IPMs are preoccupied with deceased lay tenants of the crown and other feudal lords, not therefore, with undying religious corporations, but nevertheless monastic estates and advowsons do occur. A handful of leases, tithe disputes, and other landed matters crop up in the proofs of age.

The proofs also illuminate other aspects of monastic life outside the cloister. It was a late medieval commonplace that a monk 'out of his cloystre ... is likned till a fish that is waterlees'.[43] This geographical restriction was firmly rebutted by the religious themselves, even the enclosed orders, who knew well that they had estates to run, rents to collect, supplies to bring in, repairs to undertake, servants to employ, and all the other business affairs of important corporations that demanded the activity of cellarers, other obedientaries (officials), and superiors beyond the precinct. Often, therefore, obedientaries missed the church services, the burden of which was shouldered by the cloister brethren or sisters who were not officers. Friars, of course, lived in the world. Moreover, superiors (abbots and priors) had their own lodgings – sleeping and dining quarters separate from the common dormitory and refectory – the households to manage them, often other residences, and frequently estates separate from those of their monasteries. They were the public faces of their institutions. Chaucer's fictional lady prioress, attended by another nun and a chaplain (the nun's priest), went on a pilgrimage that necessitated mixing with lay people of both genders, various social ranks, eating and sleeping away from her priory. Chaucer's monk, the superior of a cell (a small dependent monastery), who often resided outside his priory, engaged with society, hunted, and went on pilgrimage. Cellarers and other obedientaries had rented properties to run, purchases to make both wholesale and retail, and employees to supervise. Monks and nuns outside their cloisters were familiar sights. Satirists deplored such departures from the original *Rule* and wanted the religious enclosed once more.

Proofs of age offer glimpses of monks outside the cloister. A limited range of themes are illuminated, but they occur nowhere else. Abbots and priors did not travel unaccompanied: servants, squires, and, especially, household officers, attended them at christenings. Moreover, a considerable number of monastic superiors are named and dated, supplementing even the comprehensive list

[43] *Works of Geoffrey Chaucer*, ed. F.N. Robinson, 2nd edn (London, 1957), 19; see also *Piers Plowman: the B Version*, ed. G. Kane and E. Talbot Davidson (London, 1975), 425 (Passus X 305–11). My former student Kay Stevenson showed this to be a commonplace.

published in 2008 by Professor David Smith.[44] Not all, however, appear authentic. All those named relate in some way, by date and topic, to the baptisms on which the proofs of age are focused.

Monastic churches were frequented by lay people. Baptisms could take place there. However, even the great normally took their new-born babies to the parish church for baptism: even to Bolton parish church rather than nearby Bolton priory. Out of 427 baptisms recorded in the proofs of age between 1377 and 1447,[45] only three were staged in monastic churches. Thus Robert de Vere, the future duke of Ireland, was christened at Earl's Colne priory (Essex) in 1362, Margaret Tretherf (née St Aubyn) at the Minoresses in London in 1415, and Ellen Sumpter in the baptistery at St Botolph's priory in Colchester in 1413.[46] This contrasts with other vital events, such as funerals/burials and marriages, which aristocrats quite commonly located in abbeys and priories. Patrons of monasteries often made the monastic churches into their hereditary burial place, such as the De Veres at Colne priory, the Bohuns at Llanthony Prima, the Mortimers at Wigmore abbey (Salop.), the De Clares and Despensers at Tewkesbury abbey (Gloucs.), and the earls of Salisbury at Bisham priory (Berks.).[47]

Proofs of age illuminate monasticism in two principal ways. First, some illuminate the aristocratic connections of the regular clergy and, indeed, the aristocratic circles in which they moved. They were often godparents and guests who were invited by or related to the parents, the feudal tenants-in-chief, who were generally aristocratic. Second, the proofs record other monastic details recalled by the witnesses to help them date the baptism. Sometimes these latter did relate to people attending the christening, often they did not, but all shed light on the social connections and memories of the witnesses rather than of the baby's parents.

Proofs of age sometimes record who conducted the christening, although often they leave unclear whether the priest was the rector/vicar, curate, or some other chaplain. Just occasionally outsiders undertook the task. In 1381 it was Henry Wakefield, bishop of Worcester, who baptised Richard Beauchamp, the future earl of Warwick, at Salwarpe (Worcs.). Four religious performed the actual christening. It was right at the start of his priorate that Adam Leverinton, prior of the Gilbertine mother house at Sempringham (Lincs.), baptised Henry Beaumont at

44 *Heads of Religious Houses: England and Wales*, iii, *1377–1540*, ed. D.M. Smith, 3 vols (Cambridge, 2008).

45 Many of these were younger sons and daughters, who later succeeded, which suggests that all offspring enjoyed the same welcome to Christianity. If so, this sample needs magnifying several times over to include all the parents' live births, even those that did not result in maturity.

46 *CIPM*; xv.889; xxii.415, 830.

47 M.A. Hicks, 'English Monasteries as Repositories of Ancestral Memory', in *Monuments and Monumentality across Medieval and Early Modern Europe*, ed. M. Penman (Donington, 2013), 229–30.

Folkingham (Lincs.) in 1381.[48] In 1425 the Cistercian abbot of Pipewell baptised William, future Lord Zouche, at Harringworth (Northants.).[49] In 1409 Prior Walter of Clifford (Here.) baptised Richard ap Harry at Turnastone.[50] An anonymous canon of Torre baptised Joan Wibbury at Tormaham in Devon in 1424.[51] It was far more common to act as godparents, even though religious were not meant to fulfil this office.[52] The majority of godparents were laymen or laywomen, relatives or friends of the parents. These religious were selected by the parents of the baby – because the individuals were personally known to them, on friendly terms, and respected by them. The baptism of Richard Beauchamp performed by Bishop Wakefield featured two Benedictine abbots, of Evesham and Pershore, as godparents. Altogether monks and canons acted as godparents on 37 occasions in these proofs of age: at approximately 1% of baptisms. With one exception, an anonymous canon of Alnwick in 1395,[53] all these godfathers were monastic superiors except for Nicholas [Stratton], prior of the abbey of Muchelney, in 1380 (and he became abbot in 1398).[54] This surely is because it was the abbots and priors who moved in high society in the provinces, who were known personally to the local aristocracy, and who were respected by them.

Fifteen of the 39 religious houses that supplied superiors as godparents were Benedictine.[55] All but Pilton and Deerhurst (which did not survive till the Reformation) were categorised as greater monasteries worth over £200 a year in 1536. Four godparents were Cistercian abbots, of Ystrad Marchall (Wales), Newnham (Devon), Pipewell and Revesby (Notts.), two priors were Cluniacs (Clifford (Here.) and Wenlock (Salop.), there were three Premonstratensian abbots from Alnwick (Northum.), Croxton (Leics.), and Torre abbeys (Devon), two Gilbertine priors from Chicksand and Sempringham (Lincs), two Arrouasian abbots from Lesnes (Erith, Kent) and Missenden (Beds.), and ten Augustinian priors.[56] That seventeen headed houses of canons regular is not perhaps surprising, as such canons often retained some parochial responsibilities. Only one Carthusian godparent, the prior of the more strictly secluded eremitic house at

48 Smith, *Heads of Religious Houses*, I, 604; *CIPM* xviii.998.

49 *CIPM* xxii.526. The abbot was either Thomas Burton or Stephen Ryshippe, Smith, *Heads of Religious Houses*, iii, 320.

50 *CIPM* xxiii.598. Not recorded by Smith, *Heads of Religious Houses*, iii, 234.

51 *CIPM* xxv.298.

52 J. Garrett, 'Spiritual Kingship, Godparenthood and Proofs of Age of Heirs to Northumberland Estates, 1401–1472', *Northern History* xlix (2012), 197.

53 *CIPM* xix.897.

54 *CIPM* xviii.858; Smith, *Heads of Religious Houses*, iii, 53.

55 Abbotsbury (Dors.), Bath cathedral priory, Colchester St John's abbey, Deerhurst (Gloucs.), Evesham (Worcs.), Gloucester St Oswald's priory, Malmesbury (Wilts.) and its cell Pilton (Dev.), the alien priory of Loders (Dors.), Milton (Dors.), Muchelney (Soms.), Pershore (Worcs.), Peterborough (Northants.), Selby (Yorks.), and Tavistock (Dev.).

56 Breamore (Hants.), Chacomb (Northants.), Colchester St Botolph (Essex), Darley (Derb.), Drax (Yorks.), Kenilworth (Warw.), Launceston (Corn.), Maiden Bradley (Wilts.), Newark (Notts.) and Plympton (Devon).

Witham (Soms.), officiated. Two categories are wholly missing. No friars were godfathers. Were they not asked – an indication perhaps that it was not in aristocratic circles that they operated – or, alternatively, did friars refuse such invitations? The other category was superiors of female orders, abbesses and prioresses, none of whom acted as godmothers. This could be put down to sexism, that fathers did not select nuns; but mothers seem also to have exercised some choice in godparents and did not pick them either. More probably the absence of nuns indicates that abbesses and prioresses did not interact much with aristocratic ladies. Remember the expectation that female houses were more strictly enclosed, and also the sheer poverty that many non-Benedictine nunneries endured. The poorest male monasteries also supplied few godfathers to the aristocracy whose heirs were most commonly proved of age.

It was an onerous responsibility to be a godparent, the making of the new-born infant into a Christian capable of salvation, and carried it with it responsibilities thereafter. Few of these superiors lived to see their charges come of age. Whilst many came from the immediate locality to the ritual, all needing to drop any other activity in order to attend at once, some did come from further afield. Certainly they did not come unaccompanied. The proofs record that servants came with the prior of Kenilworth in 1377, the esquires John Power on behalf of the prior of Worcester in 1382 and Robert Irthingborough with the abbot of Missenden in 1384, a donzel with the abbot of Dore and the juror John Micheldever with the prior of Muchelney.[57]

A substantial christening gift was expected of godparents that befitted the status of the baby and the religious house. John Prior of Worcester gave a silver goblet worth £5 in 1382; Thomas Culling, abbot of Tavistock [1381–1402], gave a gold cup decorated with gold latticework containing £10 and another £1 to the nurse;[58] John Legge, Cistercian abbot of Newnham [1391–] gave a silver gilt cup worth £5 with £10 of money in it;[59] John Shealdon, prior of Plympton [1378–88] gave £20; William Forrester, the Augustinian prior of Deerhurst [1399–], gave a silver cup with cover, 6*s* 8*d* to the wet nurse, and two silver vessels of sweet wine; and the abbot of Torre gave £2 and to the wet nurse a further 6*s* 8*d*. Apparently a gift to the wet nurse was normal: the abbot of Milton also gave 6*s* 8*d* to the godmother in 1433. These were substantial sums, especially if multiplied: the Deerhurst gift – and the priors are recorded officiating twice – may have been a substantial chunk of the priory's income. Three superiors were tackled on the christening day by fathers of other new-born infants: summoned as guest to the christening of Joan Wibbury in 1424, the abbot of Torre did actually stand sponsor also to the sons of John Fursse and John Strecche, both baptised in the

57 *CIPM* xviii.855, 858. No John was prior at this date; Walter Legh was 1370–88, Smith, *Heads of Religious Houses*, iii, 86.

58 *CIPM* xviii.855; xxi.149; Smith, *Heads of Religious Houses*, iii, 86.

59 Smith, *Heads of Religious Houses*, iii, 316; *CIPM* xx.130.

same church on the same day, and gave the latter £1.[60] Another abbot of Milton (Dors.) in 1361 at Dawlish declined, on the spurious ground that he could not act twice in one day.[61] Was the cost of being a godparent a reason for refusing this honour?

All the data so far was imparted by the witnesses – for whom evidently the presence in their church of abbots and priors was unusual enough to be worthy of remark. All such references relate to baptisms, whether the superiors conducted the service or were godparents. They are never reported in other guises, conducting marriages, funerals, or masses, presumably because they never fulfilled these functions in parish churches. In their monastic churches they did. The choice of baptiser and godparent lay with the parents of the aristocratic baby and reveals something of the integration of monastic superiors into provincial aristocratic society. Religious also appeared on four occasions in disputes that were arbitrated in parish churches at the same time as baptisms. These were in their capacities as landlords and tithe holders.[62]

There are a considerable number of other references to religious that do not relate directly to the christening, but were aides memoires for the proof jurors. These offer insights into the society from which the jurors were drawn – which was less socially selective. Seldom aristocratic, never women or clergymen, such jurors ranged from the middling sort to mere labourers and menial domestics. The religious were attached to 21 different monasteries – half the number who supplied godparents – and were significantly different. Only six houses feature on both lists. There were Benedictine houses – Colchester St John, Dorchester (Oxon.), Malmesbury, a Cluniac house (Wenlock), and the Minoresses, but there were no Gilbertines or Carthusians or alien houses. Also on this list are the Cistercian houses of Bordesley (Warw.), Fountains and Salley (Yorks.), the Augustinian priories of Carlisle (cathedral, Cumb.), Daventry (Northants.), Haughmond (Salop.), Launde (Notts.), Studley (Worcs.), and Thornton (Lincs.), and the Premonstratensians of Torre (Devon). There were two nunneries, Arthington and Nuncoton (Yorks.), and five friaries – the three Franciscan houses of Babwell, Exeter, and Salisbury, and two Carmelite houses.[63] Not only were there fewer to be categorised as major houses and from enclosed orders, but they included, in the canons regular and friars, orders that had more pastoral missions.

Eleven jurors had sons who professed as monks, canons, or friars. Three did become friars, but nobody else is recorded as joining poorer houses. Several indeed

[60] *CIPM* xviii.855; xx.130; xxi.149, 875; xxi.149; xxi. 418; xxiv.418; xxv.132, 298. Smith, *Heads of Religious Houses*, ii, 172; iii, 86, 316.

[61] *CIPM* xv.663.

[62] See M. Hicks, 'Reconciling Disputes: The Evidence of the Proofs of Age 1360–1447', www.mappingthemedievalcountryside.ac.uk

[63] *CIPM* xv.660, 893; xvi.947; xviii.311; xix.785; xxii.228, 363; xxiii.309, 310, 721; xxv.127, 614.

joined major houses – Malmesbury, Colchester St John, and Dorchester abbeys (all Benedictine), Wenlock priory, Carlisle cathedral priory, and Haughmond abbey (Augustinian). On this evidence no class bar excluded the middling sort from monasteries that offered comfortable livings, but did the hordes of poorer houses recruit from below the level of such jurors? Five elections of monastic superiors are noted, two prelates with different surnames from those jurors who remembered them from Carlisle cathedral priory and Dorchester abbey, and two prioresses of the Yorkshire nunneries of Arthington and Nuncotom. Agnes (née Willesthorp) was sister of a juror. Elizabeth Skipwith was presumably a relative of the baby William Skipwith:[64] further evidence perhaps that the impoverished northern nunneries recruited from an unexpectedly elevated social group, the wealthy Anglo-Saxon abbeys being confined to the South. Thomas Blisworth, brother of the wife of Thomas Stotsbury esquire, was made Augustinian abbot of Chacomb in 1401.[65] Similarly John Clyve's brother-in-law John Langridge became prior of the charterhouse of Witham in 1400.[66] That aristocrats also entered religion and quite frequently became superiors is revealed by their family genealogies, but they do not feature in the proofs of age. Five witnesses reported burials in monastic churches: three sisters and a grandmother in the male houses of Daventry and Launde and in two friaries, the Franciscans of Salisbury and the London Carmelites, and Robert Malinson at Thornton abbey in 1408.[67] If not indicating that such burial sites were commonplace, they do indicate once again that juror families could aspire to such burial locations.

A dozen other references perpetuate casual meetings in churchyards, visits to monasteries to visit particular inmates, a meal given by the abbot of Bordesley to the prior of Studley, the purchase of a horse, and leases, the everyday encounters of everyday society. Clearly it was not unusual for aristocrats to encounter monks outside their cloisters, whether deliberately or accidently.

One final point, however. There are no references to religious in the final calendared volume, covering 1442–47. Is this significant – evidence perhaps of a drastic fall in the reputation of religious superiors or the visibility of religious in everyday society? – or merely a statistical quirk. There are only 27 proofs of age for this quinquennium. An answer may emerge when the IPMs for 1447–85 are calendared.

64 *CIPM* xv.419, 893; xxv.127, 614. Agnes was not recorded in Smith, *Heads of Religious Houses* iii, 624. However a Katherine Wilestrop was prioress 1475–84, ibid. iii, 624.; for Skipwith, abbess 1440, see ibid. iii, 677.

65 He is not recorded and rather unlikely, as Edmund Thorpe was abbot 1371–1411 and Thomas Brackley was abbot 1412–18, Smith, *Heads of Religious Houses*, iii, 409.

66 *CIPM* xxi.871, 876.

67 *CIPM* xv.656; xxiii.308, 316, 415, 419.

III

Another quite different area that the proofs of age illuminate is the material possessions of late medieval aristocrats: for the baby was already, or in time became, heir to a feudal estate, however small. The font itself belonged to the parish and was a fixture in every parish church, but the decorations for the church, the torches of wax (and torch-holders), the water jug and bowl for washing of hands, the wine-holder and beakers that were necessary accoutrements to late-medieval christenings were supplied by the infant's family, often explicitly brought in procession from the neighbouring manor house.[68] Such vessels were often explicitly silver: for humbler babies they may have been pottery or treen and the tapers dipped in tallow. Moreover, the office of godparent carried with it the expectation of christening gifts: two cups of silver or adorned with silver were especially common.[69] One or four or even six cups are less usual: perhaps all drank from the one silver goblet at Morpeth Castle in 1408.[70] Although far from systematic, therefore, and indeed far from comprehensive, the proofs of age indicate a universal set of rituals, with some regional variations, and the availability and penetration of some manufactures, some at least imported. Of course English bees did produce wax, but it was imported wax from Poland that was traded in largest quantities.[71]

Wine is another commodity that features commonly in proofs of age. Normally it was served to the godparents in the church after the service,[72] sometimes also to others at the ceremony,[73] either in the church or gathered outside. Red wine was for general consumption; a sweet wine – a more expensive luxury – apparently for the godparents only. For some, any kind of wine was a special drink with which they were unfamiliar. At Edvin Loach (Worc.) in 1392 the intoxicated witnesses could scarcely walk from the church.[74] Sometimes wine was specially purchased for the mother[75] or laid up for her churching. Indeed the quantities donated towards the churching, a whole pipe of 128 gallons on three occasions, suggest that churchings could be much larger celebrations than the baptism itself.[76] Unlike baptisms, they could be scheduled precisely in advance. Perhaps such gifts also anticipated difficulties in obtaining supplies 40 days hence. Wine

68 E.g. Burpham (Surr.), Colwich (Staffs.), Barton Blount (Derb.) and Stoke Poges (Bucks.), *CIPM* xxi.370, 875, 948; xxv.227.

69 E.g. *CIPM* xix.655; xxii.223, 363, 672, 674, 678, 679, 680; xxiii.395, 416, 593, 717; xxiv.267–9, 273–4, 395, 562; xxv.128, 131.

70 *CIPM* xxiv.724.

71 W.A. Harwood, 'Trade and Consumption Patterns in Central Southern England: The Supply of Iron and Wax to Winchester College', *Southern England* xxix (2007), 14.

72 *CIPM* xxi.758; xxii.223, 226.

73 *CIPM* xix.655; xx.270; xxi.875, 882, 948; xxii.363.

74 *CIPM* xx.263.

75 *CIPM* xvii.1319; xxv.295.

76 *CIPM* xix.780; xvi. 196, 241.

was a topic commonplace enough to become stereotyped. There are quite a few duplicate testimonies.[77] Most are more individual. A few indeed are so remarkable that it is not surprising that they were remembered. In 1372, for instance, William Hammond dropped one of the two jars of wine he was carrying and was beaten in consequence by his master, Jude Sireby. Moreover, John Shilston, riding in search of sweet wine from Bigbury to Plymouth across an inlet of the sea, was nearly drowned by the rising tide.[78]

The proofs of age cast light on the wine trade by answering the question how did the wine reach the christening.

Historians are quite well informed about the supply side of the wine trade. The customs levied by the English government have enabled wine imports to be charted in total year by year and port by port, e.g. Bristol, Exeter and Dartmouth, Plymouth and Fowey.[79] Whereas 50,000 gallons of Gascon wine was carried overland from Southampton – and not infrequently 100,000 – the comparative imports of sweet wine were 1,000 gallons a year, rising on occasion to 2,500.[80] Substantial amounts of this luxury product were consumed, but much less is known about consumption than about supply. Few of the accounts kept by great households survive today, and indeed the most systematic, of Durham cathedral priory and Cambridge university colleges,[81] were hardly representative. Distribution and consumption are areas where proofs of age can make a small but significant contribution.

Because Gascon wine was carried by sea to a range of ports, directly or by coastal shipping, it was readily accessible almost everywhere as the proofs of age, which cover the whole country, demonstrate. For south-central England, the remarkable Southampton brokage books record the transmission of such wine overland to 167 destinations both close by and as far afield as Bristol, Gloucester, Coventry, and London. This was bulk traffic. On arrival at the designated destination, the wine was decanted into smaller casks or more diminutive receptacles for delivery to smaller towns, to customers such as aristocratic fathers, for sale at the market, or for consumption in taverns. Very few consumers took whole tuns. Wine was heavy: it ceased to be economic to carry it overland further than 50 miles.[82] Moreover, Southampton's trading hinterland for wine ended where such other ports as Poole (Dors.), Exeter (Devon), and Bristol held sway.

What happened thereafter is documented in part by the proofs of age, which reveal wine consumption as routine throughout the kingdom, from the metropolis and great cities like Bristol to the extremes of the kingdom such as the Lizard,

[77] E.g. *CIPM* xxii. 226, 227, 229; xxi. 882, 923, 925, 948.

[78] *CIPM* xvii.573; xix. 343; xxvi. 146.

[79] *Studies in English Trade in the Fifteenth Century*, ed. E Power and M.M. Postan (1933), 330–60.

[80] Harwood, 'Commodities: Wine', 12.2, 12.14.

[81] M. Threlfall-Holmes, *Monks and Markets. Durham Cathedral Priory 1460–1520* (Oxford, 2003); J.S. Lee, *Cambridge and its Economic Region 1450–1560* (Hatfield, 2005).

[82] Ibid. Maps 5 and 6.

the marches of Wales, and many other rural locations. Some insight into the retail wine trade also emerges from the accounts of those English towns and other institutional customers (like Winchester College) that entertained royal judges on circuit and royal courtiers, whose favour they sought, and their own legal counsel with gifts of wine (and often fish), the wine measured in small numbers of gallons.[83] Winchester College purchased its communion wine in smaller parcels, gallons, from local suppliers, some of whom – like John Coteler – received large consignments by cart from Southampton as recorded in the brokage books.[84] Remember that medieval wine had a short shelf life: it did not keep and needed to be consumed within a year. There was no point in stockpiling large quantities in one's cellar for future years. The aristocratic parents of the babies in the proofs of age did drink wine at least occasionally – hence the large numbers of butlers recorded in the proofs of age. For christenings they needed to draw on what they had to hand or purchase it locally at short notice. Usually they had stocks of the few gallons required – measures, vessels, gallons – failing which they could be purchased retail in every locality. Sometimes ale was provided, on at least one occasion mead, together with bread, cake, or miller bread.[85]

Trade in the rarer sweet wines was different. Clarey, osey, Romney, bastard, malmsey, tyre, hippocras had been imported in smaller quantities, through fewer ports, and were more costly. Originating in the Mediterranean and Atlantic islands, the sweet wines were conveyed to England principally by the Italians, for whom Southampton was the main port of entry. The Italians did not frequent ports west of Southampton or north of London. From Southampton, sweet wines were carried to only fourteen destinations.[86] Surely therefore sweet wines percolated as a matter of course in smaller quantities than Gascon wine to far fewer locations and retailers? Yet sweet wine was normally served at these christenings. Fathers of new-born babies had often to secure supplies at short notice, frequently from quite far away.

A few proofs cast light on the specifics of supply. Every aristocratic christening required wine, and that wine was not necessarily in stock: indeed the more luxurious sweet wines were almost certainly not in stock. How did wine reach the extremities of the kingdom? All of it came by sea, from Gascony or the Mediterranean, to such ports as Bristol, London, and Southampton, but what then? It was wine probably shipped to Southampton (but possibly Poole in Dorset) and carted to Wimborne (Dors.) that was retailed 'off the shelf' for

[83] E.g. M. Hicks, *Edward V: The Prince in the Tower* (Stroud, 2003), 63; Alexander Brondarbit has used such data to chart the efforts of the Cinque Ports to ensure intercession by their chosen power-brokers, 'Cultivating Power in Yorkist England: Political Patronage and the Cinque Ports, 1461–1485', *Southern History* 37 (2015), 29–39.

[84] Harwood, 'Commodities: Wine', 88; see also A.R. Brondarbit, 'Cultivating Power in Yorkist England: Political Patronage and the Cinque Ports, 1461–1485', *Southern History* 37 (2015), 29–30, 34.

[85] *CIPM* xviii.1123; xix. 342; xxi.370; xxii.368, 561, 823; xxiv.267.

[86] Harwood, 'Commodities: Wine', 125.

a christening at Canford near Poole. Bigbury in North Devon was supplied from the nearby South Devon port of Plymouth, and Tawstock from the almost adjoining North Devon port of Barnstaple, both apparently stocked by sea. A father at Lockington in the East Riding of Yorkshire bought his wine at Beverley, which in turn must have been supplied from Hull. The wine for two christenings at Chillingham in Northumberland was purchased in Newcastle: not at the much closer market towns of Alnwick, Morpeth, Rothbury, or Wooler, where, presumably, sweet wine was not in stock. Ordinary wine was imported direct at both Hull and Newcastle and was customed there. There were several links even in this simple chain from vineyard to goblet. How did the wine consumed at Wichenor in Staffordshire arrive? It was bought in the cathedral city of Lichfield, a substantial town with a market and a range of tradesmen. But Lichfield itself was almost as far from the sea in England as it was possible to be. Was it supplied with wine via the rivers Trent and Humber via Hull and to them by sea via London from Gascony and the Mediterranean? The wine consumed at Pentridge (Here.) was procured from the minuscule centre of Monnington on the River Wye.[87] Presumably it had come upriver from Bristol via Chepstow and was transhipped at the point where the River Wye ceased to be navigable. Wine, even sweet wine, *could* be obtained everywhere, sometimes from small suppliers in very small centres, who might nevertheless handle substantial amounts. All these middlemen took their cut, of course. The pipe of red Gascon wine that John Ulshowe at Holme in Spalform (Yorks.) procured in 1423 cost the substantial sum of £5: this £10 per tun compares with £4 to £7 per tun current at Southampton.[88] Wine was more of a luxury commodity inland than at the quayside.

IV

The testimonies in the proofs of age were prompted by the demand for reminders that located baptisms in time. The christenings themselves were special occasions of course, especially these instances that involved local notables – peers, landlords, masters, and employers – and especially grand ceremonial. What was remembered varied: the later witnesses often further amplified those that had already testified. It follows that there are many proofs of age that make no reference to bastard feudalism, to the regular clergy, or to the drinking of wine. Those that did provide a snapshot, sometimes of the remarkable, more often of the commonplace. Collecting these memories together provides insights to these three topics: never enough to reveal the whole topic, but often enough particular perspectives on it that are available nowhere else. Deller's paper (chapter 9) indicates the range of material. More can be made of this scrappy material when it is properly collated with other sources and secondary literature. This chapter

87 *CIPM* xvii 1319; xix. 342, 780, 784, 999; xix 780, 999; xxvi 146
88 *CIPM* xxvi.241; Harwood, 'Commodities: Wine', 119.

has revealed how the gentry aped the retaining of their superiors, when and how familiar were monks in local society, and how exotic wines had penetrated into the most remote locations. Future full-scale studies of bastard feudalism, the religious, and the wine trade will now need to take account of the proofs of age. These three studies, however, are mere samples of the potential of this under-exploited source. There are other topics that they can be made to illuminate that deserve further exploration.

12

The Administration and Efficiency of the Inquisitions Post Mortem Process: A Case Study of Northumberland

Janette Garrett

Government in late medieval England was a highly advanced system for its time and one of the most sophisticated in Europe.[1] From its centre at Westminster, the king's command travelled to the most remote areas of his realm. Nevertheless, the government lacked the infrastructure to function independently in the shires. There the operation of government and administration relied on the voluntary participation of the local landed élites. Moreover, Professor Ralph Griffiths has argued, the capacity of English kings was limited by the geography of the kingdom. Much of the realm was too distant, too large, too complex and too expensive to be governed effectively.[2] Historians' understanding of the government of England's most northerly county has suffered particularly from this notion of remoteness and royal weakness. Yet the county of Northumberland outside the liberties was no different from any other shire in terms of the range of officials who were appointed to protect the king's interests and to manage affairs in his name.[3] Professor Anthony Pollard has explored this subject in relation to key officers in north-eastern England during the second half of the fifteenth century, the period of greatest interest.[4] This chapter takes another perspective on the relationship between periphery and centre by exploring how Northumbrian society interacted with royal administration through the lens of the IPM process. The local officer was the escheator, an office last comprehensively examined more than half a century ago.[5] The distance in geographical miles between Northumberland

[1] A.L. Brown, *The Governance of Late Medieval England 1272–1461* (London, 1989), 1. I would like to thank Professor M. Hicks for his help in the preparation of this chapter; and Dr D. Newton and Professor A.J. Pollard for their earlier comments on the work from which it is taken.

[2] R.A. Griffiths, 'The Provinces and the Dominions in the Age of the Wars of the Roses', in *Estrangement, Enterprise and Education in Fifteenth-Century England*, ed. S.D. Michalove and A.C. Reeves, 2nd edn (Stroud, 1998), 1–25.

[3] H.M. Jewell, *English Local Administration in the Middle Ages* (Newton Abbot, 1972), 100–2, 145–7, 153–7, 182–99.

[4] A.J. Pollard, *North-Eastern England during the Wars of the Roses: Lay Society, War and Politics 1450–1500* (Oxford, 1990), 144–72.

[5] E.R. Stevenson, 'The Escheator', in *The English Government at Work, 1327–36*, ed. J.F. Willard et al., 3 vols (Cambridge, Mass., 1940–50), ii.109–67.

and Westminster, this paper suggests, is too rudimentary and inadequate a measure. This paper uses the Northumberland IPMs to survey firstly the management of the process at a local level and secondly its interaction with chancery at Westminster. The proofs of age are specifically excluded from discussion.

I

Northumberland's escheators were leading gentry who often acted as sheriffs and justices of the peace. Normally they served for one year only.[6] Exceptions were William Strother of Bolton, who acted for more than four years, taking the place of successive escheators who failed to account, and Robert Rhodes, who was in post for three consecutive years from November 1434 to 1437.[7] Some also held high office in Newcastle. Laurence Acton was selected escheator for Northumberland in November 1431, the only county position that he ever held, but he juggled this responsibility alongside his work as the town's MP and its mayor for the second time. A few had specialist knowledge through a professional career, for example the lawyers Robert Whelpington and Robert Rhodes. Robert Wetwang had held a lower rank in local government as a searcher of ships in Newcastle and along the north-eastern coast. John Beer had developed relevant skills elsewhere as customer of Berwick and receiver of the castle and lordship of Bamburgh.[8]

The escheator's workload was quite light – normally between one and three inquisitions *post mortem* per term of office – but the random nature of mortality meant that there was no guarantee. Even the busiest period, during March to October 1422, resulted in just seven new IPMs and two supplementary proceedings. In practice, an escheator's responsibilities commenced and terminated a little later than the dates of appointment enrolled on the Fine Rolls suggest. Edward Bertram, for example, conducted an IPM for Joan Bromflete on 3 November 1434, the same day that Robert Rhodes was identified in Westminster as his replacement. Time was needed for the new escheator to be sworn before an official handover could take place, which seems to have taken between two and three weeks.

The IPM process began after the death of the feudal tenant with the issue by chancery by a writ *diem clausit extremum (dce)* commanding the escheator to seize the individual's property held and to convene an inquisition *post mortem*, after which the escheator conveyed his findings to chancery at Westminster.

6 Carpenter, 'Introduction', *CIPM* xxii.9.

7 *List of Escheators*, List and Indexes ix (1909), 107.

8 *List of Escheators*,107; C.H. Hunter Blair, 'The Mayors and Lord Mayors of Newcastle upon Tyne', *Archaeologia Aeliana* 4th ser. 18 (1941), 14–5; idem, 'Members of Parliament for Newcastle upon Tyne', loc. cit. 4th ser. 14 (1937), 37–8, 44–5; *CFR 1437–45*, 16; *CPR 1441–46*, 206, 219, 235.

Whenever the heir was of full age, chancery issued a writ for livery of seisin to the escheator to transfer possession of the estate from the crown to the heir.

At least in theory, the first tasks for the escheator upon receiving a writ *dce* were to arrange a suitable location to hold an inquisition and to request the sheriff to summon a jury. In the interests of transparency, IPMs were held in 'open places'. Northumberland's IPMs were arranged at eleven locations. The towns of Alnwick, Corbridge, Morpeth, and Newcastle were utilised throughout the period to varying degrees. The royal castle at Newcastle was by far the most frequently used venue, which no doubt added gravitas to the proceedings. Less frequently, inquisitions were held at market towns to the north and west of Newcastle. Morpeth was the base for seventeen gatherings, Alnwick for eight, and Corbridge in Tynedale for ten.[9] Sites based in more northerly areas were chosen on just one or two occasions. Two IPMs were also conducted south of the river Tyne, at Newbiggin and Hart, for members of the aristocratic Beauchamp and Clifford families, whose lands the crown still regarded as part of Northumberland rather than of the palatinate of Durham.[10] Unfortunately, IPMs taken outside the walls of the royal fortress at Newcastle do not specify the actual meeting place. The crown and substantial landholders may have made space available within major castle complexes at Alnwick, Bamburgh, Morpeth, Rothbury, and Wark-on-Tweed, but evidently suitable accommodation was available in market towns. Rooms may also have been found at village inns.[11]

As the popularity of Newcastle as a meeting place indicates, IPMs were not always held near the estates of the deceased. Thomas Heselrigg, for example, had held the manor of Eslington and half the vills of Whittingham, Thrunton, and Barton, all within nine miles of Alnwick, but his inquisition was taken at Newcastle. Local jurors might face a considerable trek to fulfil their duty, although any annoyance may have been mitigated a little by the opportunity to attend to a variety of private matters in the town. Nor were IPMs necessarily convened close to the tenant's lands or at Newcastle. Although William Young's sole estate was the manor of Throckey, approximately six miles west of Newcastle, his inquisition was held at Corbridge in Tynedale, twice that distance. John Clavering had possessed the manors and vills of Calally and Yetlington, approximately eight and a half miles west of Alnwick, yet his IPM was held more than twenty miles away to the south, at Morpeth. Some IPMs are notable because the selected locations were so far away from the late occupier's property. Eleanor Ask had held a third of the manor of Jesmond, but her IPM was executed more than thirty miles further

9 E.g. *CIPM* xx.551; xxi.862; xxii.390.

10 *CIPM* xviii.775; xxvi.435.

11 C. Dyer, 'The Value of Fifteenth-Century Inquisitions *Post Mortem* for Social and Economic History', *IPM Companion*, 111. Almost a third of the total IPMs held outside Newcastle took place on the town's respective market day and the figure rises to a half for all those conducted at Morpeth, see S. Letters, *Gazetteer of Markets and Fairs in England and Wales to 1516*, 2 vols, List and Index Society Special Series 32–33 (Kew, 2003), ii, 268–73.

north, at Alnwick. Emma Craster's holdings consisted of the manor of Dilston and property at Corbridge in the west of the county, yet her IPM was conducted at Morpeth, in the east, which even by the most direct route, as the crow flies, is some forty miles.[12] Such distant venues were probably selected for the convenience of the escheator.[13] Although a statute of 34 Edward III had required the findings of an inquisition to be indented to prove a jury had been present, only a quarter of all Northumberland IPMs taken between 1422 and 1447 comply with the requirement. Where they are not indented, it cannot therefore be safely deduced that jurors were excluded from the process. A number of possible scenarios have been put forward in explanation. It is impossible anyway to tell whether IPMs held at the TNA that are now unindented were always so: seals were subsequently removed, and so may have been the indenting. Even an indented return is not in itself unassailable proof that a jury attended an inquisition. The *Paston Letters* relate an instance where an IPM had not been taken, but credence was given to the pretence in the submission of an indented return.

A few local IPMs suggest that malpractice was more widespread. Sir John Widdrington (d.1444), cannot have held the manor of Widdrington (and other properties) of Henry Lord Scrope of Upsall, who had been executed for treason in 1415; it was of Scrope's brother John (d.1452) that he actually held it. The jurors also found Widdrington to have held other lands in Cresswell and Ellington of John Lord Welles, who died in 1421, and three waste husbandlands in Newton-on-the-Moor of Sir John Hastings, dead since June 1440. The IPM for Sir Robert Ogle (d.1436), likewise indented, makes numerous references to Henry Percy of Atholl as his landlord, but Percy had died four years before, and found that the manor of Unthank was held of Philip Lord Darcy, although he was buried in 1418. Ogle's inquisition was one of two taken on the same day by the county escheator, Robert Rhodes, at Newcastle; the other was for John Lord Greystoke. Did Rhodes, perhaps, in reality take only one IPM for Greystoke? Possibly not even that, since Greystoke's IPM also details that he also held land of Atholl.[14] Whilst such examples may indicate how irrelevant and even forgotten feudal tenures had become, they suggest that no proper inquiry was held. If the indented IPMs reviewed above are fictitious, local residents had connived with the escheator in applying their seals. Such discrepancies also raise some uncertainty about the involvement of the sheriff, who should have summoned a jury.

Where a jury was present, its role was to endorse the findings of the IPM rather than to supply information.[15] IPMs were most likely to have been informed by the family of the deceased, perhaps with the assistance of estate officials and legal

12 *CIPM* xviii.212; xx.847; xxii.20, 671; xxiii.194.

13 M.L. Holford, '"Thrifty Men of the Country"? The Jurors and their Role', *IPM Companion*, 207.

14 *CIPM* xxi.358, 862; xxiv.61b, 498, 694; xxv.468; xxvi.223; *A History of Northumberland*, ii (1), 373; *Northumberland County History* vii, 130.

15 Carpenter, 'Introduction', *CIPM* xxii.20–22.

advisers. Whilst the jury at the initial IPM for John Hawkswell failed to name his heir for want of information from the his next of kin – an aunt who had joined an enclosed order of nuns and thus renounced her rights of property – a subsequent inquisition proved more successful. On this occasion Hawkswell's heir was named as Sir William Heron and various genealogical relationships were given to support his claim, particulars that were almost certainly provided by Heron himself.[16] It is reasonable to deduce that the important letters patent 'shown to the jurors' which pardoned John Lord Clifford and his wife, Elizabeth, 'all gifts, alienations and acquisitions of land' were provided by the couple.[17] Close similarities in the various IPMs for John Duke of Bedford suggest that relevant information was assembled and digested by one of his officials before being distributed to county escheators. The majority of statements regarding his heir have an identical sentence structure and contain the term '*viz*' (*videlicet*). Admittedly, the actual wording in the returns does differ, but they provide four descriptions of Bedford's heir, Henry VI, as 'our lord king', 'the current lord king', 'the most excellent prince and lord', and 'son of the illustrious' Henry V.[18]

Whether items recorded as 'shown to jurors' were actually produced on the day is, perhaps, open to question. IPMs for William Tempest conducted in Northumberland and Yorkshire both refer to his charter, dated 1443, that was presented to the jury. Tempest's Northumbrian IPM was held at Newcastle on 21 April 1444, followed by another taken at York three days later, on 24 April. This charter may well have been delivered to the inquisition at York, since the names of the nine trustees are given in identical order in each return.[19] Then again, the Yorkshire escheator may simply have reproduced these details from sight of the Northumberland IPM. Was it a coincidence that both returns were delivered to chancery on the same day?

Arrangements were almost certainly in place between some county officials for the return of documents. IPMs for Joan Neville that were held concurrently in Newcastle and Northumberland on 9 January 1441 were handed to chancery on the same date, and on another occasion two IPMs for John Belasis were delivered simultaneously, although the inquisitions had been taken a month apart.[20]

Escheators generally delivered an adequate return following an inquisition, but some submissions proved unsatisfactory. Chancery generated fourteen directives demanding further attention. Twelve writs required greater explanation of information provided in a previous return or particulars that had been omitted from it. One such order highlighted a dating error as 'the feast of St Gregory the Martyr was unknown', but the remainder concentrated on the main lines of investigation: the deceased's estates and identification of the heir. A writ *melius inquirendo* for

16 *CIPM* xxi.475–6.
17 *CIPM* xxi.955.
18 *CIPM* xxiv.520–52.
19 *CIPM* xxvi.213–14.
20 *CIPM* xxv.367–8, 515–16.

Helen Ogle requested more information about her property at Lorbottle and the amount of service. The writ *melius sciri* for John Musgrave asked for a manorial extent of Heaton (a survey consisting of a description and valuation of the estate). In the case of John Hawkswell a writ *plenius certatori* wanted the name of his successor.[21] The only example where the findings were challenged relates to John Lord Latimer, who held more land than was specified. Ten new jurors were sworn for Latimer's second inquisition,[22] which implies a renewed effort to provide an accurate return.

II

It was 'generally in the interests of an adult heir that the whole process be carried out as speedily as possible'.[23] What did this mean in practice? While the substance of IPMs has attracted considerable attention, the mechanics and efficiency of the administrative system have been largely neglected by historians of the fifteenth century. What little has been written highlights great variations. The whole process from a writ *dce* (ordering an inquisition) to the return of the findings of the inquisition could take from less than a month to over a year. And in 1440 the time that elapsed from the date of the writ ordering an inquisition to the date that it was held varied from nine days to almost two years.[24]

Work on the chronology and transmission of writs has largely concentrated on fourteenth-century England, utilising crown records and episcopal registers. J.F. Willard highlighted a major obstacle for researchers by detecting that the dating clause on royal letters was not necessarily the date of despatch.[25] Eugene Stevenson surveyed the following two aspects of writ-driven administration:

(1) The time that elapsed from the death of a tenant-in-chief to the issue of a writ for an inquisition and its execution.
(2) The dates on which escheators were ordered to seize and deliver property to a successor, and the periods that they accounted for at the exchequer.

In relation to the process resulting in the execution of an IPM, Stevenson found that the 'promptness with which the work was done' was 'testimony to not only the efficiency of the escheator's office but also of the king's post', though he also acknowledged inconsistencies therein and numerous records where inquisitions were not held for several months. Although Stevenson did not summarise his

21 *CIPM* xix.2; xxi.420, 476.
22 *CIPM* xxiii.473.
23 Carpenter, 'Introduction', *CIPM* xxii.16.
24 Carpenter, 'Introduction', *CIPM* xxii.13; C. Noble, 'Writs and the Inquisitions Post Mortem: How the Crown managed the System', *IPM Companion*, 190.
25 J.F. Willard, 'The Dating and Delivery of Letters Patent and Writs in the Fourteenth Century', *BIHR* x (1933), 2–3.

findings, an examination of his sample shows that inquisitions took place between 5 and 129 days from the date shown on the ordering writ, with an average of 35 days.[26] No geographical breakdown was supplied. The sample proves somewhat flawed, as none of the selected records includes shires north of the Humber. Stevenson's interpretation of efficient communication between centre and locality therefore glosses over the subject of distance.

But geography was not the sole determinant of the speed of communication. Chancery experienced widespread difficulty in obtaining information from escheators during the early fifteenth century, which resulted in further legislation. A statute of 1429 (8 Henry VI, c. 16) ordered that with effect from Easter 1430 escheators must submit returns within a month of taking an inquisition, under a £40 penalty for default.[27]

The calendared IPMs contain 119 abstracted returns of IPMs and consequent proceedings concerning Northumbrian tenants-in-chief held between 1399 and 1447.[28] What proportion of the original archive this material represents is impossible to estimate: unfortunately the calendars cannot provide a complete account of the process. In some instances information relating to key stages simply does not exist. How and when chancery received the news of a tenant's death that instigated the production of a writ *dce* is not recorded. The dates on which county escheators received chancery writs are also unknown. Records of writs ordering livery of seisin appear in the Fine and Close Rolls, but there are no details of the date on which these orders were executed. There are, however, three fixed documented points: the date of the writ *dce*; the date of the first inquest; and the date of the writ ordering delivery of seisin. These three dates can thus reveal how many days elapsed between each phase and the overall amount of time from the beginning of the documented process to its end. There are 55 calendared inquisitions taken for Northumbrian tenants-in-chief between 1399 and 1447 that resulted in an award of seisin to the deceased's partner, an adult heir/heiress or any coheiresses, trustees or grantees documented in the Fine and Close Rolls within a particular reign. This structure provides a basis for a sensible analysis of routine administration, as it provides a more comprehensive view of the process than one restricted to heirs and it avoids the possibility of significant distortion of the figures that would result from any extreme delays.

Table 12.1 codifies this data. The poorest performance in terms of the duration of the process was in the time of Henry IV, with an average of 301 days. By comparison, it took three times longer during his reign to complete the administration than it did during the reign of his son, Henry V, which produced a total figure of 101 days, and twice as long as that during the reign of his grandson, Henry VI, which produced a figure of 154 days.

26 Stevenson, 'Escheator', 122.

27 'Henry VI: Parliament of September 1429, Text and Translation', ed. A. Curry, in *PROME*, item 56.

28 The rest of this paper is based on *CIPM* xviii–xxvi.

Table 12.1 The progress of selected Northumbrian IPMs between 1399 and 1447

Reign	Average number of days from date of writ *dce* to date of execution	Average number of days from date *dce* executed to date of writ of seisin	Average total days
Henry IV	106	195	301
Henry V	52	49	101
Henry VI	60	94	154

Evidently the system worked most efficiently under Henry V. The figures for each phase during his reign are almost equal, which suggests that crown administration was working at an optimum level in terms of relaying and acting upon information received. In the first phase chancery produced a writ for an inquisition that was dispatched to the county for action; the second phase operated in reverse, with the county transmitting the findings of an inquisition to chancery for action in the production of a writ of seisin. During the reign of Henry VI the timescale for completion increased by half the time from the level achieved in his father's era. The detail of the two phases shows that the amount of time taken between the date that the writ was executed and the date of writ of seisin almost doubled, but it is impossible to isolate the location of the delay. Escheators may have been slower in making their returns, or chancery may have taken longer to produce and dispatch the writ of seisin.

There were occasions when the duration of the process was outside the direct control of the chancery or the escheator. It took more than four years to complete the administration for William, son and heir of Henry Heton. William was a minor at his death on 27 September 1401, leaving his three sisters as coheiresses to his estate that had been taken into the crown's hand. A writ to hold his inquisition was dated 12 February 1404, when his eldest sister, Joan, was fifteen and married to Robert Rutherford. She was already a little older than the minimum age to succeed to part of her late brother's estate, set at fourteen for married females. Her siblings, Elizabeth and Margaret, were still minors, then aged twelve and nine, respectively. A long interval of more than three years passed. A writ for Joan's proof of age, ordering the escheator to take an inquisition to confirm her age, was dated June 1407. The cause of the delay appears to have been a local wrangle over rights of lordship and, specifically, the wardship of Heton's daughters, which reached the courts in 1407 for a judicial decision. Presumably, a writ for proof of age had not been sued out at an earlier stage as a safeguard against the challenge, which left the estate in the hands of the crown. The first award of seisin for one of William's sisters was made in May 1408. Even if this particular record is disregarded, the duration of the process under Henry IV is still the lengthiest for any Lancastrian king.

In order to assess the impact of distance, the figures for Northumberland have been compared against those for the southern county of Berkshire in Table 12.2.

Table 12.2 Comparison of the progress of selected IPMs for Northumberland and Berkshire between 1399 and 1447

Reign	County	Average number of days from date of writ *dce* to date of execution	Average number of days from date of execution to date of writ of seisin	Average total days
Henry IV	Northumberland	106	195	301
	Berkshire	22	48	70
Henry V	Northumberland	52	49	101
	Berkshire	35	80	115
Henry VI	Northumberland	60	94	154
	Berkshire	57	41	98

In Northumberland the duration of the process was lengthiest under Henry IV at 301 days, whereas in Berkshire it took just 70 days, the shortest of any reign. The figures for the average total number of days for both counties under Henry V are close, but in Berkshire the timescale had actually increased by 45 days from that achieved in Henry IV's reign. Administration was not at its weakest in either county during the reign of Henry VI, but occupied the middle ground at 154 days for Northumberland and 98 for Berkshire.

As the best figure for Northumberland was an average of 101 days during the reign of Henry V and that for Berkshire was 70 days during the reign of Henry IV, the effect of distance on the whole process was 31 days, or one month. Since information was communicated between locality and centre twice during the process, each phase took approximately an additional 15 days to complete in relation to Northumberland.

What impact did the statute of 1429 have on the duration of the process? The aggregated figures for the reign of Henry VI discussed earlier have been separated out to show the position before and after Easter 1430, when the statute came into effect.

Table 12.3 provides a comparison for Northumberland and Berkshire prior to the statute. Shown in this way, the completion figures are worse than those presented earlier for Henry VI's reign, at 154 days for Northumberland and 98 for Berkshire. Clearly, there was a balancing act in the aggregated figures, with shorter periods compensating for longer timescales. The increase is located in the second phase, from the date of execution to writ of seisin.

Table 12.4 shows the situation after the introduction of the statute, which did result in a reduction in the timescale of the process in both counties. In Northumberland the average duration was reduced by nearly three months, which infers that escheators had generally been dilatory in the past. In Berkshire the reduction was less significant, approximately two weeks. Overall, it was an improvement, but the timescale had been bettered in both counties during earlier reigns.

Table 12.3 Comparison of the progress of selected IPMs for Northumberland and Berkshire, 1399–Easter 1430[29]

Reign	County	Average number of days from date of writ *dce* to date of execution	Average number of days from date of execution to date of writ of seisin	Average total days
Henry VI	Northumberland	61	159	220
Henry VI	Berkshire	53	52	105

Note: This comparison is based on six returns for Northumberland and sixteen for Berkshire.

Table 12.4 Comparison of the Progress of Selected IPMs for Northumberland and Berkshire, post Easter 1430–47

Reign	County	Average number of days from date of writ *dce* to date of execution	Average number of days from date of execution to date	Average total days
Henry VI	Northumberland	61	73	134
Henry VI	Berkshire	60	31	91

III

Following routine records relating to IPM processes thus provides a more nuanced interpretation of the notion of distance between locality and centre. This exercise has shown that royal administration moved at different rates under Lancastrian kingship and, despite the significant changes at Westminster, this function of the bureaucracy was not at its worst during the reign of Henry VI.[30] As the figures for the reign of Henry V demonstrate, the IPM process took a little longer to expedite in Northumberland than in Berkshire, but it was no more difficult for the crown to govern the peripheral shire of Northumberland than the central shire of Berkshire.

[29] Easter, a moveable feast, fell on 16 April 1430.

[30] Cf. C. Carpenter, 'Henry VI and the Deskilling of the Royal Bureaucracy', in *The Fifteenth Century ix: English and Continental Perspectives*, ed. L. Clark (Woodbridge, 2010), 1–37.

13

Late Medieval Land Disputes and the Manipulation of the Inquisitions *Post Mortem*

SIMON PAYLING

This is very much a preliminary study of a complex subject, and it is largely based on a series of case studies that may or may not be meaningfully representative. Its argument may thus fall into the modern confusion of thought that indicts an entire system for what may be only its occasional failings. Nonetheless, in the case of the inquisitions *post mortem* these failures were important, at least when conceived in terms of individual cases.

Taken on the deaths of tenants-in-chief or of tenants of mesne lords in royal wardship, inquisitions had two main purposes, namely to discover royal rights, which had a particular value when the heir was a minor, and to identify the heir or heirs and so secure the formal transmission of the lands held in chief into the next generation. There are thus two distinct themes in discussing the manipulation of inquisitions. The first, partially discussed by Bean in his *Decline of English Feudalism* of 1968, relates to those inquisitions that were designed either to inflate or, more commonly, to diminish the feudal rights of lords, principally, of course, those of the greatest lord, the crown.[1] The second theme, the subject of this paper, concerns those that were intended illegitimately to promote the claim of one individual to land over that of another.

Such manipulation played an important part in many land disputes, for inquisitions had a crucial role in the transmission of property both within and between families. They determined the title to land which, in the first instance at least, was acknowledged by chancery and upon which livery of seisin was awarded. It is the contention of this paper that they were ill-adapted to discharge so important a role. Such a contention would not have surprised contemporaries. A statute of the reforming Parliament of 1429–30 (8 Hen. VI, ch. 16) spoke of the daily disinheritances which occurred through the dishonesty of escheators who for '*lour propre gayne*' took inquisitions, '*favourablement et noun duement*' by juries not empanelled, as law demanded, by the county sheriffs.[2]

[1] Bean, *Decline*, 200–220. I am grateful to the Trustees of the History of Parliament Trust for their permission to draw on material to be published by the History of Parliament Trust in *The Commons, 1422–61*, ed. L.S. Clark (forthcoming c.2017).

[2] *SR* ii.252–3.

Even, however, leaving aside these problems of the integrity of escheators and improperly empanelled juries, there were two general problems with the inquisition system. First was its reliance on jurors, who, even when properly empanelled, were generally drawn from, at best, the margins of gentry society.[3] Not until 1509 (1 Hen. VIII, ch. 8) did statute lay down an income qualification for inquisition jurors, and even then it was placed at a modest 40*s* a year.[4] The lack of social robustness of juries made it difficult for them to resist the blandishments of the influential and self-interested. The second problem related to the scale of the task that, in contentious circumstances, the jurors were asked to undertake. They were required to make a judgment as to title at a time when the ever-developing complexity of the law governing the descent of land made 'true title' an increasingly subjective concept. It is not, therefore, surprising that their findings seem to have favoured the interested party which, independent of the merits of the rival claims, best exploited the inquisition system.

I

To understand how such exploitation worked, one needs first to address the vexed and much-debated question of how the returned inquisitions were compiled. As has long been realised, it was a convenient fiction that inquisition findings were a function of the unprompted local knowledge of the jurors. Charles Crump of the Public Record Office concluded as long ago as 1924 that the inquisitions were probably based on a written statement to the escheator's office by the heir or other interested party; and thus that what he called the 'secret' of the inquisitions 'must be sought in the materials used by the experts who drew them up, and not in the institution of the sworn inquest'.[5] Later research has confirmed this insight. In general, the jurors were simply called upon to validate, in routine fashion, the uncontested evidence produced before them by the deceased's family.[6] When there was no contention about either the descent of the lands to the heir or their division between heir and widow, the only losers in respect of any falsehood were the crown or mesne lords, who might be deprived of lands that should have passed into their wardship.[7] But when the descent of the deceased's lands was open to question, the jurors played a more critical and contentious part. Sitting before a relatively minor local official in the escheator, they were far more open to the exploitation of local influence than a jury called upon to rule on a plea of land

[3] M. Holford, '"Thrifty Men of the Country"? The Jurors and Their Role', in *IPM Companion*, 201–21.

[4] *SR* iii.4–5.

[5] C.G. Crump, 'A Note on the Criticism of Records', *Bulletin of the John Rylands Library* viii (1924), 144.

[6] C. Carpenter, 'General Introduction', *CIPM* xxii.20–23; M. Holford, '"Thrifty Men"', 201–21.

[7] M. Hicks, 'Introduction', in *IPM Companion*, 18–21.

in the much more formal solemn presence of the justices of Common Pleas or of assize. A petition of the 1470s makes the point by posing a question that invites the answer yes:

> Please it your lordshippes to pondre and considre whether a mater tried betwix party and party by the affirmatiff and the negatiff pro et contra to fore Jug[es] assigned aught to be taken of gretter evidence [and] effecte or an office (in other words, an inquisition) called a fore an Escheatour through (the petitioner adds in case their lordships should be in any doubt) the cantelouse labour and exhortacion of a desseyuable persone.[8]

Had the petitioner cared to be more specific he might have made another point. In a plea of land the action of attaint, which threatened stern penalties to jurors who gave false verdicts, discouraged jurors from adopting a casual attitude to truth; jurors in inquisitions *post mortem* were not subject to that action. In one sense it was appropriate that this should have been so, for inquisition juries were faced with a difficulty that jurors in pleas of land did not share. The latter, in coming to a verdict, were posed with a single question that had emerged from a debate among learned serjeants-at-law, presided over by even more learned judges, on the merits of the competing claims; those in an inquisition *post mortem* were faced, when the property was in dispute, with a more difficult undertaking. In theory, they had themselves to do the work of the serjeants and judges and, with only the legal expertise of the escheator to draw upon, come to a judgment on the deceased's legal estate, whatever the difficulties and contradictions of the settlements that regulated the descent of the lands into the next generation.

In the vast majority of cases, these difficulties were more theoretical than real. Most property was not the subject of dispute, its descent being uncontentious and uncontested. Yet, when there was a dispute, the jurors found themselves under a strong temptation simply to accept the evidence placed before them by the most powerful or most adept of the rival claimants. They had little option but to do so, and this reveals the central weakness of the inquisition system. This weakness had significant potential consequences. In the long term the successful prosecution of a claim depended as much upon the construction of a strong title as it did upon acquisition of the physical possession of the disputed property. Paradoxically, this illustrates the strength of late-medieval property law: that law, sometimes haltingly but generally effectively, protected 'true title'. But the very necessary premium the law placed on such title prompted disputants to resort to fraud in the pursuit of a title that had at least the appearance of legal truth, and a tempting target for such frauds was the inquisitions and their jurors.

[8] S.J. Payling, '"A Beest envenymed thorough ... covetize": an Imposter Pilgrim and the Disputed Descent of the Manor of Dodford, 1306–1481', in *The Fifteenth Century*, x, *Parliament, Personalities and Power – Papers Presented to Linda S. Clark*, ed. H. Kleineke (Woodbridge, 2011), 25. In 1424 Serjeant Rolf opined, '*un Enquest d'office n'este si haut si come un chose trie per verdit de Enquest*': *Les Reports des Cases*, ed. J. Maynard (London, 1678–80), Hil. 2 Hen. VI, f. 7, pl. 2.

Since the success of such fraud in inquisitions arose out of the total dependence of the juries on evidence placed before them by interested parties, it is important to ask how this 'evidence' was produced and how it was then translated into the final text of the inquisition returned into chancery. It is a limitation of the surviving evidence that almost nothing is known of how medieval jurors deliberated, but, in the case of those at inquisitions *post mortem*, there are some sporadic indications. The texts of the inquisitions themselves not infrequently refer, as proof of the truth of their findings, to the production of relevant deeds and letters patent before the jurors. In the sixteenth century these documents were not infrequently reproduced in full in the text of the returned inquisition, but in the fifteenth century they are simply cited as evidence of a conveyance and, in respect of lands held in chief, as evidence that that conveyance had been made with the necessary royal licence. Records from outside the inquisitions themselves add detail. There is enough to prove that interested parties or their counsels routinely made representations before the jurors. A statute of 1509 laid down that escheators at inquisitions were to 'suffre every Persone to geve evydence openly in ther presence' on pain of £40, and that this was well established as proper practice at an earlier date is clear from the Year Book record of 'Hugford's case' in 1487. The forthright serjeant-at-law, Thomas Kebell, remarked (as though it were an established fact) that at an inquisition held on a *diem clausit* writ anyone could come to show title and thus, if one who was heir neglected to appear and was not returned as heir, that was his fault.[9] The injunction of a statute of 1361 (34 Edw. III, ch. 13), repeated in one of 1445 (23 Hen. VI, ch. 16), that inquisitions be held '*en bones villes, overtement et nemie en prive*', probably reflects this notion that an inquisition should offer an opportunity to declare their interest in the deceased's lands.[10]

Beyond this, one is drawn into more speculative realms. It is hard to believe that the jurors, having taken evidence, both written and perhaps oral, then drafted the return themselves, perhaps drawing on the escheator or his staff's knowledge of the necessary diplomatic. In any event, some returns, particularly those in complex and disputed cases, show clear signs of much more professional drafting. Since there is nothing to suggest that the inquisitions were ever composed in chancery from information supplied by the escheator, it is tempting to conclude that these complex returns were drawn up by the counsel of an interested party and then produced before the jurors for their approval. There is one well-known instance when this, or something very like it, certainly happened. On the death of John Paston in 1466 a draft inquisition, which still survives, was drawn up providing a detailed summary of the deceased's claim to the estates of Sir John Fastolf. This draft then formed the basis of the inquisition returned into chancery.[11]

9 E.W. Ives, *The Common Lawyers of Pre-Reformation England: Thomas Kebell* (Cambridge, 1983), 240; *Les Reports des Cases*, Hil. 2 Hen. VII, f. 12, pl. 14.

10 *SR*, i.368; ii.343.

11 Holford, '"Thrifty Men"', 203. For another potential example: idem, '"Notoriously Unreliable": The Valuations and Extents', in *IPM Companion*, 121, n.

Another tantalising letter of a few years later provides a more detailed picture. It seems that, on the death of his mother, Thomas Stonor delegated the task of drafting her inquisition *post mortem* to his lawyer Thomas Mulle, sending him the relevant instructions in a bill. Mulle, however, expressed reluctance, asking instead that Stonor should either come himself with a copy of the relevant deeds or else send 'a pleyn cope of al your dedes seth the dethe of your ffader'. The lawyer probably found the instructions in the bill inadequate and wanted better information. All this may be taken to imply that the drafting of inquisitions was a routine part of a lawyer's work.[12]

The texts of inquisitions give indirect but unmistakeable evidence in support of this conclusion. Some are so detailed and well ordered that it is impossible to believe that they arose out of the presentation of evidence before jurors who then, with or without the escheator's help, reduced that evidence to the form demanded by the writs. Take the Lancashire inquisition on the death of Thomas Lord de la Warre, in 1427. This runs to 3,000 words and presents, with admirable clarity, each of the many settlements relevant to the descent of each component of de la Warre's extensive holdings in the county. Whoever drafted it had before him all the relevant deeds or copies of them, from which he cited only the details precisely relevant to the proper division of the lands. No doubt such a compilation was within the scope of an escheator with an organised mind and perhaps a modicum of legal knowledge. But that is not the point here, for it is clear that the return was not drafted in the office of the Lancashire escheator. That return, together with those made by the juries in the several other counties in which de la Warre held lands, show signs of having only a single drafting source. Taken together, they appear to have been professionally drawn up in answer to one principal question: how should the inheritance be divided between the common-law heir, John Griffin, the last lord's second cousin once removed, and Sir Reginald West, the last lord's nephew of the half blood, who was heir-in-tail under a final concord of 1331 and under charters of an even earlier date?[13] In this case there is no reason to suppose that the returns did not give a complete and even-handed picture. Nonetheless, the fact that multiple inquisitions could be prepared collectively rather than individually, county by county, further gives the lie to the notion that inquisitions were the work of individual juries.[14]

Further, and much more importantly, collective drafting gave room for coordinated manipulation. Take as an example the inquisitions returned on the death of Elizabeth Lady Fitzhugh, who, like de la Warre, died in 1427. Jurors in Lincolnshire and four other counties made returns, in detailed and *mutatis mutandis* identical terms, supporting the claim, questionable but not baseless, of Ralph Lord Cromwell, to a moiety of the ancient inheritance of the Marmyon family. Each of these returns, in the legal logic of their arrangement, has the

12 *Stonor L & P* i.105.

13 *CIPM* xxii.782–9; *CP* iv.151–4.

14 Holford, '"Thrifty Men"', 203.

unmistakeable marks of professional drafting, and they must have been drafted by Cromwell's legal staff.[15] How, indeed, could they not have been? To assume otherwise is to postulate an impossible chain of events: that is, that Cromwell's representatives persuaded each of the five juries individually of the validity of their lord's claim and then each of those juries drafted inquisitions in exactly the same terms in support of that claim.

It seems fair to conclude that, in complex cases, the jurors were not simply presented with deeds and other evidences that they were invited to judge and interpret. They were, rather, presented with the texts of inquisitions for their approval. This would explain why they never returned equivocal answers as to the deceased's legal estate, and it brings us back to Crump's acute observation that the 'secret' of the inquisitions 'must be sought in the materials used by the experts who drew them up'.[16]

It would, however, be unwise to assume that, in contentious circumstances, the rival parties simply drew up conflicting inquisitions and then competed for the validation of the jurors on the day of the inquest. There is some evidence to suggest a more sophisticated process in which those inquisitions deemed likely to be contentious were preceded by a period of negotiation between rival claimants. Hicks has cited what might be seen as indirect evidence of this process at work. On the death of Henry Beauchamp, duke of Warwick, in June 1446, his distant kinsman, Sir John Beauchamp of Powick, laid claim to the earldom of Warwick as the duke's heir male. After an examination of the Beauchamp archive had yielded nothing in support of his claim, Sir John agreed 'to applie hem with alle his fauour to the good expedicion' of the duke's inquisitions *post mortem* so that the inheritance might be secured to the duke's infant daughter.[17]

A chancery petition of the 1430s provides some much more direct evidence. On the death of the wealthy Cumberland esquire, William Stapleton of Edenhall, in 1432 his widow fell into dispute with her stepson, another William Stapleton, over the extent of her dower and jointure entitlement. An attempt was thus made to come to a compromise in advance of the inquisitions. The execution of the writ of *diem clausit* was put in suspense pending the arbitration of the husbands of the heir's four sisters. In this case arbitration failed: the heir had the writ secretly executed, with juries in Cumberland and Westmorland under-enumerating his father's properties in order to deny his stepmother her legitimate dower.[18] The point here, however, is not the failure of the arbitration but the fact that it was tried. In many other instances an award or some other form of compromise in advance of the inquisition must have determined the form of the return, as it

15 S.J. Payling, 'Arbitration, Perpetual Entails and Collateral Warranties in Late-Medieval England', *Journal of Legal History* xiii (1992), 41–6; *CIPM* xxiii.81–90.

16 Crump, 'Criticism of Records', 144.

17 M. Hicks, 'Between Majorities', 36, from C81/1546/14.

18 C1/70/85; *CIPM* xxiv.85–6. This case is discussed in detail in Payling, 'William Stapleton', in *The Commons, 1422–61*.

probably did, for example, in the case of those made on the death of Lord de la Warre.

II

The second part of this paper is concerned with some specific examples where the inquisition system was exploited in the furtherance of one claim over another.[19] In these cases the inquisition findings emerged not out of a compromise, but from a conflict resolved in favour of one party over the other. The first two of these relate, like the Stapleton case, to the difficult relations that generally prevailed between stepsons and stepmothers, and both involve stepmothers who had been treated with more than ordinary generosity by the heir's father.

The first example is the most revealing, in that one does not have to infer what lay behind the findings of the inquisition from a combination of surviving deeds and what is known of the family situation. A letter survives that clearly reveals the nature of the heir's subterfuge to deny to his stepmother what his father had given her. Late in his life the wealthy Nottinghamshire knight Sir Robert Strelley made a second marriage and chose to compromise the interests of his adult son and heir by, in 1435, levying a final concord settling on his new wife a life interest in the family's *caput honoris*, the manor of Strelley near Nottingham. Not surprisingly, after his death three years later, his son was anxious to undo a conveyance that, should his relatively young stepmother long survive, threatened both his wealth and his hereditary place in local affairs. An earlier conveyance gave him the necessary pretext. In about 1400 his grandfather, Sir Nicholas, had conveyed the bulk of the family property, including the manor of Strelley, to a group of feoffees including the Derbyshire lawyer Peter de la Pole. The young Robert now sought to show that these feoffees had remained seised until after the death of his father, in other words, that they were seised when the final concord was levied, thus rendering it void. This, at least, is the conclusion to be drawn from a letter from Pole to Strelley dated on 12 January 1439. Pole stated, in reply to Strelley's inquiry, that he did not remember reconveying the lands to Sir Nicholas, and concluded by saying what his correspondent wanted to hear, namely that if any deed of re-enfeoffment was produced he would disavow it unless it was sealed

[19] To the examples cited below, others could added, most notably the inquisitions taken on the death of the infant daughter of the duke of Warwick, in 1449: M. Hicks, *Warwick the Kingmaker* (Oxford, 1998), 42–8. For some of the others: S.J. Payling, 'Legal Right and Dispute Resolution in Late Medieval England: the Sale of the Lordship of Dunster', *EHR* cxxvi (2011), 30n.; Payling, *Nottinghamshire*, 209–11; R. Virgoe, 'Inheritance and Litigation in the Fifteenth Century: The Buckenham Disputes', *Journal of Legal History* xv (1994), 23–40; *Plumpton Correspondence*, ed. T. Stapleton (Camden Society iv, 1839), lxxxvii–lxxxviii; C. Carpenter, 'General Introduction', 7–8, 15, 28; *Armburgh Papers*, 5–9; *RP* iii.633–4; *CIPM Hen. VII*, ii.14; SC8/204/10200.

with his seal of arms or signet.[20] The first stage of Robert's plan was complete; a judicious intervention in his father's inquisition *post mortem* was the second stage. The jurors in that inquisition, convened only four days after Pole had written his letter, gave an account that served his interest. They referred to the feoffment made by Sir Nicholas; described Pole as the only survivor of these feoffees; and claimed that Robert's father had entered on Pole's possession to levy the 1435 fine. This was almost certainly not true. The jurors in the inquisition *post mortem* of Sir Nicholas, taken only nine years before, made no mention of feoffees and stated that he died seised of all his estates. This statement is supported by a surviving deed of 1405 by which Pole and his co-feoffees granted Sir Nicholas the manor of Strelley and all else they had of his feoffment.[21] All this invites only one conclusion. Faced with the very damaging prospect of the *caput honoris* of the family coming into the hands of his stepmother, Strelley suborned first the forgetful Pole and then the jurors in his father's inquisition. Given that his stepmother was alive as late as 1460, it was as well for him that he was able to do so, and the inappropriateness of the 1435 settlement gave the colour of justification to his resort to subterfuge.[22]

In this case it is just about possible to suggest that the inquisition findings were the product of the usual compromises between widow and heir, and that the findings were simply the legal solution to the formal extinction of the widow's interest contingent on some financial or other compensation to her. But it seems unlikely. In the next example there is no possibility that any compromise was involved. Here exactly the same tactic – that is, the denial of a father's seisin – was employed in a very much more important and famous dispute involving a stepmother. In this case the threat to the heir was even greater than it had been to Strelley, for the father's provision was not just for the second wife but for her issue. In 1442 John Talbot, first earl of Shrewsbury, levied a fine settling his valuable lordships of Blackmere in Shropshire and Painswick in Gloucestershire on himself and his second wife, Margaret Beauchamp, in joint tail general. In the Shropshire inquisition taken after the earl's death at the battle of Castillon in 1453, the new earl, eldest son of the first marriage, subverted this settlement by having a jury return that his father had not been seised when this fine was levied. The legal estate, it was alleged, was then vested in the last surviving feoffee of the first earl's brother, Gilbert Lord Talbot, who had been killed at the siege of Rouen in 1418. Other evidence shows that this was a fabrication. In fact, Gilbert had never held Blackmere, the legal estate of which had been remained through-

20 SC 1/51/68.

21 *CIPM* xxiii.484; xxv.232; *CAD* vi.C4724; C146/8246. When, in the reign of Henry VIII, the lands of the family were disputed between the heir male and the heirs general, the former claimed that the 1405 re-enfeoffment was a forgery, but the only evidence he cited in support of his claim was Pole's letter: SP 1/243, f. 120.

22 *CAD* vi.C6832. In September 1439 Pole quitclaimed to Robert all his right in the lands he had by Sir Nicholas's feoffment and declared that he had not previously made any re-enfeoffment: C146/9991.

out his life in the hands of his mother's feoffees who, after Gilbert's death and before the levying of the fine, had conveyed to the first earl. The fine was, in short, a legal conveyance and should have been effective, but the second earl avoided its consequences through a false inquisition finding. He was no doubt helped by the fact that the escheator who convened the inquisition was Thomas Horde, one of his legal counsel.[23]

Although, however, false or distorted inquisition findings were employed within families, often to the disadvantage of widows, they were more commonly used (or at least employed in a greater variety of ways) in inheritance disputes, that is, in cases were the identity of the heir to a specific property was the subject of contention. The famous dispute over the great lordship of Dunster in Somerset provides an example of a claimant acting so expeditiously on the writ of a *diem clausit extremum* (*dce*) that he prevented his rival claimants from laying their evidence before the inquisition jurors or drafting their own version of the return. In 1376 Elizabeth Courtenay, widow of Sir Andrew Luttrell, had purchased from Joan Burghersh, widow of John Lord Mohun, the reversion, expectant on Joan's death, of Dunster for the princely sum of 5,000 marks (£3,666 6*s* 8*d*). The sale was a controversial one. Not only did it involve the disinheritance of Joan's three daughters, but the rights of those daughters were, arguably at least, protected by an entail in tail general made by a deed of 1346. The purchaser's son, Sir Hugh Luttrell, was thus well aware that he would have great difficulty in establishing title when Joan died. Providentially for him, when that event occurred on 4 October 1404, he was MP elect for Somerset. Two days later, the day that Parliament assembled, *dce* writs in respect of Joan's lands were issued from Coventry, where Parliament was sitting, and there is no reason to doubt that it was Sir Hugh who obtained them. There is also no reason to doubt that it was he who, on 10 October, sued out a writ directed to the escheator of Somerset ordering him to act expeditiously. Five days later the escheator did as he was ordered, holding inquisition at Taunton by a jury including several of Sir Hugh's associates.[24]

Unsurprisingly the jury's findings were entirely supportive of the Luttrell title: it returned that Lady Joan died seised under the terms of the fine of 1376, one of the feet of which they reported to have seen. This is not to suggest that the jurors were guilty of making an untrue return, only that, had they been subject to the

[23] A.J. Pollard, 'The Family of Talbot, Lords Talbot and Earls of Shrewsbury in the Fifteenth Century (Bristol University, Ph.D. thesis, 1968), 54–62; CP25(1)/293/70/262; C139/154/29. In this case, as well as that of Sir Robert Strelley, the use of inquisitions to negate settlements by final concord was a legally elegant one. The operation of the statute of fines of 1299 (27 Edw. I, ch. 1) meant that neither the earl nor Strelley could plead the seisin of the feoffees against the fine. Under that statute no heir to a party to a fine could overturn a fine by claiming that his ancestor, as party to the fine, was not seised. Had they sued in Common Pleas, they would have had to rely on the surviving feoffee acting as plaintiff, a complication they both avoided.

[24] Payling, 'Legal Right', 29–30.

lobbying of the coheirs, who could have shown them the tail general entail of 1346, they might have made a different one. This finding gave Sir Hugh a crucial advantage in the dispute that he was not subsequently to lose.

The Dunster case illustrates the problem alluded to earlier, namely the grave difficulties jurors faced when questions of title were at issue. Even if the facts presented to them were complete and they were intent on impartiality, the legal rights and wrongs of opposing titles were often beyond easy resolution. In the Dunster case, the judges later found themselves divided upon the merits of the competing titles. Nevertheless, in this particular case, the inquisition finding, although not returning the full facts of the respective claims, served a legal right. The same might be said, although with less confidence, in respect of the findings engineered by Lord Cromwell on the death of Lady Fitzhugh. He had a respectable claim to the lands he sought, and the arbitrated settlement that emerged from the inquisitions resulted in an equitable division. In other cases, like the Strelley one, the inquisition findings served to undo a settlement that did not accord with some general perception of how lands should be divided within families. Yet there are other examples where the inquisition findings simply served to perpetrate, in the short and sometimes the long term, a simple injustice.

A late fourteenth-century case provides a striking example, both in the fact that it resulted in the near-total disinheritance of the right heir and in the blatant method employed to secure that disinheritance. On the death in 1375 of Gwenllian, the last representative of the ancient family of Keynes of Dodford (Northamptonshire), her common-law heir was her unmarried paternal aunt, Elizabeth. There was, however, a complication: Elizabeth had departed on pilgrimage to the Holy Land and it was not known whether she was alive or dead. This unusual circumstance provided an opportunity to a courtier, Sir William Brantingham, whose brother, the bishop of Exeter, had been Gwenllian's guardian. He had inquisition juries in Northamptonshire and three other counties return Elizabeth as Gwenllian's heir, subverting the complication of her absence by producing before the juries a woman claiming to be the recently returned pilgrim. This, at least, is the allegation made by the disinherited Keynes heirs in a petition presented to the 1377 Parliament. Brantingham then sued out a pardon from the crown for a series of unlicensed entries and conveyances by which he had supposedly acquired from Elizabeth all the lands of the Keynes family. He claimed that she had entered these properties without suing livery of seisin; and that she, a woman who was already dead, had then granted them to him in fee. In short, he exploited the inquisition system to have Elizabeth returned as heir, and then claimed directly in chancery that he had her title. As a result of this truncated process, it was no longer necessary for chancery to issue letters to the various escheators ordering the livery of seisin to a dead woman, a proceeding that would have revealed Brantingham's fraud. Ten years later, to give further protection to his title, he instigated a new campaign of false inquisitions, designed to convert his title to one derived not only from Elizabeth but also from one of the disinherited coheirs, Gwenllian's second cousin Margaret Ayot. In 1385 and

1386 inquisitions *post mortem* were belatedly convened in respect of the dead pilgrim Elizabeth: the juries dated her demise to November 1376, in other words after she had supposedly conceded her inheritance to Brantingham, and falsely returned Margaret, whose title Brantingham had already acquired, as her heir.[25]

The delay of more than ten years between Elizabeth's death and the holding of inquisitions *post mortem* would, even if nothing else was known of the particular facts of this case, arouse suspicion of some irregularity. Such inquisitions, that is those held more than a year after the deaths of their subjects, were convened not on writs of *diem clausit* but on those of *mandamus*. Both writs posed the same questions, and the latter had an obvious application in the preservation of royal rights, particularly in respect of concealed wardships. Yet, as in the Brantingham case, they also had an application in land disputes. When *mandamus* was used to protect royal rights, it was invoked in those cases where a tenure in chief had been concealed; when it was used in land disputes it generally involved the false assertion of such a tenure.

Long ago, Peter Lewis cited a clear example of the practice. In 1431 Sir John Fastolf bought the Norfolk manor of Titchwell from John Roys, the widower of its heiress, Margery Lovell, who had died seven years before. The seller's right to sell was questionable, not least because the manor was bound by an entail. This provided an opportunity for the courtier Sir Edward Hull, whose wife was a distant kinswoman of Margery Lovell. In the autumn of 1448 Hull sued out a *mandamus* in respect of the long-dead Margery and an inquisition returned that his wife was one of the two coheirs to the manor of Titchwell under an ancient entail. Further, according to the jury, the manor was held in chief and Margery had entered it without suing livery. This gave the crown the necessary pretext to seize the manor and to grant it to farm to Hull for as long as it should remain in royal hands. The whole proceeding was a fraud. Hull's wife was a Lovell but she was not the deceased's heir-in-tail; the descent given her in the inquisition was a fabrication; and the manor was not held in chief but, rather, of William Lord Lovell, representative of the main branch of the Lovells. Fastolf was almost certainly right in his contention that the inquisition was forged by a hostile escheator. Not until after Hull's childless death in 1453 was he able to undo the damage, when a new inquiry rightly found that the manor was not held in chief.[26]

25 Payling, 'Imposter Pilgrim', 24–30.

26 P.S. Lewis, 'Sir John Fastolf's Lawsuit over Titchwell, 1448–55', *Historical Journal* i (1958), 1–20; A. Smith, 'Litigation and Politics: Sir John Fastolf's Defence of his English Property', 63–4. In another case, the manor of Stretton-en-le-Field in Derbyshire was disputed between 1439 and 1465 through a series of writs of *mandamus* ordering inquiries into the lands of a tenant who had died in the reign of Edward II: M. Jurkowski, 'Law and the Politics of Property during the Wars of the Roses: the Dispute over Stretton-en-le-Field in Derbyshire and Leicestershire' (unpublished typescript).

III

In conclusion, what do these rather random examples tell us? The majority of inquisitions *post mortem* involved property that was not in dispute either within a family or between one family and another. Thus the total dependence of the jurors on information provided to them by the family of the deceased, most commonly either the heir or the widow, posed no particular difficulty. If any interest was compromised it was that of the crown, with juries too ready to accept a family's account of, for example, a feoffment that would keep lands out of royal wardship, and with escheators little minded to restrain that indulgence.

Where, however, there was dispute the jurors were faced with a grave difficulty. They were, in effect, being asked to decide questions of title without the expert assistance provided to jurors in pleas of land in the common law courts. Sometimes the problem was taken out of their hands in advance of the inquisition: the disputing parties came to a compromise and produced before the jurors a return that was acceptable to both parties. On other occasions, however, the jurors were suborned into returning a verdict that damaged the interests of one party.

Of course, such findings did not mark a final defeat for the loser. If the crown's rights were invoked to deprive a tenant of his land, as in the Titchwell case, or an heir of his inheritance, the aggrieved party, under the terms of a statute of 1360, could challenge the findings on the common law side of chancery and have the matter tried before a jury in king's bench. In other cases, the effect of a false return was either overturned by a subsequent action at common law or, as in the case of Cromwell's claim against the Fitzhughs, modified by arbitration.

Nonetheless, it cannot be denied that a favourable inquisition finding could provide a disputant with a vital tactical advantage in a dispute, as it did for Sir Hugh Luttrell in respect of Dunster and the second earl of Shrewsbury in respect of Blackmere. In the most extreme of cases, an inquisition could be exploited in the creation of an entirely contrived title, to the permanent disinheritance of the right heirs. The success of Brantingham's machinations over the Keynes inheritance may have owed much to unusual circumstances, but it is unlikely that that success represents a unique case.

Index

Key: bp = bishop; c = countess; d = duke/ duchess/ daughter; e = earl; ld = lord; s = son; w = wife/widow

Lightning Source UK Ltd.
Milton Keynes UK
UKOW06n1445251116
288558UK00007B/76/P

9 781783 270798